PAKISTAN
IN
PERSPECTIVE

1947–1997

PAKISTAN IN PERSPECTIVE
1947–1997

Edited by
Rafi Raza

OXFORD
UNIVERSITY PRESS

OXFORD

UNIVERSITY PRESS

Great Clarendon Street, Oxford OX2 6DP

Oxford University Press is a department of the University of Oxford.
It furthers the University's objective of excellence in research, scholarship,
and education by publishing worldwide in

Oxford New York

Auckland Cape Town Dar es Salaam Hong Kong Karachi
Kuala Lumpur Madrid Melbourne Mexico City Nairobi
New Delhi Shanghai Taipei Toronto

with offices in

Argentina Austria Brazil Chile Czech Republic France Greece
Guatemala Hungary Italy Japan Poland Portugal Singapore
South Korea Switzerland Turkey Ukraine Vietnam

ISBN 978-0-19-579775-6

First published by Oxford University Press, 1997
First paperback edition, 2001

Third Impression 2007

Typeset in Times
Printed in Pakistan by
Colortone Graphics, Karachi.
Published by
Ameena Saiyid, Oxford University Press
No. 38, Sector 15, Korangi Industrial Area, PO Box 8214
Karachi-74900, Pakistan.

CONTENTS

Fiscal Deficit.

p. 203.

EDITOR'S NOTE

The authors, who are recognised specialists in their own fields, have written in broad terms for the general reader. They have expressed their own views, and have not had the opportunity to see each other's contributions. The editor does not subscribe to some of the views put forward.

Is should be noted that a few of the statistics quoted in the chapters may vary according to the source relied on by the author; this particularly applies to the present population and social indicators because of the absence of a census in Pakistan since 1981. In the text, figures for years mainly relate to fiscal years, that is, from 1 July to 30 June of the following year. The period covered in the book ends in May 1997.

The spellings of names and places are as used today. Thus, for example, it is Mao Zedung and not Mao Tse Tung, Beijing and not Peking, and similarly Dhaka, Sindh and Balochistan. They have been changed accordingly even in quoted passages.

The contributors and the editor have decided to forego remuneration and royalties. All the proceeds from the book will be donated to the Edhi Foundation.

5 May 1997
Karachi.

BIOGRAPHICAL SKETCHES OF CONTRIBUTING AUTHORS

Dr Muneer Ahmad has a Ph.D. from Munster University, Germany. He has served on the faculty of Punjab University, Lahore, as Chairman of the Administrative Science Department, Director of the Centre for South Asian Studies, and as a member of its Senate and Syndicate. He has also been a Research Fellow at the University of Columbia and Visiting Professor at Western Michigan University.

He is the author of several significant research reports, including 'The Civil Servant in Pakistan', 'Legislatures in Pakistan' and 'Aspects of Pakistan's Politics and Administration'.

Aftab Ahmad Khan has had a distinguished career as a civil servant and has held numerous important appointments both in Pakistan and abroad from 1958 to 1989. These have included being Secretary to the Government of Pakistan for Finance, Economic Affairs, Defence and Establishment, and Chairman of the Pakistan Banking and Finance Service Commission. He has also acted as Governor of the Islamic Development Bank and alternate Governor of the Asian Development Bank and World Bank. He has led Pakistan's delegations to many international meetings and conferences on economic, development and social issues.

He read Economics at Punjab University, Lahore, and holds a Masters degree in Public Administration from Harvard.

He is now an economics consultant and writes regularly on national and international economic problems.

Rafi Raza was born in 1936, read Jurisprudence at Brasenore College, Oxford (1954-57), and was called to the Bar (Inner Temple) in 1958. He has practised as a corporate and constitutional lawyer, and has been a legal consultant to international organizations.

He was associated with Zulfikar Ali Bhutto in forming the Pakistan People's Party in December 1967, and was its constitutional law expert. In December 1971 he became Special Assistant to President Bhutto and played a key role in all major political and diplomatic developments, particularly the framing of the 1973 Constitution. He was a Senator (1973-77) and Federal Minister for Production and Industries from 1974 till March 1977. In 1990, he was Minister for Production in a caretaker Cabinet.

He is the author of *Zulfikar Ali Bhutto and Pakistan: 1967-1977,* Oxford University Press, Karachi, 1997.

I. A. Rehman is the Director of the Human Rights Commission of Pakistan. He has been Chief Editor of *The Pakistan Times,* Lahore-Islamabad, and is a prominent journalist and columnist. His notable publications include 'Jinnah as a Parliamentarian', 1977, 'Arts and Crafts of Pakistan', 1983, and 'Pakistan under Siege', 1990.

He serves in an honorary capacity in several fields apart from human rights, including the National Commission on History and Culture, the Pakistan Environmental Protection Council, and Pakistan National Council of the Arts.

Dr Nafis Sadik is the Executive Director of the United Nations Population Fund and holds the rank of Under-Secretary-General. As Secretary-General of the International Conference on Population and Development in September 1994, she was instrumental in focusing world attention on the urgent need to address collectively the critical challenges ahead and interrelationships between population and development.

Dr Sadik holds a Doctor of Medicine degree from Dow Medical College in Karachi. She is the recipient of many prestigious awards for her contributions to advancing the cause of women and to addressing the complex issues related to population growth, its distribution and migration. She is currently President of the Society for International Development and is the recipient of many honorary degrees. She has written numerous articles for leading publications in the family planning, health and development fields.

Abdul Sattar has been a career diplomat in the Foreign Service of Pakistan and has held important ambassadorial posts, notably in India and the Soviet Union. He has been Foreign Secretary and served as Foreign Minister in a caretaker Cabinet in 1993.

He was educated at Punjab University, Lahore, and at the Fletcher School of Law and Diplomacy in Massachusetts. He has received a MA degree in Geography and in International Law and Diplomacy.

He has contributed regular columns on foreign affairs and is the author of several articles in important publications, including 'Nuclear Issues in South Asia', 'The Simla Agreement—Negotiations under Duress' and 'Afghanistan—From Jihad to Civil War'.

INTRODUCTION
The Genesis of Pakistan
Rafi Raza

Pakistán came into existence on 14 August 1947—the first State in recent history created on the basis of religion. The founding fathers, fearing Hindu domination, had emphasized the separateness of the Muslims from the Hindus of the subcontinent of India—'Two Nations'—mainly in social and cultural terms. The later stress on Islamic ideology and the assertion that it alone could bind together in nationhood a geographically and ethnically divided Pakistan was undermined by dismemberment and the emergence of an independent Bangladesh in 1971.

To comprehend the motivation for the creation of Pakistan, it is necessary to examine the events leading up to its establishment and the aspirations of the Muslims which it reflected. The following brief outline serves three purposes: to provide a background for those not familiar with the genesis of Pakistan, to indicate some of the main developments which have, historically, helped shape Muslim consciousness, and to touch upon the present situation.

The early Muslims in India were conquerors, traders, settlers and converts. The first invasion was of Sindh in 711 by Muhammad Bin Qasim who, after defeating Raja Dahir, captured Multan in 713. The Ghaznavids came from the north-west in 1001, subjugating Multan by 1010; they were followed by the invasion of the Ghors in 1175, again aimed at Multan.

Muslim permanence was eventually established in the thirteenth century by several dynasties of the Sultanate that ruled Delhi. In this period, when India embraced many religions and cultures, of which the principal was Hindu, the Sufis played an important part in spreading Islam through their identification of God with the Universe, a concept which helped accommodate the views of others. The Sultanate of Delhi was succeeded by the Moghul Empire after the invasion of Babar in 1526, and its expansion brought the Muslims into undisputed leadership, particularly in northern India.

The third Moghul Emperor, Akbar, who ruled from 1556 to 1605, adopted an eclectic approach to provide a single framework for his subjects of different faiths and common ground for all religions. The failure of his short-lived policy led to a puritanical reaction, especially under his great-grandson, Aurangzeb, and the movement for orthodox Islam. A rapid decline in Muslim power followed the death of Aurangzeb in 1707; the Empire had suffered as a result of his long and expensive campaigns against the Marathas and in the Deccan, while his Hindu subjects had been alienated by his intolerance. Even in Bengal, effective Muslim rule was curtailed in 1757. The prevailing disorder and absence of proper central government provided the British East India Company with a ready opportunity to expand and gain control. The failed uprising of 1857 against the British resulted in the final eclipse of the Moghul Empire, and direct British rule in India.

British suspicion of the Muslims, particularly after 1857, was accompanied by increased patronage of the Hindus. The Muslims' sense of exclusion led them to reappraise their role in the subcontinent. From this emerged a Muslim renaissance, whose leading figures included Sir Syed Ahmed Khan. A new political awareness began to grow, and, as a consequence, the Muslim League was established in Dhaka in 1906. Its aims were, *inter alia*, 'To protect and advance the political rights and interests of the Mussalmans of India, and to respectfully represent their needs and aspirations to the Government.' The same year Mohammad Ali Jinnah joined the Indian National Congress, which had been formed earlier in 1885. He formally enrolled as a member of the Muslim League in 1913.

The main concern of the Muslim League was how to achieve effective political representation when the Hindus outnumbered the Muslims by three to one. The demand for separate electorates for the Muslims was a natural outcome. This was secured under the Indian Councils Act of 1909 through the Minto-Morley Reforms proposed by Lord Minto, the Viceroy of India, and Lord Morley, the Secretary of State for India. However, the Muslims soon received a reversal when, in 1912, the partition of Bengal by Lord Curzon in 1906 was set aside. Under this partition, which had been made merely as an administrative convenience, the Muslims had in fact gained; they formed the majority in the newly constituted province of Eastern Bengal and Assam, the latter having been separated from Bengal in 1874.

The outbreak of the First World War gave a new impetus to Indian political aspirations, and soon both Hindus and Muslims participated in the formation of the All-India Home Rule League in August 1916. Later that year, in November, cooperation between the two communities reached a new high in Lucknow where sessions of both the Muslim League and Congress were held. Under the Lucknow Pact, the Muslim League undertook to work with the Hindus to achieve freedom, while Congress accepted the demand for separate electorates and allowed the Muslims weightage in excess of their numbers. This created confidence among the numerically smaller Muslim community, and Mohammad Ali Jinnah was hailed as the 'Ambassador of Hindu-Muslim unity'. The following year he became President of the Bombay branch of the Home Rule League. Another important unifying factor at the time was the Khilafat Movement, a Muslim cause which Congress fully supported. Jinnah's subsequent disillusionment with Congress led him to leave the Home Rule League at the end of 1920, and subsequently Congress, because, as he correctly predicted, Mahatma Gandhi's efforts 'to generate coercive power in the masses would only promote mass conflict between the two communities'.[1]

Meanwhile, in response to growing political agitation, on 20 August 1917 the Secretary of State for India announced Britain's new policy 'to provide for the increasing association of Indians in every branch of Indian administration, and for the gradual development of self-governing institutions, with a view to the progressive realization of responsible government in British India as an integral part of the British Empire'. The 'Constitution' that emerged in the form of the Government of India Act, 1919, proved insufficient and did not stem the tide of Indian demands. These came to a climax in 1929 in the call of Congress for independence.

Earlier, in 1927, the British Government had appointed a Commission consisting of British Members of Parliament, led by Sir John Simon, to report on the functioning of the 1919 Act. The Commission included no Indians. In protest, an All-Party Conference was convened which in turn appointed a committee under Motilal Nehru (Jawaharlal's father) to examine various constitutional issues. The Nehru Report, published in August 1928, proved a major turning point for Muslims because it rejected the Muslim League proposals, which had earlier been agreed. Jinnah pleaded in vain for separate electorates to avoid 'civil war'. For him, this became 'the parting of the ways'.[2]

The Report of the Simon Commission was published in 1930. Three Round Table Conferences were convened in England between 12 November 1930 and 17 November 1932 to consider proposals for a new Indian Constitution. Congress refused to be represented at the first, and Jinnah was not invited to the third. In fact, in September 1931, he decided to settle in London to pursue his law practice before the Privy Council, returning to India in October 1935 to become President of the Muslim League. By then the British Parliament had passed the Government of India Act, 1935; two of its main features were the introduction of a federal system and a considerable degree of autonomy for the provinces.

The next major development took place after the 1937 elections to the Provincial Assemblies held under the 1935 'Constitution'. The Muslim League remained ill-organized despite Jinnah's recent return. It had only initiated a programme for mass contact from April 1936, and this weakness was reflected in its poor results, securing less than a quarter of the 485 seats reserved for Muslims, of which Congress contested

58 and won 26. Congress, which was in a minority only in Bengal, the Punjab and Sindh, formed ministries in eight provinces, where it decided against coalitions. Instead of minimizing the differences between the two major communities, and providing a propitious beginning to the process of self-rule in India, it only thereby exacerbated the divide. The rift was highlighted by Jawaharlal Nehru's remark in March 1937 that 'There are only two forces in India today, British imperialism, and Indian nationalism as represented by the Congress'; to which Jinnah retorted, 'No, there is a third party, the Mussalmans'.[3]

After its ministries took office in July 1937, the uncompromising attitude of Congress confirmed among Muslims the fear of Hindu domination, and they turned increasingly to the Muslim League. Even earlier, similar concerns had been expressed, most notably by Allama Muhammad Iqbal in his Presidential Address to the All-India Muslim League annual session at Allahabad on 29 December 1930. He referred to Islamic polity as 'a social structure regulated by a legal system and animated by a specific ethical ideal', which had been 'the chief formative factor in the life history of the Muslims of India'. He visualized what eventually became Pakistan:

> I would like to see the *Punjab, the North-West Frontier Province, Sindh and Balochistan amalgamated into a single State* (emphasis added)...in the best interests of India and Islam. For India it means security and peace resulting from an internal balance of power; for Islam, an opportunity...to mobilize its laws, its education, its culture, and to bring them into closer contact with its own original spirit and with the spirit of modern times.[4]

Iqbal was the poet-philosopher of Pakistan, a name that was coined by Chaudhri Rehmat Ali in England in January 1933. It meant 'Land of the pure'. The letter 'P' stood for the Punjab, 'A' was for the Afghan Frontier, or the North-West Frontier Province, 'K' represented Kashmir, while 'S' symbolized Sindh and 'Tan' Balochistan. Bengal was included by neither Iqbal nor Rehmat Ali.

The post-election period witnessed communal riots and serious efforts to reorganize and reorientate the Muslim League. With the outbreak of the Second World War, there was a swift and dramatic change in the Indian political scene. As a condition for cooperation in the war effort, Congress demanded immediate independence from a beleaguered Britain. Jinnah pressed for the right of self-determination for Muslims, and hailed as deliverance the resignation of the Congress ministries in November 1939. His principled leadership played a major part in making the Muslim League a dominant force in Indian politics, particularly from 1937.

The next landmark was the Twenty-seventh Session of the All-India Muslim League at Lahore in 1940. In his Presidential Address, Jinnah elaborated on the real nature of Islam and Hinduism:

> They are not religions in the strict sense of the word, but are, in fact, different and distinct social orders... The Hindus and the Muslims belong to two different social philosophies, social customs, and literature...and indeed they belong to two different civilizations, which are based mainly on conflicting ideas and conceptions...and derive their inspiration from different sources of history... To yoke together two such nations as a single State, one as a numerical minority and the other as a majority, must lead to growing discontent and the final destruction of any fabric that may be so built up for the Government of such a State.[5]

While refering to the Muslims of India as 'a nation by any definition', he cited the Balkan Penninsula and Czechoslovakia as other examples of States incorporating different religions and ethnic groups.

On 23 March 1940, the second day of the session, a resolution was moved which later came to be known as the 'Lahore Resolution' and the 'Pakistan Resolution', although the term Pakistan itself was not mentioned. It affirmed that no constitutional plan for India would be either acceptable or workable unless 'Geographically contiguous units are demarcated into regions...[so] that the areas in which the Muslims are numerically in a majority, as in the North-Western and Eastern zones of India, should be grouped to constitute Independent States.'[6] Islam itself found no mention, but reference was made to the protection of 'religious, cultural, economic, political, administrative and other rights and interests' of all 'minorities in these units'.

The British Government tried to ensure peace in the subcontinent by sending a mission led by Sir Stafford Cripps, which offered Dominion Status and India's right to secede after the war. This was rejected by Gandhi as a 'post-dated cheque on a tottering bank'. When attempts to find a solution finally failed, Congress passed the 'Quit India' resolution on 8 August 1942. Instead of the planned mass movement of non-cooperation and non-violence, death and destruction resulted from the arrest of Congress leaders the following day. Jinnah insisted on non-violent and constitutional procedures, and seized this opportunity to consolidate the League's position.

Further significant developments followed Lord Wavell's installation as Viceroy on 20 October 1943. After nearly two years of frustrating discussions with the British Government, he was finally permitted to announce on 14 June 1945 that he would invite Indian leaders to discuss the establishment of a new Executive Council which, apart from the Viceroy and the Commander-in-Chief, would be entirely Indian, and have equal representation of Muslims and caste Hindus, as distinguished from Scheduled Caste Hindus. The Council would work under the 1935 Act, but would consider framing a new constitution for India. As a consequence, the Simla Conference commenced on 25 June 1945, but it eventually failed because of Jinnah's insistence that only the League could nominate Muslims to the Council. Wavell, however, persisted in his efforts, which were aided by the election in the United Kingdom of a Labour Government favourable to India's independence.

On 21 August 1945, Wavell announced that elections would be held by the end of the year, and, four weeks later, that Britain would allow full self-government in India. The elections to the

Central Legislative Assembly foreshadowed the division to come: the goal of Congress was to maintain the unity of India and it won 91.3 per cent of the votes in non-Muslim constituencies; the aim of the League was to achieve the exclusive right to represent the Muslims, and thus create Pakistan, and it secured 86.6 per cent of the votes cast for the Muslim seats.[7] Unlike in 1937, Jinnah and the League were now undisputed leaders of the Muslims in India. They were in a strong position to press their demands before the British Cabinet Mission, and proposed at the League Legislators' Convention in Delhi in April 1946 that the only formula to 'maintain internal peace and tranquility' required

> That the zones comprising Bengal and Assam in the North-East and the Punjab, North-West Frontier Province, Sindh and Balochistan in the North-West of India...be constituted into a sovereign independent State and that an unequivocal undertaking be given to implement the establishment of Pakistan without delay.

It is noteworthy that in the Delhi Resolution the emphasis was also on Muslims as 'adherents of a faith which regulates every department of their lives (educational, social, economic and political) whose code is not confined merely to spiritual doctrines and tenets or rituals and ceremonies, and which stands in sharp contrast to the exclusive nature of Hindu Dharma Philosophy...'[8]

This was the first specific demand for the State of Pakistan and for separate constitution-making bodies, one each for 'the people of Pakistan and Hindustan for the purpose of framing their respective constitutions'. It was made just prior to the arrival in India of the British Cabinet Mission, comprising Lord Pethwick-Lawrence, Sir Stafford Cripps and A.V. Alexander, to find agreed principles for a new constitution on India attaining independence. The Cabinet Mission and Wavell met the Congress and League leaders on 5 and 6 May, and, ten days later, announced a plan proposing a federation consisting of

(1) north-west regions with significant Muslim majorities, (2) Bengal and Assam, and (3) the remaining provinces with Hindu majorities. The Constituent Assembly was to be elected on a communal basis by the Provincial Legislative Assemblies and the representatives of the Princely States which joined the federation. Each province could opt out of this arrangement after the first elections. The Muslim League accepted but Congress refused to accept parity of representation either in the Council or the Legislature, claiming that this was against the principles of democracy. Jawaharlal Nehru also asserted that Congress would have the right to modify the plan after independence. As a result, Jinnah withdrew his acceptance. With the failure of the Cabinet Mission, Jinnah for the first time departed from legal methods and called for 'Direct Action'. Massive communal riots followed from 16 August 1946 in Bengal and other areas, which confirmed the view that the two major communities of India could not live together.

Prime Minister Clement Attlee sent Lord Mountbatten as Viceroy in March 1947 with a view to expediting independence. On 3 June 1947, Mountbatten announced his plan for the partition of the subcontinent; this conceded Pakistan but excluded from it East Punjab and West Bengal. In those areas where the will of the people had to be ascertained, as in the NWFP and the district of Sylhet, referenda were held. Mountbatten appointed Boundary Commissions to demarcate the division in Bengal and the Punjab. One result of this was the unfair, if not unscrupulous, provision of a corridor for India to Jammu and Kashmir; the problem of that State has since bedevilled relations between India and Pakistan. Both Congress and the Muslim League accepted the Partition Plan, though neither was satisfied with it.

Pakistan came into existence without receiving its fair share of assets as one of the two successor States that emerged from British India. Unlike India, it lacked a ready-made national government. It also had to cope with a far larger influx of refugees amidst communal rioting and killing that resulted in the death of hundreds of thousands of Muslims. Despite all the difficulties, there was no doubt in the minds of Pakistanis at the time that the country was there to stay, a beacon for Muslims throughout the world. Everyone was full of confidence and enthusiasm. It was India that asserted that such a country could not survive; indeed, some analysts attributed India's acceptance of Partition to its belief that Pakistan would not last. Within twenty-five years the country was dismembered, the result of both our own mistakes, and India's intervention followed by its invasion in 1971. This gave rise to renewed concerns about the future survival of the remaining half of the country, though these were at the time soon dispelled.

Pakistan is now a country of about 140 million people, comprising four Provinces and the Federally Administered Tribal Areas. The Punjab has more than half the total population, with its capital, Lahore, consisting of 6 million. It is followed, numerically, by the Province of Sindh, its capital being Karachi with over 10 million people, then by the North-West Frontier Province and Balochistan, with their capitals of Peshawar and Quetta respectively. The country's strategic importance is underlined by its situation at the head of the Arabian Sea, flanking the entrance to the Persian Gulf region with its oil riches, and commanding the sea-lanes between Europe and the Indian Ocean. It is at the crossroads of the Muslim World which ranges from north-west Africa on the Atlantic to Indonesia on the Pacific rim, and can emerge as a gateway to the newly-established Central Asian Republics. It has a border to the north with China and Afghanistan consisting of some 370 miles, with Iran to the west and India to the east.

Apart from its geopolitical significance, the country is potentially rich in agriculture and natural resources, with an enterprising people capable of sacrifice and hard work. Yet today there are many, both inside and outside the country, who wonder despairingly whether Pakistan is a 'failed State' and can continue to survive. However, the following chapters, outlining some important aspects of the first fifty years, show Pakistan remains a viable State. They provide a framework for reappraisal, pointing out the pitfalls of the past and the way ahead for a more prosperous people. Clearly, success depends on the ability of Pakistanis to recapture the enthusiasm of the founding fathers in pursuing the goals of a democratic and modern Muslim State, implementing the call of Quaid-i-Azam Mohammad Ali Jinnah for 'Faith, Unity and Discipline'.

NOTES

1. K.M. Munshi, *Pilgrimage to Freedom,* Bharatiya, Vidya Bhavan, Bombay, 1967, p. 18.
2. Henry Hector Bolitho, *Jinnah, Creator of Pakistan*, Murray, London, 1954, pp. 94-95.
3. Michael Brecher, *Nehru, A Political Biography*, Oxford University Press, London, 1959, p. 231.
4. Syed Sharifuddin Pirzada, ed., *Foundations of Pakistan—All India Muslim League Documents: 1906-47,* National Publishing House Limited, Karachi, 1970, Vol. II, pp. 159-60, with the previous quotations at p. 154.
5. Ibid., pp. 337-38.
6. Ibid., p. 341.
7. V.P. Menon, *The Transfer of Power in India*, Orient-Longmans, Calcutta, 1957, quotes these figures at p. 228.
8. Syed Sharifuddin Pirzada, ed., op. cit., pp. 512-13.

CHAPTER 1

CONSTITUTIONAL DEVELOPMENTS AND POLITICAL CONSEQUENCES

Rafi Raza

The constitutional history of Pakistan reflects the tortuous and chequered course of the country since Independence in 1947. The dominant and overriding role of constitution-making, and its intertwinement with political developments, becomes apparent in any analysis of this fifty-year period.

The nation has had three 'permanent' Constitutions, introduced in 1956, 1962 and 1973, the first two of which were abrogated, and the third suspended, and later significantly amended, under Martial Law. There have been two formal 'interim' Constitutions, in 1947 and 1972, and for long periods the country has been governed by 'constitutional' arrangements under Martial Law. Failure to achieve a constitutional *modus vivendi* in 1971 between East Pakistan and the provinces of the West Wing, which now comprise Pakistan, resulted in a bitter civil war, the dismemberment of the country and the creation of Bangladesh. The efforts of several leaders to constitutionalize their personal positions and their immediate requirements of power contributed to exacerbating this sad state of affairs. Even during the periods of constitutional governance, no norms were followed. Up to 1958, there were numerous changes of government without elections or a vote of no confidence. Throughout, several governments have been removed, dismissed or suspended, both at the federal and provincial levels, and the National and Provincial Assemblies dissolved, by executive fiat.

All manner of experiments have been either made or contemplated in dealing with important constitutional issues in Pakistan. These complex questions included such concerns as the federal structure and the quantum of provincial autonomy; the role of religion in the State and whether the minority religious communities should have electorates and candidates separate from the Muslim majority; the issue of direct or indirect elections and the related subject of universal or limited franchise; the question of a presidential or parliamentary form of government and the division of power between the executive and the legislature; fundamental rights and the right to property in the context of 'Islamic socialism'; the role and independence of the judiciary; national language; and, most important, Martial Law.

It would require a longer and more detailed treatise to cover all these subjects adequately. Here, the intention is to concentrate on certain basic issues which affected the main body politic of the nation. Accordingly, it is proposed to provide an overview of Pakistan's constitutional history in order to set the problems in proper perspective; to focus on three main aspects of the 1973 Constitution, namely, the federal structure, Islam and the State, and the executive authority; and to outline the constitutional amendments under the last Martial Law, the decisions of the Supreme Court, and subsequent developments. This analysis will also describe the failure of the two Wings of Pakistan to reach a satisfactory equilibrium in 1971, and how the country has suffered as a consequence of recurrent attempts to pursue or consolidate personal and political power.

Pakistan's Constitutional History

From 1947 to Martial Law in 1958

Under the Indian Independence Act of 1947, Pakistan inherited a quasi-federal parliamentary system. Section 8 laid down that, until a constitution was framed, the interim arrangement for the country would be as set out in the Government of India Act, 1935. The 1935 Act was based on the Report of the Simon Commission, 1930. It consisted of 14 parts and 321 sections, with 10 schedules, the longest-ever legislation passed by the British Parliament. Pakistan has since been governed by a series of similarly detailed basic laws, none of which has been given proper effect. The most important feature of the Simon Commission Report was the proposal for a federal system, for which the following reasons were given:

> We recognize that a change from a unitary to a federal system is unusual... The answer is to be found in the peculiar features of the Indian problem.
> India is gradually moving from autocracy to democracy...[and] the practical difficulties of applying the principles of western democracy to so large a unit as British India were insuperable...
> A further reason is that it is only in a federal structure that sufficient elasticity can be obtained for the union of elements of diverse internal constitution and of communities at very different stages of development and culture... The authors of the Montagu-Chelmsford Report stated that the process on which they were engaged was not that of federalizing India, but the antecedent one of breaking up the old structure before building the new... We desire to complete this preliminary process and at the same time lay down the broad lines of the future federation.[1]

Following Independence, the first Constituent Assembly of Pakistan consisted of indirectly elected or nominated members—44 from East Bengal, 22 from the Punjab, while Sindh had 5, the North-West Frontier Province 3, and Balochistan 1, with the remaining 4 from the Princely States and other areas. The representatives of the first four provinces were elected by their Provincial Assemblies which had been formed in 1946. The East Wing accommodated non-Bengali leaders of the Pakistan Movement among their number.

During the early period, the new country faced innumerable problems of governance, coping with a vast influx of refugees from India, and the question of survival itself. It was thus understandable that the task of constitution-making was not its first concern. Moreover, the Founder of the Nation, Quaid-i-Azam Mohammad Ali Jinnah, an outstanding statesman and lawyer, died on 11 September 1948. It was indeed not until March 1956 that the first Constitution was adopted. No constitution meant no national elections, and this was to prove disastrous for the new State. Such delay had little excuse. Even though the Assembly was slowed down in its deliberations by its dual function as a legislating and constitution-making body, it met as a constituent body for only 57 days in 6 years.

The main contribution of this Assembly was to pass the Objectives Resolution on 7 March 1949, which set out the framework for the future constitution. In this it made specific mention of Islam. Earlier, when the All-India Muslim League meeting in Lahore in 1940 first formulated the idea of a separate homeland for the Muslims of the subcontinent, the resolution of 23 March had contained no such reference. The 1949 Objectives Resolution provided, *inter alia*:

> Whereas sovereignty over the entire Universe belongs to God Almighty alone and the authority which He has delegated to the State of Pakistan through its people for being exercised within the limits prescribed by Him is a sacred trust;...
>
> Wherein the principles of democracy, freedom, equality, tolerance and social justice, as enunciated by Islam, shall be fully observed;
>
> Wherein the Muslims shall be enabled to order their lives in the individual and collective spheres in accord with the teachings and requirements of Islam as set out in the Holy Quran and the Sunnah (Traditions of the Holy Prophet (PBUH))...[2]

Shortly thereafter, on 12 March 1949, the Assembly appointed a Basic Principles Committee (BPC), which, in turn, formed three main sub-committees for subjects considered important, (1) the federal and provincial constitutions and the distribution of power, (2) franchise and (3) the judiciary. By 7 September 1950, when the BPC presented its interim report, only the first of these sub-committees had submitted its recommendations on the federal structure.

A federal arrangement is difficult to evolve and operate even in the most favourable circumstances. As Felix Frankfurter put it, 'Of all the laws ordering the political life of a nation the federal system is the most complicated and subtle. It demands most flexible and imaginative adjustment for harmonizing national and local interest.'[3] In the case of a geographically divided Pakistan—with the majority of the population in the smaller East Wing, while the West Wing possessed the military-bureaucratic base of the Punjab—the task of evolving a suitable federal structure proved beyond the imagination of the politicians and constitution-makers. The BPC's interim report and the attempts that followed can best be described as a 'numbers game' to balance the two Wings, mainly through a process of 'parity'.[4] In this, the Punjab and East Bengal were the chief protagonists.

The interim report of the BPC recommended in clause 30 that 'there should be a Central Legislature consisting of two Houses: (1) the House of Units representing the Legislatures of the Units, (2) the House of People elected by the people', though their composition was not fixed. The representatives of the Punjab had proposed that both Houses should be about the same size, particularly as the two were to have equal powers in terms of clause 39. These proposals were deferred till the BPC sub-committee on franchise agreed in late 1951 that 'there should be parity as a whole between the two Wings of Pakistan'. Subsequently, in August 1952, the BPC itself proposed a different scheme for the two Houses, which would have been to the disadvantage of the Punjab; its representation was to be in percentage terms, but neither in the context of Pakistan nor of the West Wing. Instead, based on East Bengal's reduced position under the parity proposal, the Punjab with a population of about 22 million as against East Bengal's 50 million, was to have 90 seats compared to East Bengal's 200 in a House of People consisting of 400 members; and 27 seats in the House of Units, whereas East Bengal would have 60. It meant that the other

West Wing provinces combined, although numerically less than the Punjab, would have a proportionately larger representation of 110 and 33 respectively in the two Houses. East Bengal tried to gain the support of the smaller West Wing provinces for this formula, contained in clauses 38 and 43 of the BPC's final report, but no agreement could be reached because of growing opposition from the Punjab, which soon surfaced in other forms.

Within months, on 17 April 1953, Governor-General Ghulam Mohammed, in exercise of his 'inherent' powers, summarily dismissed Prime Minister Khwaja Nazimuddin, a prominent Bengali politician. His replacement, Mohammad Ali Bogra, another Bengali, was recalled from the United States, where he was Pakistan's Ambassador.

Prime Minister Mohammad Ali Bogra presented a fresh formula to the Constituent Assembly: parity in the combined chambers, with 175 members from each Wing. Both chambers were to have equal powers, at least 30 per cent of the members from each Wing were required to concur in votes of no confidence against the Prime Minister, and in certain other important measures, and the Governor-General and Prime Minister would have to belong to opposite Wings. The last of these proposals was subsequently dropped. The debate continued into 1954, mainly between East Bengal and the Punjab. The latter feared East Bengal would dominate the centre, and suggested that the powers of the Federal Government should be confined to foreign affairs, defence, communications between the two Wings, foreign trade, currency and foreign exchange. The Punjab also promoted the idea that the West Wing provinces should be amalgamated into a single unit or a 'zonal sub-federation'. However, the Bengali representatives continued to favour the earlier constitutional proposals.

On 21 September 1954, the Assembly approved the report of the BPC with minor amendments, and adjourned till 27 October for the Constitution Bill to be prepared for final debate. Three days before it was to convene, encouraged by his earlier successful constitutional *coup* in dismissing Prime Minister Nazimuddin, the Governor-General again exercised his 'inherent' powers: he dissolved the Constituent Assembly as it could 'no longer function', and declared a State of Emergency. In these circumstances, the Prime Minister announced the following month that the Government had decided to merge the West Wing provinces and the ten Princely States of the area into a unified Province of West Pakistan, and 'One Unit', as it was commonly termed, formally came into existence. The country now consisted of two provinces, West Pakistan with a population of 40 million and East Pakistan (formerly East Bengal) with 50 million. At the time, this suited the two main protagonists. The West Wing viewed One Unit as an administrative convenience; it would save expenditure and permit concentration on development, while allowing the Punjab to remain in a dominant position. East Pakistan believed that this would contribute to a rational basis for the further devolution of power. Although it made the task of framing a constitution for a divided country easier, the unique nature of the two-unit federation sowed the seeds of separation.

In the meantime, the dissolution of the Constituent Assembly by the Governor-General resulted in the first major politico-constitutional battle before the Federal Court in the Tamizuddin Khan Case.[5] The Speaker of the Assembly challenged the validity of the dissolution of the Assembly; and the Sindh High Court held in his favour on the ground that the power of dissolution had to be dependent on a specific provision in the Constitution or statute, and was not inherent. In appeal, Chief Justice Muhammad Munir overruled, on a technicality, the decision of the High Court to issue a writ: the amendment under Section 223A of the Government of India Act, 1935, conferring the power to issue writs, was invalid as it had not received the formal assent of the Governor-General. However, the question of the dissolution of the Assembly itself was left open.

On 17 April 1955, the Governor-General referred the matter to the Federal Court, seeking its advisory opinion on various questions of law; and two days later, at the suggestion of the Court, the question was added 'as to whether the Constituent

Assembly was rightly dissolved'. On 16 May, the Federal Court advised that the Assembly had been properly dissolved:

> ...it cannot reasonably be contended that the intention of the Indian Independence Act was to foist a perpetual legislature on this country, and if that was not the intention but the Constituent Assembly did become in fact a perpetual legislature, the purpose of the Act could only be served by ordering its dissolution.[6]

In fact, following the 1954 provincial elections in East Bengal, when the ruling Muslim League party was overwhelmingly defeated, the Constituent Assembly had indeed become unrepresentative, particularly in its reflection of political power and opinion in the East Wing. Moreover, the Assembly had already taken an inordinately long time over constitution-making. Had the Federal Court limited itself to these facts and grounds, the matter might have rested there. But it also underlined the importance of the 'Doctrine of Necessity', which has since plagued the country:

> The point that arises...is whether in an emergency of the character described in the Reference there is any law by which the Head of State may, when the legislature is not in existence, temporarily assume to himself powers with a view to preventing the State and society from dissolution... This branch of the law is...the law of civil or State necessity.
> ... *Id quod alias non est licitum, necessitas licitum facit* (that which otherwise is not lawful, necessity makes lawful) and maxims *salus populi suprema lex* (safety of the people is the supreme law) and *salus republicae est suprema lex* (safety of the State is the supreme law)...[are to be] treated as part of the law. The best statement of the reason underlying the law of necessity is to be found in Cromwell's famous utterance: 'If nothing should be done but what is according to law, the throat of the nation might be cut while we send for someone to make a law'.[7]

In the Court's opinion, the 'new Assembly, constituted under the Constitution Convention Order, 1955, as amended to date, would be competent to exercise all the powers conferred by the Indian Independence Act, 1947, on the Constituent Assembly'.[8]

The second Constituent Assembly, again elected indirectly through the Provincial Assemblies, saw a new draft constitution presented on 9 January 1956, which was hurriedly passed, and came into effect on 23 March. In all, the first Constitution had taken over eight years to finalize, the longest ever in any country, although it was based essentially on the existing arrangements and the 1950 Indian Constitution.

The short-lived 1956 Constitution continued the Westminster-style, but single chamber, legislature. The National Assembly was to consist of 300 directly elected members, and an additional 10 seats were reserved for women to be indirectly elected, allowing East and West Pakistan equal representation. On one important issue, however, the question of whether the electorate should be joint or separate, opinion remained sharply divided. The Constitution left the subject to be settled by the National Assembly through legislation, after ascertaining the views of the two Provincial Assemblies. East Pakistan favoured joint electorates; the Hindus were a substantial minority in that province, but did not seek separate electorates. The Bengali Prime Minister, Huseyn Shaheed Suhrawardy, maintained that imposing separate electorates might contribute to developing fissiparous tendencies instead of welding one Pakistani nation. West Pakistan, which had a small number of non-Muslims, insisted otherwise. As a result, the National Assembly adopted both views in October 1956 by providing for joint electorates in East Pakistan and separate ones in the West Wing. Eventually, in April 1957, joint electorates were reintroduced throughout Pakistan because the task of delimiting separate constituencies proved too complex. Generally, the 1956 Constitution had little effect, and changes in government continued as before without elections or votes of no confidence.

The period prior to the 1956 Constitution, and thereafter, also witnessed the decline of the Muslim League as a political force. The early death of the Quaid-i-Azam, the assassination of Liaquat Ali Khan, the removal of Khwaja Nazimuddin as Prime

Minister, the collapse of the League in the East Pakistan elections of 1954, combined with the jockeying for personal position and power, were important factors in this loss of strength. By the time the League tried to revive its popular appeal in 1958, it was too late.

General elections were scheduled for February 1959 but, instead, on 7 October 1958, Martial Law was declared and the 1956 Constitution was abrogated. During the seven-year period following the assassination of the first Prime Minister on 16 October 1951 till Martial Law, the country had six Prime Ministers and three Governors-General. This political instability, mainly engineered, was one reason for Martial Law; the other was the ambition of General Muhammad Ayub Khan, the Army Commander-in-Chief.

Ayub Khan: 1958 to 1969

Ayub Khan took over as Chief Martial Law Administrator (CMLA) on 7 October 1958 and then, twenty days later, assumed the office of President. The military *coup* was validated by the Supreme Court in the Dosso Case:

> Thus a victorious revolution or a successful *coup d'etat* is an internationally recognized legal method of changing a Constitution.
>
> After a change of the character I have mentioned has taken place, the national legal order must for its validity depend upon the new law-making organ. Even Courts lose their existing jurisdictions, and can function only to the extent and in the manner determined by the new Constitution.[9]

Once again an extra-constitutional measure was justified on the basis of necessity. If it had been essential to adopt the doctrine of necessity, it would have been preferable to follow the 'principle of condonation and not legitimization' of illegal acts, as was done in a subsequent case.[10]

As CMLA, Ayub Khan initially ran the country almost as if it were a unitary state, with Martial Law holding total sway. Important constitutional issues of provincial autonomy, representation in the federal legislature, and those related to Islam, were relegated to the background. He proceeded to embark on his 'Basic Democracy' programme, a four-tiered arrangement with 80,000 primary units, half from each Wing, to elect their representatives at grass roots level. His next step was to legitimize and constitutionalize his rule through the decision of his nominated Cabinet to hold a referendum among these 80,000 members to secure a vote of confidence in the President, who would then formulate a new constitution and, ingeniously, if the majority were in the affirmative, 'he should also be deemed to have been elected President of Pakistan for the first term of office under the constitution to be so made'. On 14 February 1960, Ayub Khan received 75,283 affirmative votes.

He established a constitution commission to examine the 'progressive failure of parliamentary government in Pakistan' and to submit proposals for a democracy 'adaptable to changed circumstances and based on the Islamic principles of justice, equality and tolerance'. After a detailed inquiry, the commission submitted its report in May 1961, but Ayub Khan settled on an authoritarian form of presidential rule. His 1962 Constitution continued the two-unit arrangement for the National Assembly, with each Wing having 75 representatives to be elected by the same 80,000 Basic Democrats, who were also the electoral college for the President. He described it as a 'blending of democracy with discipline', but, in reality, it was constitutional autocracy as reinforced in the preamble of the Constitution: 'Now, therefore, I, Field Marshal Muhammad Ayub Khan, Hilal-i-Pakistan, Hilal-i-Jura'at, President of Pakistan, in exercise of the mandate given to me...do hereby enact this Constitution.'

The President's position under the 1962 Constitution was unassailable. The impeachment process for his removal under Article 13 required one-third of the total membership of the National Assembly to give notice in writing, setting out particulars of the charge; it then had to be passed by three-fourths of the total membership and, if it received less than half the votes, those who subscribed to the notice ceased to be members on the declaration of the result. He was also empowered, under Article 23, to dissolve the National Assembly at any time. The President's authority to declare an Emergency was unchallengeable. His veto power over legislation was extensive, allowing him to return a bill to the Assembly, and, even if it were then passed by a two-thirds majority, the President could still withhold assent and send the bill to the electoral college of Basic Democrats for a referendum under Article 27. Articles 41 and 42 further restricted the authority of the legislature to new and not recurring financial expenditures. Moreover, the legislature had no say over important appointments, unlike, for example, in the United States. In all respects, the powers of the President were both supreme and far-reaching.

This concentration of central power also impinged on provincial autonomy. Although the 1962 Constitution appeared to give greater autonomy to the provinces by introducing a single list of subjects for the federal legislature with residual authority vesting in the provincial legislatures, Article 131(2) ensured that this autonomy was minimal. It provided that, if the national interest required, in relation to '(a) the security of Pakistan, including the economic and financial stability of Pakistan, (b) planning or coordination, or (c) the achievement of uniformity in respect of any matter in different parts of Pakistan', the federal legislature would have the power to make laws not enumerated in that list. In addition, under Article 80, the executive authority in the provinces was vested in the Governor, who was appointed by and subject to the directions of the President under Article 66, and removable at will by him under Article 118. As a result, the country continued to be run almost as a unitary state.

Apart from legitimizing his constitutional position, Ayub Khan also endeavoured to gain political support. For this, he turned to the Muslim League, but only succeeded in capturing one faction which came to be known as the Convention Muslim

League. His limited success in this direction is evidenced by the fact that this group could not survive his ouster from power.

Inevitably, such excessive constitutional authority vesting in one person resulted in abuse and upheaval. It discredited the presidential system and confirmed the general view that a parliamentary form of government was appropriate for a geographically divided country. More significantly, East Pakistan suffered economic and political deprivation under the 1962 dispensation while the West Wing prospered. East Pakistani economists now promoted the 'two economies' theory, showing the separateness of the two Wings. This view gained ground following the Indo-Pakistan September 1965 War which resulted in the complete though temporary severance of communications between the two Wings. Formerly, it was claimed *vis-à-vis* India that the defence of Pakistan lay in the strength of West Pakistan, but during the 1965 War it became clear that only the threat from China averted the possibility of an Indian invasion of East Pakistan, which India in any case did not appear to seek at that time. West Pakistan could only defend itself.

In the turmoil following the 1965 War and the Tashkent Declaration which settled the terms of peace, the demand for provincial autonomy took the form of the 'Six Points' proposed by Sheikh Mujibur Rahman's party, the Awami League. This programme confined the federal authority to matters of defence and foreign affairs, the latter to be further limited by separate foreign trade and aid arrangements for the two Wings. Even for the two subjects assigned to the federal sphere, the federation would have had no taxing authority of its own and was to function through subventions from the provinces. It was a unique proposal for a federation, and, for all practical purposes, it was confederal in nature. In the East Wing, the programme was seen as a means of escaping continued economic and political domination by West Pakistan, where, in turn, it was viewed as a stepping stone to secession.

President Ayub Khan temporarily succeeded in capping the discontent in East Pakistan by arresting Mujibur Rahman and

other Bengalis, including some military personnel, in the 1967
Agartala Conspiracy Case.[11] However, Ayub's authority had
already declined in the presidential campaign of 1964, when
Fatima Jinnah, the Quaid-i-Azam's sister, led the Combined
Opposition Party against him. His position was further damaged
by the sudden acceptance of the cease-fire in the 1965 War,
which ran counter to the propaganda that had built up popular
expectations, followed by what was viewed as a 'surrender' to
India at the Tashkent Summit in January 1966. Then, in January
1968, he fell seriously ill, and never fully recovered.

Against this background, several major developments
converged by the end of 1968 to signal the end of the Ayub era.
The demand for provincial autonomy in East Pakistan,
spearheaded by the Awami League, gained momentum. In the
West Wing the emergence of the Pakistan People's Party (PPP)
under Zulfikar Ali Bhutto, who had been Ayub Khan's Minister
for eight years, provided another focus for popular unrest, with
its call for *Roti, Kapra aur Makaan* (Bread, Clothes and
Housing) catching the public's imagination. By this time, the
attitude of the army and the United States' administration
towards Ayub Khan had also changed. The army, hitherto his
power base, had lost confidence in his ability to secure the
lifting of the US arms embargo imposed in 1965. The United
States disapproved of the close relations he continued to develop
with China, and was equally upset by Ayub Khan serving notice
in April 1968 for the termination of the American
communications base at Badaber, near Peshawar, prior to the
visit of the Soviet Prime Minister, Alexei Kosygin. At the time,
the United States was unsuccessfully involved in the war in
Vietnam.

Ayub Khan recognized that the system he had imposed could
not continue, and on 17 February 1969 invited the opposition
parties to a Round Table Conference (RTC) to consider all
constitutional issues. They made their participation conditional
on certain demands, including the withdrawal of the Emergency,
which he lifted. However, conflicting demands increased,
particularly relating to the dissolution of One Unit, parity and

provincial autonomy. He further conceded, on 21 February, that he would not be a candidate in the forthcoming presidential elections. The RTC met on 10 March, but reached no conclusion after four days of deliberations. At the final session, Ayub Khan announced he would call on the National Assembly 'to make the necessary amendments to the existing constitution to convert it into a federal parliamentary system without disturbing the basis of parity and the existing distribution of powers between the centre and the provinces until such time as the directly elected representatives of the people had had an opportunity to decide these matters'.[12] At the same time, he appealed for 'collective resistance to the forces of agitation and disruption', but in vain. The RTC broke up in confusion. Z.A. Bhutto, who had been arrested in November 1968, had throughout refused to attend, and Mujibur Rahman quit the Democratic Action Committee (DAC), an eight-party opposition group which participated in the RTC.

President Ayub Khan could not accept the various demands of the unelected leaders who comprised the DAC, and, indeed, they should not have expected this from him. In the impasse, the initiative passed to the army. On 25 March, in disregard of his own Constitution which required him on resignation to hand over power to the Speaker of the Assembly, Ayub Khan wrote to General Yahya Khan, Commander-in-Chief of the Army: 'I am left with no option, but to step aside and leave it to the Defence Forces of Pakistan, which today represent the only effective and legal instrument, to take over full control of the affairs of the country'.

Yahya Khan: 1969 to 1971

Following in Ayub Khan's footsteps, Yahya Khan abrogated the 1962 Constitution and declared Martial Law. After consolidating his position, he announced, on 28 November 1969, the future constitutional arrangements under a federal parliamentary system. He promised general elections in October

1970 on the basis of one-man-one-vote, the dissolution of One Unit and maximum autonomy for the provinces consistent with the Federal Government's authority. This had far-reaching consequences. Four months later, he promulgated the Legal Framework Order (LFO) which set out the basis for the future constitution.

On the main issue of the division of powers between the centre and the provinces, the LFO provided for maximum provincial autonomy while requiring that the provinces 'shall be so united in a Federation that the independence, the territorial integrity and the national solidarity of Pakistan are ensured and that the unity of the Federation is not in any manner impaired'. It stressed that 'the Federal Government shall also have adequate powers, including legislative, administrative and financial powers, to discharge its responsibilities in relation to external and internal affairs and to preserve the independence and territorial integrity of the country'.[13] The LFO also set out such details as the contents of the preamble, Fundamental Principles of the Constitution, and Directive Principles of State Policy, but omitted a key element by failing to provide for voting procedures. As a result, in a federation where one province was numerically larger than the others combined, a one-sided arrangement could not be prevented. East Pakistan had 169 votes out of a total of 313,[14] whereas Balochistan had only 5. Despite the fact that, under Articles 25 and 27, the President was the final authority regarding the Legal Framework Order, the issue of autonomy ultimately negated the LFO and destroyed the country.

The year 1970 was spent in the electioneering process, and the polls were postponed from October to 7 December 1970 due to floods in East Pakistan. The general elections were the first ever held throughout the country since Independence on the basis of adult franchise and one-man-one-vote, and were the fairest in Pakistan's history. Although it was evident that Six Points could not be implemented within the framework of the LFO, the Awami League was allowed to propagate this programme unchallenged by the Government, and received massive public endorsement in East Pakistan. In the Punjab and Sindh, the PPP bandwagon rapidly gained momentum.

The election campaign for a constituent assembly to frame a constitution for the country presaged the ensuing division. Firstly, most political parties did not contest in both Wings: the Awami League concentrated on East Pakistan's autonomy demand, while the PPP and the Jamiat-ul-Ulema-e-Islam (JUI) had no candidates in the East Wing. Only the Jamaat-i-Islami (JI) and the Muslim League campaigned throughout the country, both unsuccessfully. Secondly, there was considerable contrast in the approach to India, with Bhutto chauvinistically losing no opportunity to attack India, while Mujibur Rahman remained conciliatory. Yet another unusual feature was that, unlike previous and subsequent elections, there were no electoral alliances in 1970. In the absence of earlier general elections based on adult franchise, there was no real measure of strength; attempts to establish alliances, even among the religious and rightist parties, failed because they were viewed as weakness or a cover for ulterior motives.

On 7 December 1970, nearly 57 million voters went to the polls, out of whom 29 million were in East Pakistan; there were 1,570 candidates from 25 political parties and a further 315 independents. The contest was for 290 National Assembly seats, as polls in some East Pakistan constituencies were postponed because of floods. The turnout was 57 per cent in East Pakistan, where the Awami League secured 75 per cent of the vote, winning 151 out of 153 seats, and a month later the remaining 9 postponed contests. The campaign was fought exclusively for the rights of East Pakistan, against exploitation by the West Wing, and this sweeping mandate for Six Points meant Mujibur Rahman could not deviate from it. In the West Wing, the voting percentage was higher in the Punjab, with 63 per cent, and in Sindh with 60 per cent, but lower in the NWFP and Balochistan. The PPP won 81 of 130 contested seats in the West Wing, with 62 out of 82 in the Punjab and 18 out of 27 seats in Sindh. Though smaller in numerical terms than the Awami League, the PPP's success was no less significant as, it crossed provincial boundaries and resulted in defeat for numerous traditionally strong candidates. In the process, the religious and rightist parties were routed in both Wings. However, national and international attention soon focused on East Pakistan, overshadowing these other developments.

Yahya Khan's military regime did not anticipate, and was dismayed by, the Awami League's absolute majority in the National Assembly, and the emergence of Bhutto as leader in the West Wing. Instead of serious discussions on critically important issues, the following three months mainly witnessed political posturing and power play, resulting in abortive negotiations on the future constitution, followed by civil war. Mujibur Rahman remained adamant on Six Points, but was prepared to allow the West Wing provinces to make their own arrangements *inter se*. He neither trusted the military-bureaucratic establishment nor did he want West Wing interference in his province. The main concern of the PPP was that, with no voting procedure prescribed in the LFO, the Awami League could frame a constitution at will, rule East Pakistan virtually separately and yet dominate the Federal Government without the West Wing's major provinces having a proper say. Reflecting this, Bhutto asserted: 'Punjab and Sindh are the bastions of power in Pakistan. Majority alone does not count in national politics. No Government at the centre could be run without the cooperation of the PPP which controlled these two provinces.'[15]

Any analysis of this period would be incomplete without touching upon the abortive negotiations on a viable constitutional arrangement.[16] The first round of discussions commenced with President Yahya Khan visiting Dhaka on 11 January 1971. Mujibur Rahman said he was 'fully satisfied' with the talks, and Yahya Khan maintained that it was up to the Awami League leader and Z.A. Bhutto to formulate a constitution. The President followed this by meeting Bhutto in Larkana, on 17 January, when Bhutto expressed misgivings about the consequences of accepting Six Points *in toto*, but agreed to hold discussions with the Awami League in an effort to secure a compromise on the future constitution.[17]

The second round of negotiations took place when Bhutto led a large PPP delegation to Dhaka on 27 January. Twin-track talks were held; Bhutto mainly dealt with future governmental arrangements and power-sharing in his direct discussions with Mujibur Rahman, while the negotiating teams of the two parties met to consider constitutional issues. No progress was made at either level. The Awami League insisted that details must follow initial agreement on Six Points, while Bhutto did not want to be denied what he considered his due role in constitution-making.

On Bhutto's return to the West Wing, a significant event occurred, the consequences of which were to prove more serious than anyone anticipated at the time. An Indian Airlines plane, the *Ganga,* was hijacked to Lahore on 30 January. The hijacking incident resulted in Delhi banning, on 5 February, all Pakistani planes flying over India. They thus had to go via Colombo to Dhaka, some three thousand miles. India had virtually won the first battle for East Pakistan. There seemed little realization among West Wing leaders that India was determined to seize the opportunity presented by the polarization resulting from the elections, and by the failure to evolve a constitutional formula.

February 1971 saw tension increase between the PPP and the Awami League. Apart from disagreement over Six Points, the date for convening the National Assembly had become a new subject of contention. A combination of events led Bhutto to change his mind on this. He sought, but did not secure, more time from Yahya Khan. On 13 February, the President announced that the Assembly would meet on 3 March. As a result, Bhutto abruptly declared that the PPP would not attend the Assembly session because the Awami League had already framed a Six Point Constitution on a 'take-it or leave-it' basis. He refused to allow PPP representatives to be in 'jeopardy' and 'double hostage' in Dhaka in the face of Indian hostility and Six Points, claiming that he wanted a transfer of power from the military but not a 'transfer of Pakistan'.[18] This proved to be the first significant public move in the tragedy that unfolded. It was followed two weeks later, on 1 March, by Yahya Khan postponing the Assembly *sine die,* which spelt the end of any trust between the two Wings.

During the intervening days, Yahya Khan held a long private meeting with Bhutto on 19 February. Two days later Yahya Khan removed his Cabinet and then, on 22 February, told a meeting of the Provincial Governors and Martial Law Administrators about his intention to postpone the Assembly session. Unknown to others, the decision was also taken for military action in East Pakistan.[19] On 28 February, Bhutto addressed a huge public meeting in Lahore, setting out his position on Six Points: apart from the question of foreign trade and aid which could not be entrusted to provincial governments, adjustments could be made on the remaining issues. He also suggested either the postponement of the Assembly session or an extension of the 120-day limit to allow time for negotiations.

Mujibur Rahman was informed about Yahya Khan's postponement decision the evening before its announcement This proved to be the beginning of the end of any meaningful and peaceful relations between the two Wings. East Pakistan erupted and the Awami League seized administrative control of almost the entire province. Taken aback by this adverse reaction, the President, on 3 March, invited the leaders of all the political parties to meet him in Rawalpindi. The Awami League rejected the invitation and, in turn, privately put forward the 'two Committees' proposal to Yahya Khan on 5 March.[20] This meant the elected representatives of the two Wings meeting separately in Islamabad and Dhaka to devise a constitution. The following day the President summoned the session for 25 March, and proceeded with his team on 15 March to Dhaka for talks with the Awami League on the 'two Committees' proposal and other constitutional issues.

The final, and what proved to be fatal, round of negotiations was held by Yahya Khan with Mujibur Rahman, and their respective advisers, from 16 to 24 March. Z.A. Bhutto arrived in Dhaka with his team on 21 March and, the following morning, the three leaders held their only brief, joint meeting. Discussions with the Awami League took place initially on the 'two Committees' proposal and the role of the National Assembly; in the end, however, the Awami League called for 'two

Constitutional Conventions', with the role of the Assembly being limited to combining the two texts into a constitution for a 'Confederation of Pakistan'. This was not acceptable to the President who represented the military, nor to Chairman Bhutto of the PPP, resulting in breakdown and armed action.

The military operation that followed on the night of 25-26 March met with early success; but the task of suppressing widespread insurrection in East Pakistan, in itself difficult, became impossible with open armed invasion by India later on 22 November. The Indo-Pakistan War extended to the West Wing on 3 December, East Pakistan surrendered early on 16 December, and the following day President Yahya Khan accepted a cease-fire on the western front. Theories abound on the causes and reasons for the separation of East Pakistan, now Bangladesh.[21] Whether this was the result of accumulated errors or deliberate actions, or the culmination of India's determination to dismember Pakistan, are not examined here because the focus is on constitutional issues. However, it is clear that the two Wings, divided by India, lacked the requisite imagination or will to achieve a viable accommodation under a federal arrangement, and domestic power play remained overwhelmingly important.

In *Zulfikar Ali Bhutto and Pakistan: 1967-1977*,[22] I concluded that the 'Confederation' proposal, regarded as treason at the time, might have been the most suitable for a geographically divided country. Whereas under the Six Points scheme the Awami League, or at least the representatives of the East Wing, would have controlled not only East Pakistan, but also the centre, for the foreseeable future, the confederal arrangement would have established the West Wing as an equal partner, and would have obviated dangers envisaged to the unity of the West Wing in the event of any breakdown in the arrangement.[23] But that was not to be. The 'numbers game' had come to a deadly end, but political power play continued to dominate the second phase of what now remained of Pakistan.

Z.A. Bhutto and the 1973 Constitution

The collapse of the Yahya regime saw the advent of the government of Zulfikar Ali Bhutto, first as President from 20 December 1971 to 14 August 1973, and then as an all-powerful Prime Minister till the military *coup d'etat* on 5 July 1977. Before examining this period, it is important to mention the decision of the Supreme Court in the Asma Jilani Case in April 1972, which held Yahya Khan's Martial Law illegal, and reversed its earlier decision in the Dosso Case, as the 'assumptions' in that case were 'not justified' and 'wholly unsustainable'. The Court stated:

> ...a person who destroys the national legal order in an illegitimate manner cannot be regarded as a valid source of law making. May be that on account of his holding the coercive apparatus of the State, the people and the Courts are silenced temporarily, but let it be laid down firmly that the order which the usurper imposes will remain illegal... As soon as the first opportunity arises, where the coercive apparatus falls from the hands of the usurper, he should be tried for high treason and suitably punished.[24]

Five years later these fine words were not followed when Prime Minister Bhutto was overthrown, and Martial Law ruled for eight years.

On taking over from Yahya Khan, Z.A. Bhutto also assumed the office of Chief Martial Law Administrator—the first civilian to hold this position. In fact, till a new constitution was approved by the National Assembly, Martial Law remained the source of legal authority. However, as a consequence, in the Asma Jilani Case, Bhutto's government was in the invidious position of having to defend the validity of Yahya Khan's Martial Law, which the PPP had earlier condemned.

After the trauma of military defeat and dismemberment under Martial Law, it was necessary to establish constitutional rule as soon as possible for the four remaining provinces which now formed Pakistan. Bhutto decided to have an interim arrangement initially, and discussions between the main political parties representing the four provinces resulted in the Accord of 6 March 1972. Pursuant to this, the interim Constitution came into force on 21 April 1972. It was based on the Government of India Act, 1935, and provided for a presidential form of federal government, while the four provinces had parliamentary systems. At the same time, Bhutto agreed to the withdrawal of Martial Law.

The discussions concerning a permanent constitution were more complex and protracted. Following the loss of East Pakistan, the task of framing a constitution for a more homogeneous West Wing might have appeared less problematic. However, several of the earlier issues had remained unresolved, and, as far as the federal arrangements were concerned, the Punjab now replaced East Pakistan as the province with a population greater than the other provinces combined. After four days of detailed negotiations between the representatives of all political parties and groups in the National Assembly, the terms of the permanent Constitution were settled on 20 October 1972. President Bhutto sought a consensus on the basic law for the country in spite of the PPP having an overwhelming majority in the existing Assembly. He conducted the meetings of 16-20 October with skill, making concessions where appropriate to the two smaller provinces of Balochistan and the NWFP. The 20 October Accord undoubtedly eased the task of constitution-making, but did not prevent power politics again coming into play. Many difficulties, both political and constitutional, occurred before the Constitution Bill was finally adopted by the members of the Assembly on 12 April 1973.[25]

The 1973 Constitution was passed, without dissent, by an overwhelming majority of the representatives of the four provinces and came into effect on 14 August 1973. It followed in substantial part the provisions of the 1956 and 1962 Constitutions. The main changes related to (1) the federal structure, (2) the executive in the parliamentary system and (3) the Islamic provisions and 'Islamic socialism'.

The Federal Structure

The 1973 Constitution introduced certain new features in the federal arrangement, most notably a bicameral legislature and a Council of Common Interests. While the 200 members of the National Assembly continued to be elected on the basis of one-man-one-vote, Article 59 provided for the smaller Senate to have equal representation from the provinces, to be indirectly elected by the four Provincial Assemblies. However, real power remained with the National Assembly because the Senate had no say on the budget or any 'Money Bill'. This expression was interpreted widely, with the Speaker of the Assembly authorized to decide what was a Money Bill. Moreover, other bills within the exclusive jurisdiction of the federal legislature could only originate in the National Assembly, which was empowered to override, by a subsequent vote, any rejection in the Senate. In matters relating to the concurrent legislative list over which both the federal and provincial legislatures had jurisdiction, a bill could originate in either House, and, in the event the two Houses did not agree, it would go to a joint sitting of Parliament (Article 71). Later, in 1985, General M. Ziaul Haq amended Articles 70 and 71, allowing all non-Money Bills to be initiated in either House.

The 20 October Accord also settled the division of legislative subjects between the federation and the provinces, conferring extensive authority on the federal Parliament. An important innovation covered such subjects of inter-provincial concern as railways, water and power, oil and gas, and the development of major industries. They had previously been dealt with mainly by the Province of West Pakistan. With the dissolution of One Unit, there was uncertainty as to how these subjects should be distributed under the new arrangement, and the Accord settled on a new Part II of the Federal List for them, which was adopted by the 1973 Constitution. The following table compares the legislative lists under various constitutional dispensations.

Comparative Legislative Lists

List of subjects	1935 Act	1956 Constitution	1962 Constitution	1973 Constitution
Federal	61	30	94 (Only 1 list)	Part I: 59 Part II: 8
Provincial	55	94	—	—
Concurrent	—	19	—	47
Residual powers		With the provinces	Provinces (but with an overriding proviso regarding national interest)	With the provinces

Bills relating to Part II of the Federal List could be introduced in the Senate, and, importantly, Article 153 established a Council of Common Interests to formulate and regulate policies for these matters. This Council was composed of an equal number of representatives of the centre and the provinces, with four Federal Ministers, including the Prime Minister, and the four Provincial Chief Ministers. It also had exclusive jurisdiction to deal with complaints and disputes over water supplies involving the Federal or any Provincial Government (Article 155), a vitally important subject, hitherto dealt with solely by the Supreme Court. The Council was subject only to Parliament in joint sitting. It provided the federating units with a common forum to consider matters of practical concern to them. However, the wide powers which had been conceded to the Council in the rush to reach the 20 October Accord ran counter to Bhutto's to concentrate authority in himself. As a consequence, only one formal meeting was held at the end of 1976 for the limited purpose of appointing a commission consisting of the Chief Justices of Pakistan and the four Provincial High Courts to recommend apportionment of the waters of the River Indus. This was intended to prevent the politically explosive water issue coming to the fore in the March 1977 elections. Because the matter fell within the exclusive constitutional jurisdiction of the Council, it had to meet. The other issues of concern to the Council were left unattended, and routine differences between the provinces were instead ironed out by a newly established Ministry for Provincial Coordination.

The 1973 Constitution met the essential requirements of provincial autonomy. However, there was potential for eroding this in the Emergency provisions (Articles 232 and 234), which allowed the Federal Government to assume powers in the provinces in the event of national or provincial Emergency. Such provisions are not uncommon in a federation, but in Pakistan they have invariably been used as weapons against the provinces, particularly those governed by parties opposed to the Federal Government. Pakistan has throughout been run in a highly centralized manner, a federation merely in name. Despite expending considerable effort to achieve a delicate constitutional balance in the federal structure, Z.A. Bhutto, true to tradition, interfered in the provinces, centralized power and circumvented the federal nature of the Constitution.

The Executive

The question of whether the executive should be in a presidential or parliamentary form has repeatedly troubled Pakistan. During the first twenty-five years, the locus of executive authority changed continuously. With Independence, it vested in Governor-General Mohammad Ali Jinnah, as the Founder of the Nation. On his death, it devolved, appropriately within a parliamentary system, on Liaquat Ali Khan who remained as Prime Minister. Following his assassination, it again shifted, but this time partially, from various Prime Ministers to Governor-General Ghulam Mohammad. Following the adoption of the 1956 Constitution, President Iskander Mirza retained significant authority despite the parliamentary dispensation. After October 1958, President Ayub Khan exercised supreme power for ten and a half years, followed by Yahya Khan for nearly three years and then Zulfikar Ali Bhutto for twenty months as President.

The 1973 Constitution adopted a parliamentary system, concentrating all authority in the Prime Minister, who was specifically designated the 'Chief Executive'. A deliberate effort was made to put an end to the diarchy that existed before 1958. To doubly ensure that the President could not act independently, Article 48 stated that he had to 'act on and in accordance with the advice of the Prime Minister and such advice shall be binding on him', and all orders of the President had to be counter-signed by the Prime Minister. Previously, the President could choose as Prime Minister the person who, in his opinion, was most likely to command the majority in the National Assembly; now, the Prime Minister was exclusively elected by the Assembly. The President had been reduced to a ceremonial head who, according to one member of the opposition, 'had less power than the Queen of England and none of her glory'.

The position of the Prime Minister was further strengthened by dealing effectively with floor-crossing, a practice prevalent in previous legislatures in Pakistan. It was provided that, for a period of ten years or two general elections, the vote of a member cast against the majority of his party would not be counted in the case of a vote of no confidence or on the budget. Furthermore, the Prime Minister could only be removed by a vote of no confidence which also nominated his successor in the same resolution. In order to secure the consent of the two smaller provinces to these arrangements for the federal legislature and executive, Bhutto agreed to have the same apply *mutatis mutandis* in the provinces.

Many of these provisions concerning the executive in the 1973 Constitution were drawn from the Constitutions of the

Federal Republic of Germany and other countries with parliamentary systems. However, their cumulative effect made the Prime Minister almost irremovable.

Islamic Provisions and 'Islamic Socialism'

After twenty-five years of debate and strife, the content of the Islamic provisions was settled to a great extent by the 1973 Constitution. This provided a sense of security and stability following the separation of East Pakistan which many people felt had struck at the Islamic foundation of the country and the two-nation theory. For the majority of Muslims in the subcontinent, the creation of Pakistan had indeed been a practical implementation of the assertion that the Muslims were a separate nation from the Hindus, and entitled to a State of their own.

Once Pakistan was established, the call for an Islamic constitution followed. However, this has so far proved elusive because of conflicting views on the subject, which have made the achievement of any consensus difficult. To those who maintained that one had to look no further than the Holy Quran and Sunnah for guidance, the reply was that these provided little that was specifically related to the form of an Islamic State. There are others who claim that an Islamic State is one with Islamic laws; such an assertion, however, merely describes the laws and not the State. Moreover, there are several religious schools of thought as to what is meant by *Shariat* or Islamic law. To some, it exists only in the Holy Quran; for others, the fundamental laws of Islam were settled in the early golden age, and all that is needed today is an application of these fundamentals to the present situation. To yet another school of thought, the *Shariat* is a dynamic system where historical stages are available for guidance, and present developments are open to creative inference from a range of known facts.

Debate has long continued over whether Islam envisaged a presidential or parliamentary system, and whether the electorate should be comprised of Muslims and minorities, jointly or separately. However, Quaid-i-Azam Mohammad Ali Jinnah settled one major issue at the outset, namely, that Pakistan would not be a theocracy, with the *ulema* responsible for running the State. In February 1948, he categorically stated, 'Make no mistake: Pakistan is not a theocracy or anything like it'. Prime Minister Liaquat Ali Khan similarly declared against theocracy when speaking on the Objectives Resolution on 7 March 1949:

> I just now said that the people are the real recipients of power. This naturally eliminates any danger of the establishment of theocracy...[which] has come to mean a government by ordained priests, who wield authority as being specially appointed... I cannot over-emphasise the fact that such an idea is absolutely foreign to Islam...and, therefore, the question of a theocracy simply does not arise in Islam.[26]

Despite the fact that the Objectives Resolution was incorporated in the preambles to the 1956 Constitution, the interim Constitution of 1972 and the 1973 permanent Constitution, this did not satisfy the demand for an 'Islamic Constitution'. Under the 1956 Constitution the country was called 'The Islamic Republic of Pakistan'; and the Directive Principles of State Policy, which were not legally enforceable, called, *inter alia,* for making 'the teaching of the Holy Quran compulsory' and 'the observance of Islamic moral standards' (Article 25). The 1956 Constitution also specified that the President should be a Muslim (Article 32). Moreover, under Article 197, the President was required to establish a body for Islamic research and instruction; and Article 198 provided for a Council to make. recommendations for bringing existing law into conformity with the injunctions of Islam. As in other fields, although much was said about these provisions, there was little effort at practical implementation.

Under Martial Law in October 1958, the Republic was 'to be known henceforward as Pakistan',[27] thus dropping 'Islamic' from the name. Ayub Khan reinforced his efforts to reverse the trend towards 'Islamization' by again omitting the term 'Islamic

Republic' in the 1962 Constitution, but this was soon reintroduced under the First Amendment. He also dropped the Objectives Resolution from the preamble, and the earlier references to Islam in the Directive Principles of State Policy. More specifically, the preamble of the 1962 Constitution referred only to 'the teachings and requirements of Islam', without the words 'as set out in the Holy Quran and Sunnah' contained in the 1956 Constitution. These words were also left out while describing the functions of the Advisory Council of Islamic Ideology. Presumably, the omission of the reference to 'the Sunnah' was intended to downplay the differences among the Muslims and to curtail sectarianism. Even on the question of the Council bringing laws into conformity with the principles of Islam, Ayub's Constitution did not include the earlier explanatory note of 1956: 'In the application of this Article [198] to the personal laws of any Muslim sect, the expression "Quran and Sunnah" shall mean the Quran and Sunnah as interpreted by that sect.' Moreover, although not a constitutional measure, his Muslim Family Laws Ordinance, 1961, made certain provisions, for example a specific law relating to inheritance, uniformly applicable 'to all Muslim citizens of Pakistan'. For the rest, the Islamic provisions were similar to those set out in the 1956 Constitution, and remained equally ineffective.

The 1973 Constitution provided specifically, for the first time, that Islam was to be the State religion (Article 2). Also, for the first time, the Prime Minister as Chief Executive was required to be a Muslim, and the oath for him and the President was elaborated to the effect that:

I am a Muslim and believe in the Unity and Oneness of Almighty Allah, the Books of Allah, the Holy Quran being the last of them, the Prophethood of Muhammad (peace be upon him) as the last of the Prophets and that there can be no Prophet after him, the Day of Judgement, and all the requirements and teachings of the Holy Quran and Sunnah.

The main Islamic content was set out in Articles 227 to 231. As in the 1956 Constitution, Article 227 provided that all laws were to be brought into conformity with, and no law was to be made repugnant to, the Holy Quran and Sunnah. However, the Council of Islamic Ideology was, for the first time, to include persons with an 'understanding of the economic, political, legal or administrative problems' of the country, and at least one woman member. Thus it ceased to be a stronghold of the *ulema.* The Council had to submit its final report on Islamic laws within seven years, and annual interim reports, which were to 'be laid for discussion before both Houses and each Provincial Assembly'. Within two years of the final report, all laws were to be enacted as required by Article 227.

The Pakistan People's Party under Zulfikar Ali Bhutto came into power calling for 'Islamic socialism', and maintained that the dynamic spirit and social gospel of Islam should be incorporated in specific provisions of the Constitution. Accordingly, to reflect its aim of an egalitarian and progressive society, it was laid down in Article 3 that 'The State shall ensure the elimination of all forms of exploitation and the gradual fulfilment of the fundamental principle, from each according to his ability to each according to his work.'

In order to promote the PPP's policy of social change and nationalization, two key additions were made. First, while the right to property was protected as in previous Constitutions, Article 24(4) specified that compensation for compulsory acquisition was not to be questioned in any court. This overcame the problem of dilatory litigation which had been a major obstacle to reform, and gave Parliament the final say in determining compensation. Secondly, Parliament was further empowered, under Article 253, to prescribe maximum limits on property and to declare that any trade, business, industry or service could be wholly or in part nationalized. Although the Constitution itself could not alter society, these provisions created a framework for change to meet the needs of a developing society and to prevent delays in the implementation of any reforms.

Constitutional Amendments under Z.A. Bhutto

The basic law of every country undergoes change, some necessitated by new circumstances and others to meet specific requirements. Between May 1974 and May 1977, the Bhutto Government introduced seven amendments, which, in the main, affected the judiciary and fundamental rights. They were seriously challenged by the opposition—only the Second Amendment defining a Muslim, after the Qadianis were declared non-Muslims, was generally endorsed.

After the Government's recognition of Bangladesh, the First Amendment removed the reference to East Pakistan in the 1973 Constitution. At the same time, the Federal Government was permitted to ban political parties 'operating in a manner prejudicial to the sovereignty or integrity of Pakistan', subject only to the Supreme Court's final decision on the matter.[28]

Several members of the 1972 Constitution Committee had attached considerable importance to the provisions relating to arrest and detention under Article 10. Indeed, the PPP took pride in this liberal approach. However, in February 1975, the Third Amendment[29] extended the period of preventive detention without production before a Review Board from one to three months, and widened the definition of those working for 'the enemy'. It also facilitated the continuation of a Proclamation of Emergency under Article 232(7)(b). The Fourth Amendment was passed nine months later,[30] further curtailing the writ jurisdiction of the High Courts under Article 199 in cases of preventive detention; they were not now allowed to grant bail to a person detained or to prohibit such detention.

In September 1976, the Fifth Amendment[31] was pushed through Parliament, again restricting the powers of the High Courts under Article 199. For the first time, the judges themselves were also affected in several ways. The term of office of the Chief Justices of the Supreme Court and the Provincial High Courts was to be determined not solely by age but, as an alternative, by a fixed period; its aim was to secure changes in some of the appointments. Moreover, the

Government now had the power to transfer a judge from one High Court to another for a period of one year for which his consent was not necessary, no reason had to be given and no consultation was required. The Sixth Amendment was minor, clarifying the age for retirement of the Chief Justices under the previous amendment.

The Seventh Amendment was passed on 16 May 1977, by which time Bhutto's Government was in the midst of the agitation against the outcome of the 7 March 1977 general elections. It made provision for a referendum, because Bhutto did not want re-elections. It also tried to take away the jurisdiction of the High Courts in respect of action taken by the military from 21 April when called in aid of civil power under Article 245. This was unsuccessful and proved futile: the opposition's agitation continued, as did the demand for the repeal of all the amendments to the Constitution.

Most of these amendments were unnecessary. They damaged Bhutto's image, and merely succeeded in diluting the triumph of the 1973 Constitution. One consequence of Prime Minister Bhutto's enhanced executive authority, and the manner in which he exercised it, was that the army became the only means of ousting him. Apart from General Ziaul Haq's ambition, this contributed to the return of Martial Law. By the time the *coup* occurred on 5 July, Bhutto had deprived himself of the sheet-anchor of a consensus Constitution.

Ziaul Haq's Martial Law

Martial Law has appeared with such regularity in Pakistan that, although extra-constitutional, some comment on the subject is necessary. It was first upheld and validated by the Supreme Court in 1958 in the Dosso Case, and subsequently rejected in the Asma Jilani Case following the débâcle in East Pakistan and the fall of the Yahya regime in December 1971.

The framers of the 1973 Constitution sought to ensure that the military would not again play a political role. Article 6 provided that any attempt to abrogate or subvert the Constitution by force amounted to high treason. Article 12(2) made a specific exception to the fundamental principle of non-retrospectivity of offences and punishments in the case of such high treason from the time of the 1956 Constitution. Regarding the armed forces themselves, it was laid down that the Federal Government had 'control and command' over them (Article 243); they had to take an oath of allegiance to the Constitution, stating that they would not engage in any political activity (Article 244); and they were required to act under the directions of the Federal Government and 'in aid of civil power when called upon to do so' (Article 245).

These provisions did not prevent the military *coup* and Martial Law of 5 July 1977. Unlike the two previous Martial Law regimes, however, General Ziaul Haq did not abrogate the Constitution but suspended it—and so it remained for eight years. A document attained through near-unanimity could not be entirely discarded nor, for that matter, readily replaced with the agreement of all four provinces. As in the earlier instances, the validity of General Zia's Martial Law was determined by the Supreme Court, this time in the Begum Nusrat Bhutto Case. The Court unanimously 'distinguished' the position from the Asma Jilani Case. It placed great emphasis on General Ziaul Haq's address to the nation on the day of the *coup* when he said that the people had rejected the March 1977 election results, and only when he saw 'no prospects of a compromise', and the country was in a serious crisis, was Martial Law imposed. On the contrary, it may be noted that by this time the agitation had abated. Zia claimed that his 'sole aim' was to organize free and fair elections in October, and to transfer power shortly thereafter to the elected representatives: 'I give a solemn assurance that I will not deviate from this schedule'. Chief Justice S. Anwarul Haq pointed out

The statement correctly brings out the necessity for the imposition of Martial Law. It is also clear that this sincere and unambiguous declaration of his objectives by the Chief Martial Law Administrator was a major factor in persuading the people of Pakistan to willingly accept the new dispensation as an interim arrangement.[32]

On this basis, the Chief Justice stated, *inter alia,* that 'the 1973 Constitution still remains the supreme law of the land subject to the condition that certain parts thereof have been held in abeyance on account of State necessity', and that the CMLA was 'entitled' to perform 'all acts or legislative measures...under the 1973 Constitution, including the power to amend it'. The Court declined to set a definite timetable for the holding of elections, instead concluding

> ...in clear terms that it has found it possible to validate the extra-constitutional action of the Chief Martial Law Administrator not only for the reason that he stepped in to save the country at a time of grave national crisis and constitutional breakdown, but also because of the solemn pledge given by him that the period of *constitutional deviation* (emphasis added) shall be of as short a duration as possible.[33]

Justice Waheeduddin Ahmad stated the position pithily: the principles laid down in the Asma Jilani Case were 'not applicable to the facts of the present case' and 'the principles enunciated in the Reference by his Excellency the Governor-General will have to be invoked for solving the present constitutional deadlock'.[34]

The period of 'constitutional deviation' continued until November 1988, when party-based general elections were held, four months after General Ziaul Haq died in a plane crash on 17 August 1988. In the intervening years, he substantially amended the 1973 Constitution. As a first step, General Ziaul Haq became both President and CMLA under President's Order No. 13 of 1978. Next, he promulgated the Provisional Constitution Order, 1981. This, *inter alia,* dealt a major blow to the judiciary: it negated certain proceedings in the Superior Courts, curtailed their jurisdiction, and required each judge to take oath again under the new system while at the same time prematurely retiring a few judges.

General Zia proceeded to secure his own position through a referendum on 19 December 1984, which posed the question:

> Whether the people of Pakistan endorse the process initiated for bringing the laws of Pakistan in conformity with the Injunctions of Islam as laid down in the Holy Quran and Sunnah...and for the preservation of the Ideology of Pakistan, for the continuation of that process and for the smooth and orderly transfer of power to the elected representatives of the people.[35]

If the answer was 'Yes', the Referendum Order went on to state, then General Zia would 'be deemed to have been duly elected President of Pakistan for a term of five years'. This convoluted logic was made even worse by the 'management' of the voting result.

He then, in 1985, promulgated the Revival of the Constitution of 1973 Order,[36] under which the new Parliament was to meet in March; 'party-less' elections had meanwhile been held. This 1985 Order significantly transformed the 1973 Constitution. Even earlier, General Zia had by several President's Orders made changes in the 'suspended' Constitution, such as introducing the Federal Shariat Court through the Constitution (Amendment) Order, 1980.[37] Moreover, to further legitimize and strengthen his position as President, and the changes made in the Constitution, he agreed with his new Prime Minister, Muhammad Khan Junejo, to withdraw Martial Law upon Parliament adopting the Eighth Amendment to the Constitution.[38] As the Eighth Amendment revised some of the previous changes made through President's Orders, it is only necessary to examine those provisions which are still in effect, or continued to be so till repealed in 1997.

Main Amendments under Ziaul Haq's Martial Law

The main thrust of these amendments was to give the President greater powers in the revived parliamentary system under the 1973 Constitution. Before analysing this issue, four other matters merit comment.

Firstly, the Eighth Amendment specifically affirmed the Proclamation of 5 July 1977 imposing Martial Law, and also all other President's Orders and Martial Law Regulations, particularly mentioning the Referendum Order, 1984, the Revival of the Constitution of 1973 Order, 1985, and other amendments to the Constitution. It added that all these Martial Law measures 'shall, notwithstanding any judgment of any court, be deemed to be and always to have been validly made, taken or done and shall not be called in question in any court on any ground whatsoever'. This formed Article 270A of the Constitution, and, as a consequence, several of these Martial Law Orders and Regulations could only 'be amended in the manner provided for amendment of the Constitution'.

Secondly, the Federal Shariat Court was established, under a new Chapter 3A of the Constitution, to 'examine and decide the question whether or not any law or provision of law is repugnant to the Injunctions of Islam'. The qualifications for appointment as judges of this Court were similar to the other Superior Courts. Curiously, appeals from the Shariat Court were to be heard by a Shariat Appellate Bench of the Supreme Court, consisting of three Muslim judges and not more than two *ulema*. Instead of establishing a parallel system of courts through the creation of a Federal Shariat Court, similar Shariat Benches could just as readily have been set up in each existing High Court. However, this was a part of Zia's 'Islamization' programme, and to this end he also defined non-Muslims and introduced separate electorates for them. In addition, he amended Article 62 which now required that a Muslim member of Parliament should 'not commonly [be] known as one who violates Islamic Injunctions', and should have 'adequate knowledge of Islamic teachings and practices obligatory duties prescribed by Islam as well as abstains from major sins'.

Thirdly, a new Article 2A was inserted to make the 'principles and provisions' of the 1949 Objectives Resolution a 'substantive part of the Constitution'. The text of this Resolution, which was set out in a new annex to the Constitution, deceptively omitted the word 'freely' in connection with minorities professing and practising their religions and developing their cultures. This was despite the fact that the Resolution, including this word, still remained in the preamble to the Constitution. It was originally a declaration of intent of how the Constitution should be made. Since the Constitution had already been framed, the main purpose of this addition could only have been one of two alternatives; either to complicate the implementation of the revived 1973 Constitution, by giving effect to this 'supra-constitutional' Resolution, or to restrict the effect of the earlier Supreme Court decision in the Asma Jilani Case. The Chief Justice had stated in 1972 that, if a *grund-norm* were necessary for Pakistan, there was no need to look to Western legal theorists:

> Our own *grund-norm* is enshrined in our own doctrine that the legal sovereignty over the entire universe belongs to Almighty Allah above, and the authority exercisable by the people...is a sacred trust. This was the immutable and unalterable norm which was clearly accepted in the Objectives Resolution.[39]

However, following the insertion of Article 2A, the Supreme Court in 1992 rightly held that, by making the Resolution a 'substantive' part of the Constitution, it did not become supra-constitutional but only an 'essential or integral· part of the Constitution possessing the same weight and status as other parts of the Constitution which are already a substantive part thereof'.[40]

Finally, on the political front, the Muslim League was once again revived by Prime Minister Junejo and others. They were encouraged by General Zia, who promoted this party in order to keep in check the PPP.

Powers of the President after the 1985 Amendments

The 1973 Constitution, as previously noted, gave the Prime Minister total authority. The amendments of 1985 attempted to correct this position but, particularly in one respect, tilted too much in the direction of the President in a parliamentary dispensation. Because they were made under General Zia's Martial Law, they have been largely condemned, even though they mainly adopted provisions similar to those in the earlier 1956 Constitution, the Indian Constitution and in the constitutions of other countries with parliamentary systems, such as Australia, Germany, Ireland and Italy.[41] As these amendments have been, and remain, the subject of considerable debate, they require some elucidation. They can conveniently be categorized under three heads: (1) general, procedural or merely formal, (2) those relating to certain appointments in the President's discretion, and, importantly, (3) provisions regarding the removal of the Prime Minister and the dissolution of the National Assembly.

Many amendments were in the general and procedural category. For example, the electoral college for the President was expanded to include, in addition to Parliament, the four Provincial Assemblies, with equal votes for each province irrespective of size. This broad-based election is similar to that in India, Ireland, Italy and Germany. Next, the amended Article 46 provided that the President had the right not only to be informed by the Prime Minister on all administrative and legislative matters, but could refer back for reconsideration by the Cabinet any decision of the Prime Minister or a Minister made without Cabinet consideration. This followed the Indian Constitution where, however, the President's powers were limited to decisions only of Ministers. Although under the amended Article 48(1) the President was required 'to act in accordance with the advice of the Cabinet or the Prime Minister', he could call on the Cabinet or the Prime Minister to reconsider any advice tendered, but was bound to act on advice after such reconsideration. A similar provision was introduced earlier in

India through the Constitution (Forty-fourth Amendment) Act, 1978, in respect of the advice of the Council of Ministers but not the Prime Minister.

A further change under Article 48(6) permitted the President 'in his discretion', and not only on the Prime Minister's advice, to refer any matter of national importance to a referendum. Several other constitutions contain such a provision. It has been used only once in Pakistan, in December 1984 by General Zia, and is not significant as the consequences of a referendum are unspecified in terms of enforceability. Then, the amended Article 50 reintroduced the concept of the President being part of Parliament, as under the 1956 Constitution, and in India (Article 79), Australia and Ireland. Similarly, the revised Article 46 provided for the President to address and send messages to Parliament; the position is the same in India and Italy. Moreover, under Article 75 as amended, the President was authorized to refer back for reconsideration by Parliament any bill, other than Money Bills, but could not withhold his assent after Parliament in joint sitting passed it by a simple majority. The same, or wider, powers exist in India, Australia and Italy.

Several amendments, mainly procedural, were made in Articles 90 and 91. However, the omission of the reference to the Prime Minister being the 'Chief Executive', and other provisions which concentrated power in him, were important. Now, under the amended Article 91, the Cabinet was 'to aid and advise the President'. The provisions of Article 91 and 48(1), when read together, are the same as the Indian Constitution (Article 74), following its Forty-second Amendment in January 1977.

In Pakistan, efforts were made to allow the President greater power under these provisions. Reliance was mainly placed on the amended Article 90(1) which provided that 'The executive authority of the Federation shall vest in the President and shall be exercised by him, either directly or through officers subordinate to him, in accordance with the Constitution.' It is, however, noteworthy, that this amended provision is identical to Article 53(1) of the Indian Constitution and Article 39(1) of our 1956 Constitution. While introducing the original Constitution Bill in the Indian Parliament, B.R. Ambedkar clearly described the position of the President:

> He is the Head of the State but not of the Executive. He represents the Nation but does not rule the Nation... The President of the Union will be generally bound by the advice of his Ministers. He can do nothing contrary to their advice; nor can he do anything without their advice.[42]

Although all executive action is taken in the name of the President, he does not exercise the function individually or independently. Thus, for example, even where the Constitution requires the 'satisfaction' of the President in the exercise of any power or function, this does not involve his individual satisfaction, but that of the President in the constitutional sense, in other words, the satisfaction of the Cabinet or the Prime Minister on whose aid and advice the President exercises his powers and functions. As will be considered subsequently in the context of the Supreme Court's decisions, the Court in its short order of 4 December 1996 held that the President must act on advice under Article 48(1) in respect of the appointments of judges to the Superior Courts.[43]

The President's power to 'act in his discretion' related mainly to certain important appointments, including the Chief Election Commissioner under Article 213, the Chairman of the Federal Public Service Commission under Article 242(1A), and the Chiefs of the armed forces under Article 243(2)(c). While the first two positions could be regarded as non-political, the appointments of Service Chiefs has a significant bearing on a civilian government's control of the armed forces. However, in all these cases, parallels can be found in other parliamentary systems. On the other hand, the President had to appoint the Governors 'after consultation with the Prime Minister' (Article 101), and not the Cabinet.

However, on the question of the removal of the Prime Minister and the dissolution of the National Assembly, the

President's powers to act 'in his discretion' were considerable under Article 58(2)(b). Upon such dissolution, Article 48(5) provided for the President 'in his discretion' to fix a date within ninety days for the holding of general elections, and to 'appoint a caretaker Cabinet', without any qualifications specified. This provision has no real equivalent in ordinary parliamentary systems.

To understand the significance of these amendments, the original provisions of the 1973 Constitution first require consideration. Under Article 91, the Prime Minister had to be elected by the National Assembly. In all circumstances, even on resignation, he continued to hold office until a new Prime Minister was elected. In a vote of no confidence, his successor had to be named, and, in his absence, or on death, the 'most senior Federal Minister' assumed his functions till the Prime Minister returned or a new one was elected. These provisions, contained in the original Articles 91, 93, 94, 95 and 96, requiring a Prime Minister at all times, were omitted in 1985.

Under the amended Article 91 clause (2A), after 20 March 1990, the President would invite that 'member of the National Assembly to be the Prime Minister who commands the confidence of the majority of the members'. Clause (5) added that he was to 'hold office during the pleasure of the President', but this 'pleasure' was not to be exercised unless the President was 'satisfied that the Prime Minister does not command the confidence of the majority of the members of the National Assembly', and the Prime Minister then had to secure a vote of confidence. If, thereafter, no member could obtain a majority, the President could dissolve the Assembly under Article 58(2)(a). The supremacy of the Assembly remained intact to this extent. However, clause (2)(b) of Article 58 provided that the President could also dissolve the National Assembly 'in his discretion' where, in his opinion, 'a situation has arisen in which the Government of the Federation cannot be carried on in accordance with the provisions of the Constitution and an appeal to the electorate is necessary'

The ad hoc nature of the 1985 amendments was apparent from the very placement of these provisions in the Constitution: the action under Article 58(2)(b) of removing an elected government and dissolving a National Assembly was set out in Chapter 2, whereas its consequences were spelt out in the earlier Chapter 1, Part III, in Article 48(5). Moreover, there were three different references to caretaker arrangements at the national level, namely, in Articles 48(5)(b), 91(3) and 94. The power conferred by Article 58(2)(b) was exercised by a President on four occasions between 1988 and 1996. How the Supreme Court has interpreted these amended constitutional provisions now needs to be considered.

The Supreme Court and Post-1985 Governments

In the three leading cases involving the imposition of Martial Law, the variance in the Supreme Court's decisions has been noted. The position is not dissimilar in the four cases concerning Article 58(2)(b). In this short overview, it is not feasible to comment in depth on each decision; this narrative is confined to setting out briefly the political events, the Supreme Court's interpretation of the Constitution, and the consequences.

On 29 May 1988, President Ziaul Haq removed the Government of Prime Minister Junejo and dissolved the National Assembly. He appointed a caretaker Cabinet, without a Prime Minister, and promised 'party-less' elections. Within three months he died, leaving acting President Ghulam Ishaq Khan to hold elections in November. The Supreme Court decided that it was a fundamental right of political parties to contest elections,[44] which were not to be 'party-less' as envisaged by General Zia. The dissolution itself gave rise to the first decision of the Supreme Court on the question of Article 58(2)(b) in the Saifullah Khan Case. The Court held that the discretion conferred on the President by this provision was not absolute but qualified:

Thus, if it can be shown that no grounds existed on the basis of which an honest opinion could be formed, the exercise of the power would be unconstitutional and open to correction through judicial review...

The circumstances that the impugned action has political overtones cannot prevent the Court from interfering therewith.[45]

The Court exercised its power of judicial review though it had not in the past questioned a similar clause relating to Emergency under Article 234 in the event that the 'Government of a Province...cannot be carried on in accordance with the provisions of the Constitution'.

The dissolution by General Zia was held to be unconstitutional, but the Court did not restore the Assembly. Instead, fresh party-based elections were allowed. On this point, an important consideration was that, in the dissolved Assembly, political parties had not been permitted to contest and, moreover, the petition itself had been filed late, after the death of General Zia.

The Supreme Court also underlined the need for a Prime Minister to head a caretaker Cabinet: 'The absence of Prime Minister from a caretaker Cabinet alters for the period under discussion the very character of the Constitution from a Parliamentary democracy to a Presidential system of Government'.[46] This, however, did not fully take into account that, unlike other provisions and particularly the preceeding clauses (1) and (4) of Article 48 itself which distinguish between the Cabinet and the Prime Minister, clause 5(b) thereof refers only to 'a caretaker Cabinet'. The Court did not note that there are periods contemplated by the amended Constitution when there is no Prime Minister or even acting Prime Minister, for example, following a successful vote of no confidence, and prior to the election for a new Prime Minister or the dissolution of the Assembly.

These considerations notwithstanding, there can be no doubt regarding the importance of the caretaker arrangements. A vital constitutional element for the exercise of the President's

extraordinary power under Article 58(2)(b) was that 'an appeal
to the electorate is necessary'. Free and fair elections were
envisaged. However, the very fact that the President could
remove a government for not acting in accordance with the
Constitution, placed him in a position adversarial to the party
removed. Moreover, caretaker executives have frequently
exercised the power of temporary legislation through
Ordinances, and ·thus affected elections. Although no
qualifications or limitations were specified by the Constitution
for a caretaker government, clearly a strictly neutral arrangement
was required to ensure free and fair elections. To provide a
buffer between the President and the removed party, a Prime
Minister was necessary at the head of a caretaker Cabinet, and
not the President as General Zia apparently believed.

In the November 1988 general elections, Benazir Bhutto's
PPP secured the largest number of seats but not a majority in
the National Assembly. Article 91(2) as amended in 1985
empowered the President, till 20 March 1990, to appoint a Prime
Minister. As a consequence, the arrangement arrived at saw
Benazir Bhutto as Prime Minister in December and Ishaq Khan
elected as President. They often disagreed and, twenty months
later on 6 August 1990, the President dissolved the National
Assembly and removed the Prime Minister on several grounds.
The dissolution order avoided the legal lacuna pointed out by
the Supreme Court in the Saifullah Khan Case. Accordingly,
the Supreme Court in the Tariq Rahim Case upheld the
President's Order against Benazir Bhutto, and rejected the
arguments that acts such as 'horse-trading of elected
representatives, corruption and nepotism, violation of
constitutional provisions, e.g., not summoning the Council of
Common Interests, all have been taking place in the past'. It
proceeded to hold that

> ...once the evil is identified, remedial and corrective measures
> within the constitutional framework must follow. Public
> functionaries holding public power in trust, under oath to discharge
> the same impartially and to the best of their ability, must react.
> They cannot and must not remain silent spectators.

The Court concluded that some of the grounds 'may not have been sufficient to warrant such an action. They can, however, be invoked, referred to and made use of along with grounds' which 'by themselves are sufficient to justify the action taken'.[47]

Following the general elections, on 6 November 1990 Nawaz Sharif became Prime Minister, the first from a purely business background. He led a coalition government with the Muslim League as the principal party. Both he and President Ishaq Khan had earlier worked under General Zia and had opposed Benazir Bhutto. However, by 1993, disagreements arose between them, mainly over the powers of the President under the Eighth Amendment, resulting in the Prime Minister's removal and the dissolution of the National Assembly on 18 April 1993. The grounds for dissolution were not unlike those for removing Benazir Bhutto. Some less significant reasons were omitted, and new grounds were advanced, including the mass resignations of opposition parliamentarians, and even some Ministers, and the inability of the President and Prime Minister to work together.

The Supreme Court accepted Nawaz Sharif's petition which was filed directly under its original jurisdiction, and not first in the High Court. This was done in terms of Article 17(2), which provided that every citizen had the 'right to form or be a member of a political party', and the Court held that this comprised the right not only to

> ...contest elections under its banner but also, after successfully contesting the elections, the right to form the Government if...in possession of the requisite majority... Any unlawful order which results in frustrating their activity, by removing it from office before the completion of its normal tenure would, therefore, constitute an infringement of this Fundamental Right.[48]

Three main aspects of the decision in the Nawaz Sharif Case are important. First, the Court held that the

...belief that the President enjoys some inherent or implied powers besides those specifically conferred on him under Article 46, 48(b), 101, 242(2A) and 243(2)(c) is a mistaken one... In view of the express provision of our written Constitution...there is no room for any residual or enabling powers inherent in any authority established by it besides those conferred upon it by specific words.

It reiterated that 'the system of Government envisaged by the 1973 Constitution is of the Parliamentary type wherein the Prime Minister as Head of the Cabinet is responsible for the Parliament, which consists of the representatives of the nation', and went on to state that the Prime Minister is not 'in any way subordinate to' the President. Secondly, on the question of Article 58(2)(b) itself, the Court followed the Saifullah Khan Case and not the Tariq Rahim Case:

Article 58(2)(b) of the Constitution empowers the executive head to destroy the legislature and to remove the chosen representatives. It is an exceptional power provided for an exceptional situation and must receive...the narrowest interpretation.[49]

It held against the President, 'after carefully examining the gravamen of each ground' and finding that 'not one of them can be validly relied upon to sustain the order of dissolution'; though, as the lone dissenting judge pointed out, there was 'no difference in the case of Khwaja Ahmed Tariq Rahim and in the present case, so far [as] allegations, grounds for dissolution and material produced in support thereof are concerned'. Finally, on the subject of the relief to be granted, the decision in the Saifullah Khan Case was revised:

On hindsight, I now think that after having found the action of the dissolution of the National Assembly was not sustainable in law, the Court should not have denied the consequential relief and ought to have restored the National Assembly.[50]

Nawaz Sharif resumed as Prime Minister on 26 May 1993. The events of this period are recent but worth recalling to demonstrate the extent of political manœuvring and mistakes that resulted in the army once again becoming overtly the dominant force. In the brief time Nawaz Sharif was out of office, his nominee as Chief Minister of the Punjab was replaced by the Speaker of the Punjab Assembly. On Nawaz Sharif's unprecedented reinstatement, had there been any degree of restraint, he might well have continued as Prime Minister with a weakened Ishaq Khan completing his remaining months as President. However, within days, the struggle for power resulted in the Chief Ministers of the Punjab and NWFP advising that their Provincial Assemblies be dissolved and fresh elections held. The Lahore High Court declared the dissolution of the Punjab Assembly to be illegal; within an hour, the Chief Minister again advised his Governor to dissolve the Assembly. The President had just previously refused to approve such action on the Governor's initiative. Since the Prime Minister did not know this, differences between them increased. Nawaz Sharif secured a resolution of Parliament declaring an Emergency in the Punjab on 29 June. This resolution could not be implemented, and the Prime Minister received a second setback when, on 14 July, the Peshawar High Court upheld the order of dissolution of the NWFP Assembly. To avert a threatened 'long march' on Islamabad, and continued deadlock, the army intervened. As a result, on 18 July, the President and Prime Minister, and with them the four Governors and Chief Ministers, were replaced, permitting fresh elections to the National and Provincial Assemblies.

After the general elections, Benazir Bhutto again became Prime Minister. She strengthened her position by having her party colleague, Farooq Ahmed Leghari, elected as President, and, with the army impartial, she appeared to be well-entrenched. However, among other mistakes, her choice of judges to the Superior Courts was such that, after years of suffering appointments of judges without proper 'consultation', the Supreme Court asserted itself in what is known as the Appointment of Judges Case:

The words 'after consultation' employed *inter alia* in Articles 177 and 193 of the Constitution connote that the consultation should be meaningful, purposive, consensus-oriented, leaving no room for complaint of arbitrariness or unfair play. The opinion of the Chief Justice of Pakistan and the Chief Justice of a High Court as to the fitness and suitability of a candidate for judgeship is entitled to be accepted in the absence of very sound reasons to be recorded by the President/Executive.[51]

This, together with the Court's findings on other points such as the appointment of 'acting' and 'ad hoc' judges, and respect for seniority, deprived the Prime Minister of considerable patronage and authority. It reflected the independence of the judiciary.

When Benazir Bhutto did not fully comply with this judgment, the President sought the Supreme Court's opinion on whether he could proceed in the appointment of judges without the Prime Minister's advice, and, as noted earlier, the Court ruled that the President could not act independently, except in matters where the Constitution specifically so allowed. This decision had little practical relevance because the Appointment of Judges Case gave the Chief Justices concerned a virtually decisive role. However, had the Court favoured the exercise of such powers by the President, its implications for other provisions of the Constitution would have contributed considerably to a conceptual change towards greater independent or inherent powers for the President. In this and other cases the Court has laid stress on the parliamentary dispensation.

On 5 November 1996, President Leghari removed Prime Minister Benazir Bhutto and dissolved the National Assembly under Article 58(2)(b); the grounds included the non-implementation of the Appointment of Judges Case, corruption, maladministration, and large-scale denial of human and fundamental rights. Benazir Bhutto challenged the order of dissolution. On 29 January 1997 the Supreme Court in its 6 to 1 decision followed its earlier judgment in the Tariq Rahim Case, and upheld the dissolution of the Assembly.

An analysis of the earlier three judgments and the Court's short order in the Benazir Bhutto Case[52] relating to Article 58(2)(b) shows that, on several issues, they did not provide certainty. No clear guidelines emerged for the President to exercise his discretion and, in reality, the Supreme Court in judicial proceedings made the final decision.

There is an inherent danger in involving the Courts in too many politico-constitutional cases, and in expecting them to solve our numerous political problems. That apart, they too have reversed, revised or 'distinguished' their earlier decisions, and have not ensured the continuity which is a prerequisite of stability. Judicial activism is in many respects commendable, particularly in the field of human rights, the protection of the environment and the assertion of the independence of the judiciary. However, a disturbing aspect of the political cases has been highlighted by the allegation of provincial bias, which is particularly worrying in the context of a federation.

In a recent case in which the constitutionality of the Eighth Amendment was challenged, thereby placing on the Supreme Court the onus of striking down an amendment made by a Parliament elected on a non-party basis and under Martial Law, the Court acted with correct circumspection. Its short order of 12 January 1997 stated:

> The Eighth Amendment was inserted in the Constitution in 1985, after which three elections were held on party basis and the resultant parliaments did not touch this amendment which demonstrates amply that this amendment is ratified by implication and has come to stay in the Constitution.[53]

However, a noteworthy feature of Chief Justice Sajjad Ali Shah's judgment of 4 April was his observation that Parliament can '...make any amendment in the Constitution...as long as basic characteristics of federalism, parliamentary democracy and Islamic provisions as contained in the Objectives Resolution...are not touched'.[54] It remains to be seen how these qualifying words will be applied in the future, particularly in view of clauses (5) and (6) of Article 239 which lay down that no amendment shall be called in question in any court and that 'there is no limitation whatever on the power' of Parliament to amend any provision of the Constitution.

Differences between the President and Prime Minister mainly arose over the exercise of power in the context of the Eighth Amendment, resulting in recourse to Article 58(2)(b) on four occasions in a period of eight and a half years. During this time there have been three Presidents, Zia, Ishaq Khan and Leghari, while Ishaq and Wasim Sajjad served as acting Presidents over long periods in 1988 and 1993 respectively. There have also been ten Prime Ministers, including caretaker ones, namely, Muhammad Khan Junejo, Benazir Bhutto, caretaker Ghulam Mustafa Jatoi, Nawaz Sharif, caretaker Balakh Sher Mazari, a reinstated Nawaz Sharif, caretaker Moin Qureshi, again Benazir Bhutto, caretaker Malik Meraj Khalid, and now Nawaz Sharif, while President Zia and acting President Ishaq Khan were, for over six months in 1988, their own caretaker executive authority.

From 1985 the parliamentary system has not worked properly, echoing the experience of the earlier period of 1951-58. In part, this was due to Article 58(2)(b). For that matter, the presidential form of government has also not succeeded despite its existence for fifteen years from 7 October 1958 to 14 August 1973, and then for another eight years under General Zia. Indeed, this has been the case with all four executive Presidents: Ayub Khan was prepared to abandon the presidential system he had established, under Yahya Khan the country was dismembered, Z. A. Bhutto had to reintroduce the parliamentary system to achieve a consensus on the 1973 Constitution, and Zia's efforts to have a party-less system were reversed and, recently, several of his constitutional amendments have been repealed.

In fact, in the past fifty years, only Zulfikar Ali Bhutto completed his first elected term as Prime Minister. Within months of the 7 March 1977 elections he was ousted, and hanged on 4 April 1979. The Quaid-i-Azam died in September 1948 and the first Prime Minister, Liaquat Ali Khan, was assassinated in 1951. All other executive Presidents and Prime Ministers

have been prematurely removed, while General Zia died in
suspicious circumstances in a plane crash. This, in short, has
been the constitutional and political history of the country.

1997 Constitutional Amendments

In the elections held on 3 February 1997, Nawaz Sharif and his
Muslim League party secured an overwhelming victory. In his
first speech as Prime Minister he focused on the economic crisis
facing the nation, and on benefits for the common man, rather
than on constitutional issues. Soon, however, he decided to
repeal some provisions of the Eighth Amendment; this was done
by Parliament on 1 April.

This Thirteenth Amendment[55] to the Constitution removed
some significant powers conferred on the President by the Eighth
Amendment, and in particular sub-clause (b) of Article 58(2).
The frequent use of the latter introduced no real change but
contributed to political instability. The arguments advanced that
it prevented Martial Law from being imposed, acted as a 'safety
valve' and allowed for 'checks and balances' are not sustainable.
It is domestic and international opinion rather than any
constitutional mechanism that prevents Martial Law. Indeed, in
July 1993, when Article 58(2)(b) had failed, the army intervened,
and, without imposing Martial Law, the legislative assemblies
and all the executive authorities at the federal and provincial
levels were replaced, and elections held. No constitution can
provide effective checks and balances when the system itself
fails.

Three further changes were introduced by the Thirteenth
Amendment. Firstly, Article 112(2)(b), which applied to the
provinces in a way similar to Article 58(2)(b), was repealed.
Secondly, Article 101 was amended to provide that the President
appoints the Governors 'on the advice of', instead of 'after
consultation with', the Prime Minister. Thirdly, control of the
armed forces under Article 243 was fully restored to the Federal
Government by omitting the provision that the Service Chiefs
were to be appointed by the President 'in his discretion'.

Thereafter, on 16 April, it was announced that the Federal Government was preparing further amendments, including the restoration of seats reserved for women in the Assemblies. Provision for this had been made under the 1973 Constitution for ten years, and the subsequent extension in 1985 had also lapsed. When the remaining changes introduced by the Eighth Amendment, and other provisions which have either lapsed or become redundant, are reviewed, consideration should also be given to curtailing the concurrent list of subjects over which both the federation and the provinces exercise legislative and executive authority.

Now that the country has reverted to a mainly parliamentary form of government under the 1973 Constitution, let us hope political leaders demonstrate the will to make it work. This is more important than any amendments to the Constitution. On Prime Minister Nawaz Sharif and his party lies the heavy burden of ensuring a democratic polity as Pakistan enters its sixth decade.

Some Concluding Thoughts

Constitution-making in Pakistan has consumed a disproportionate amount of time and effort with little positive result. Debate on the form of the Constitution commenced with the inception of the country, and still continues. The repeated process of rewriting the Constitution, and the manner in which power has been exercised under it, has kept the democratic dispensation in doubt, and prevented it from working properly, let alone succeeding. The Constitution should be a symbol of national identity and integration, but our failure to achieve these essentials has left us seeking a substitute in the Constitution— making it an end in itself.

Certain circles have continued to promote the idea that a presidential dispensation provides a panacea for Pakistan's ills. They do not adequately take into account that, despite its desirability in some respects, it can have detrimental consequences in a federation where one province has a larger population than the others combined. In any event, it is not merely a question of whether a presidential or parliamentary form of government is most suited to Pakistan. We have unsuccessfully tried both, though mainly in somewhat extreme forms. The 1985 amendments endeavoured to avoid the concentration of excessive executive authority in one person, but they were not successful.

Democracy can only develop and grow at grass roots level, and cannot be imposed from the top. Such growth can best be achieved through maximum decentralization and devolution of power; indeed, elections to local bodies and local governments are as essential as those at the provincial and federal levels. Grass roots democracy will benefit the general public who have discovered, over the years, that all the fine phrases in the Constitution have no bearing on them, and are either meaningless or fraudulent, or both. A country that came into existence on the basis of a democratic vote has so far given the common man little to satisfy his democratic, social and economic aspirations. Apathy and disillusion are reflected in the fact that each election has produced a lower voter turnout than the previous one.

Questions can well be asked about this recurrent failure to make any constitutional arrangement work. If our colonial legacy were to blame, then how have countries such as Malaysia and India succeeded? Was the idea of a State based on religion essentially unworkable? This possibility too has been disproved by Israel and, more recently, Iran. Is it because the structure of the Federation of Pakistan has been inherently unbalanced, with one province either larger than the others combined, or too dominant? While this has no doubt posed problems, they could have been overcome through provincial autonomy, decentralization, and common and effective forums such as the Council of Common Interests, provided they were allowed to work by individual leaders. This brings us to the question of leadership and its failings.

The sequence of events discussed earlier clearly shows a failure of leadership, and the serious consequences that have ensued. But to attribute all our misfortunes merely to this one factor might be somewhat exaggerated. In the absence of elections in the early period, and in times of Martial Law, any effective control on our leadership has been difficult. However, in a little over eight years, Pakistan has had four party-based general elections, and it might reasonably be expected that the verdict of the people would have a controlling force on the leadership. That this has so far not been the case is in part due to Pakistan's feudal system, which has continued to survive attempts at land reform. Feudalism has tended to breed sycophancy and excessive deference to those in power, and contempt for those over whom it is exercised. The situation has further deteriorated following the emergence of big business in politics and the excessive use of money for political ends; the entwinement of wealth and political power has made the attainment of a democratic and egalitarian order even more difficult. Moreover, many business leaders, instead of rejecting feudal culture, have adopted its worst aspects. As a consequence, the executive has wielded an inordinate degree of unchecked power, a natural outcome of which is its abuse and corruption.

A reorientation in our body politic and outlook is overdue, but attempts to achieve this merely through rewriting or amending the Constitution would not be a meaningful exercise. The Constitution is mainly a legal form for a political system: in the words of Woodrow Wilson, 'the vehicle of a nation's life'. Sadly, in the past fifty years, the vehicle has made little progress in Pakistan, and the country is today still faced with the challenge that the Quaid-i-Azam addressed as early as December 1938:

> Muslims [of India]...were like men who had lost their moral, cultural and political consciousness... You have only reached that stage at which an awakening has come—your political conscience has been stirred.

...that essential quality, moral, cultural and political consciousness...become[s] the national consciousness...; that is the force I want the Muslims to acquire. When you have acquired that, believe me, I have no doubt in my mind you will realize what you want. The counting of heads may be a very good thing; but it is not the final arbiter of the destiny of nations. You have yet to develop a national self and a national individuality. It is a big task; and as I have told you, you are yet only on the fringe of it. But I have great hopes for our success.[56]

NOTES

1. The Report of the Simon Commission, 1930, Volume II, Paras 23 and 24, p. 14, and Para 27, p. 16. The Montagu-Chelmsford Reforms were introduced in 1919.
2. *Constituent Assembly of Pakistan Debates,* Official Report, Volume V, 1949, pp. 1-2.
3. Felix Frankfurter, *Mr Justice Holmes and the Supreme Court,* Harvard, 1938, p. 16.
4. 'Parity' described the equal representation, irrespective of population, given to the two Wings of Pakistan in the federal legislature. This existed under the Constitutions of 1956 and 1962.
5. Federation of Pakistan v. Moulvi Tamizuddin Khan, PLD 1955 Federal Court, p. 240.
6. Reference by His Excellency the Governor-General (under Section 213 of the Government of India Act, 1935), PLD 1955 Federal Court, p. 435 at p. 469.
7. Ibid., pp. 478-79.
8. Ibid., p. 487.
9. The State v. Dosso, PLD 1958 Supreme Court (Pak), p. 533 at p. 539.
10. Asma Jilani v. Government of the Punjab, PLD 1972 Supreme Court, p. 139 at pp. 206-7.
11. The Agartala Conspiracy Case was named after the venue, Agartala, of the alleged conspiracy with India against Pakistan.
12. *Dawn,* Karachi, 14 March 1969.
13. The Legal Framework Order, 1970, President's Order No. 2 of 1970, *Gazette of Pakistan Extraordinary* Part II, of 30 March 1970, with these two provisions contained in Article 20 Clauses (1) and (4) respectively; also PLD 1970 Central Statutes, p. 229.

14. The total number of 313 for the National Assembly included 13 seats reserved for women to be elected indirectly by the members from a province in the Assembly, and was composed as follows:

Province and Area	General seats	Women's seats
East Pakistan	162	7
Balochistan	4	1
The Punjab	82	3
Sindh	27	1
NWFP	18	1
Federally Administered Tribal Areas	7	0
Total	300	13

15. *Pakistan Observer,* Dhaka, 21 December 1970.
16. For further details of the negotiations and developments during this period, *see,* Rafi Raza, *Zulfikar Ali Bhutto and Pakistan: 1967-1977,* Oxford University Press, Karachi, 1997, pp. 47-52 and 72-81.
17. Z.A. Bhutto, *The Great Tragedy,* Vision Publications, Karachi, 1971, p. 20.
18. *See Dawn,* Karachi, and *The Pakistan Times,* Lahore, 16 February 1971, for these quotations and other details of this press conference.
19. Rafi Raza, op. cit., pp. 61-62 and 82.
20. Ibid., pp. 67, 75, 82 and 84.
21. Of the numerous books on the subject, the following are selected by the author: G.W. Chowdhry, *The Last Days of United Pakistan,* Indiana University Press, Bloomington, 1974; Rafi Raza, op. cit., Richard Sisson and Leo E. Rose, *War and Seccession—Pakistan, India, and the Creation of Bangladesh,* University of California Press, Berkeley and Los Angeles, 1990; Stanley Wolpert, *Zulfi Bhutto of Pakistan,* Oxford University Press, New York, 1993; Hasan Zaheer, *The Separation of East Pakistan—The Rise and Realization of Bengali Muslim Nationalism,* Oxford University Press, Karachi, 1994.
22. Rafi Raza, op. cit.,
23. Ibid., p. 87.
24. Asma Jilani v. Government of the Punjab, PLD 1972 Supreme Court, p. 139 at p. 243; the earlier two quotes are at pp. 179 and 183.
25. *See,* Rafi Raza, op. cit., pp. 174-79 for further details.
26. *Constituent Assembly of Pakistan Debates,* Official Report, Volume V, 1949, p. 3.

27. Laws (Continuance in Force) Order, 1958, President's Order (Post-Proclamation) No. 1 of 1958, *Gazette of Pakistan Extraordinary*, of 10 October 1958, Article 2 (1).

28. Constitution (First Amendment) Act 1974, (33 of 1974), *Gazette of Pakistan Extraordinary*, Part I, of 8 May 1974, Sections 4 and 9.

29. Constitution (Third Amendment) Act, 1975, (22 of 1975), *Gazette of Pakistan Extraordinary*, Part I, of 18 February 1975.

30. Constitution (Fourth Amendment) Act, 1975, (71 of 1975), *Gazette of Pakistan Extraordinary*, Part I, of 25 November 1975.

31. Constitution (Fifth Amendment) Act, 1976, (62 of 1976), *Gazette of Pakistan Extraordinary*, Part I, of 15 September 1976.

32. Begum Nusrat Bhutto v. Chief of Army Staff and Federation of Pakistan, PLD 1977 Supreme Court, p. 657 at p. 704.

33. Ibid., 722.

34. Ibid., p. 723.

35. President's Order No. 11 of 1984, the Referendum Order, 1984, *Gazette of Pakistan Extraordinary*, Part I, of 1 December 1984.

36. President's Order No. 14 of 1985, *Gazette of Pakistan Extraordinary*, Part I, of 2 March 1985; also PLD 1985 Central Statutes, pp. 456-98.

37. President's Order No. 1 of 1980, Constitutional (Amendment) Order, 1980, *Gazette of Pakistan Extraordinary*, Part I, of 27 May 1980; also PLD 1980 Central Statutes, pp. 89-94.

38. Constitution (Eighth Amendment) Act, 1985 (18 of 1985), *Gazette of Pakistan Extraordinary*, of 11 November 1985.

39. Asma Jilani v. Government of the Punjab, PLD 1972 Supreme Court, p. 139 at p. 182.

40. Hakim Khan v. Government of Pakistan, PLD 1992 Supreme Court, p. 595 at p. 615.

41. The following provisions may be seen by way of example: in the Indian Constitution, Articles 55(2), 75, 78(c), 79, 86, 87, 111, 155, 156 and 327(2); in the Australian Constitution, Articles 1 and 58; in the German Constitution, Articles 54(3) and 64(1); in the Constitution of Ireland, Articles 13(4) and (7), 15, 27, 28(1), 51, 87 and 92; and Articles 83, 87, 89 and 92 of the Italian Constitution.

42. *Constituent Assembly Debates*, 4 November 1948, p. 32, as cited in M.N. Kaul and S.L. Shakdher, *Practice and Procedure of Parliament*, Metropolitan Book Company, New Delhi, (Third Edition), Reprint 1986, pp. 18-19. *See also*, notes 4 on p. 18 and 1 on p. 19 thereto.

43. *See, Dawn,* Karachi, 5 December 1996, for the short order of the Supreme Court.

44. Benazir Bhutto v. Federation of Pakistan and another, PLD 1988 Supreme Court, p. 416.

45. Federation of Pakistan and others v. Haji Muhammad Saifullah Khan and others, PLD 1989 Supreme Court, p. 166 at p. 190.

46. Ibid., p. 216.
47. Khwaja Ahmad Tariq Rahim v. The Federation of Pakistan, PLD 1992 Supreme Court, p. 646; the two quotations are at pp. 660-61 and 666-67.
48. Mian Muhammad Nawaz Sharif v. President of Pakistan and others, PLD 1993 Supreme Court, p. 473 at p. 559.
49. Ibid., p. 579; the earlier quotation is at pp. 566-67.
50. Ibid., p. 565; the earlier two quotations are at p. 561 and p. 787.
51. Al-Jehad Trust through Raeesul Mujahedeen Haibib-ul-Wahab-ul-Khaimi v. Federation of Pakistan and others, PLD 1996 Supreme Court, p. 324 at pp. 364-65. *See also, Dawn Supplement* of 4 April 1996 for the full text of the judgment.
52. *See, Dawn,* Karachi, 30 and 31 January 1997, for the short order of the Supreme Court; the detailed judgment had not been announced till May 1997.
53. *See, Dawn,* Karachi, 13 January 1997, for the short order of the Supreme Court.
54. *See, Dawn,* Karachi, 5 April 1997, for extracts from this judgment; the detailed judgment has not been published in the PLD till May, but has been examined by the author.
55. *See, Dawn,* Karachi, 2 April 1997, for the text of the Thirteenth Amendment.
56. Quaid-i-Azam Mohammad Ai Jinnah's Presidential Address at the Twenty-sixth Session of the All-India Muslim League in Patna on 26 December 1938, *Foundations of Pakistan: All-India Muslim League Documents: 1906-47,* op. cit., Vol. II, pp. 306-7.

SELECT BIBLIOGRAPHY

Ali, Chaudhri Muhammad, *The Emergence of Pakistan,* Columbia University Press, New York, 1967.

Austin, Granville, *The Indian Constitution: Cornerstone of a Nation,* Clarendon Press, Oxford, 1966.

Ayub Khan, Muhammad, *Friends Not Masters, A Political Autobiography,* Oxford University Press, New York, 1967.

Callard, Keith, *Pakistan, A Political Study,* Macmillan Company, New York, 1957.

Constitution-Making in Pakistan, 1973, published by the National Assembly Secretariat, April 1975.

Jennings, Ivor, *Constitutional Problems of Pakistan,* Cambridge University Press, London, 1955.

Kaul, M.N. and Shakdher, S.L., *Practice and Procedure of Parliament,* Metropolitan Book Company, New Delhi, (Third Edition), Reprint 1986.

Pirzada, Syed Sharifuddin, ed., *Foundations of Pakistan—All-India Muslim League Documents*, 1906-47, National Publishing House, Karachi, 1970.

Raza, Rafi, *Zulfikar Ali Bhutto and Pakistan: 1967-1977,* Oxford University Press, Karachi, 1997.

Seervai, H.M., *Constitutional Law of India,* Dasons Printers, Bombay, (Third Edition), 1983-84.

CHAPTER 2

FOREIGN POLICY

Abdul Sattar

Pakistan entered upon the world stage on 14 August 1947 with urges and aspirations founded in the history and culture of its predominantly Muslim people. Heir to a universalist civilization with an overarching sense of community that extended beyond its own territory, the nation looked forward to friendly cooperation with other countries of the world for mutual peace and progress. Its founding father, Quaid-i-Azam Mohammad Ali Jinnah, known for his intellectual integrity and emphasis on law and logic, envisioned a progressive polity. Even earlier, Syed Ahmed Khan urged the Muslim community in the nineteenth century to end its boycott of the West and assimilate contemporary knowledge in order to make up for past neglect. Allama Muhammad Iqbal, a humanist scholar deeply read in history and philosophy, used the vehicle of inspiring poetry to inculcate pride in humanity's capacity to mould its own destiny. While holding fast to its Islamic moorings, the Muslim community needed to open the door to adaptation and reconstruction in order to re-embark on the road to social and economic progress.

Solidarity with other Muslim nations was as natural as support for the just causes of nations struggling for freedom and self-determination. Bearing no bitterness toward the colonial rulers who departed in peace, Pakistan looked to the advanced nations for cooperation for the preservation of peace and promotion of economic development. Pakistani leaders also wanted peace and amity with India. Proud of having achieved Pakistan 'peacefully by moral and intellectual force',[1] they hoped that law and reason would govern relations between the two neighbouring States. They were too preoccupied by the myriad tasks of establishing the government of the new State in the midst of the turmoil of the Partition and did not want added problems. But the choice did not rest on them alone.

Foreign Policy Origins

'There is nothing that we desire more ardently than to live in peace and let others live in peace, and develop our country, according to our own lights', said Mohammad Ali Jinnah who became the first Governor-General. 'We believe in the principle of honesty and fair play in national and international dealings', he said, pledging that 'Pakistan will never be found lacking in extending its material and moral support to the oppressed and suppressed people of the world and in upholding the principles of the United Nations Charter'. Particularly solicitous of warm relations with Muslim countries, Jinnah recalled the 'deep sympathy and interest' with which the Muslims of British India followed the fortunes of Turkey 'right from the birth of political consciousness' among them. He expressed sentiments of friendship toward the United States which, he said, 'acted as a beacon of light and had in no small measure served to give inspiration to nations who like us were striving for independence and freedom from the shackles of foreign rule'.[2] Pakistan started its independent career 'without any narrow and special commitments and without any prejudices in the international sphere'.[3]

Concerning India, Pakistan's endeavour, Jinnah declared, would be to promote goodwill and friendship with 'our neighbourly dominion, Hindustan'. The Partition Plan was accepted by the leadership of the Muslim League and the Indian National Congress through a process of negotiation. Pakistan was established by the exercise of the right of self-determination by the people of Muslim majority provinces and parts of provinces, either in popular referenda or by the vote of elected Provincial Assemblies. Assuming that in future, too, Pakistani and Indian leaders could settle differences on the basis of universally accepted principles of law and justice, Jinnah saw no reason why Pakistan and India should not have good neighbourly relations.

Tension between Pakistan and India from the outset was ascribable partly to a difficult and divisive legacy, adversarial perceptions of history, differences of religions and cultures, and the clash of political aims and ideologies between the Muslim League and the Indian National Congress. But having agreed to the Partition, good neighbourly policies could have consolidated peaceful co-existence and precluded antagonistic relations. Their exacerbation, and the perpetuation of tension, were owed, in particular, to the failure to resolve disputes that arose after Independence.

Indian Congress leaders accepted Pakistan, but grudgingly, and hoped that the new State would collapse. No one epitomized the contradiction in the Congress mind more strikingly than its spiritual leader, Mahatma Gandhi. In June 1947 he agreed that the Partition was 'inevitable' but he had also declared, 'So long as I am alive, I will never agree to the partition of India'.[4] The resolution of the All-India Congress Committee, the highest organ of the party, was no less contradictory. It professed that Congress 'cannot think in terms of compelling the people in any territorial unit to remain in the Indian Union', but, in another sentence, harked back to its view that 'the unity of India must be maintained'.[5]

The Partition Plan of 3 June 1947 gave only seventy-two days for transition to Independence. Within this brief period, provinces had to be divided, referenda organized, civil and armed services personnel allocated, and assets apportioned. The telescoped timetable created seemingly impossible problems for Pakistan which, unlike India, inherited neither a capital with a government, nor the financial resources to establish and equip the administrative, economic and military institutions of the new

State. Even more daunting problems arose in the wake of the Partition.[6]

Communal rioting led to the killing of hundreds of thousands of innocent people. A tidal wave of eight million refugees entered Pakistan, confronting the new State with an awesome burden of rehabilitation. Lord Mountbatten, flattered by his appointment as the first Governor-General of independent India, abused his influence to modify the award of the Radcliffe Boundary Commission in the Punjab to give two Muslim majority *tehsils* (subdivisions) of Gurdaspur district to India in order to provide it access to the State of Jammu and Kashmir.[7] India 'dishonestly retained much of Pakistan's share of the assets of British India'.[8] Indian leaders 'persistently tried to obstruct the work of partition of the armed forces'.[9] 'What mattered to them, above all else, was to cripple and thwart the establishment of Pakistan as a viable independent state.'[10]

Suddenly, in April 1948, India cut off water supply in the irrigation canals that flowed from headworks on the rivers Ravi and Sutlej, menacing agriculture in Pakistan. Ignoring principles of international law governing international rivers, it claimed 'seigniorage' charges for the water flowing to Pakistan. Facing ruin of agriculture in the affected areas, Pakistan submitted under duress.

Kashmir Question: 1947-57

The State of Jammu and Kashmir was one of 562 Princely States which exercised varying degrees of internal autonomy under treaties with British authorities made during the period of colonial penetration. When British suzerainty over these states lapsed in 1947, the princes were advised to accede to Pakistan or India, keeping in mind that 'You cannot run away from the Dominion government which is your neighbour any more than you can run away from the subjects for whose welfare you are responsible.'[11] When the Muslim ruler of the Hindu majority State of Junagadh announced accession to Pakistan, the Indian

Government said that the decision was 'in utter violation of principles on which Partition was agreed upon and effected'.[12] It then peremptorily invaded and occupied Junagadh. Two months later, however, the Indian Government itself committed an 'utter violation' of the principle on which Partition was based when it manipulated accession by the Hindu Maharaja of the Muslim majority State of Jammu and Kashmir.

The Maharaja's collusion with the Indian Government had already sparked uprisings in his State. In Gilgit Agency, the local authority decided, with the enthusiastic backing of the people, to declare allegiance to Pakistan. The people of Poonch and Mirpur districts, home to 60,000 demobilized soldiers of the Second World War, rose in revolt and declared the formation of the 'Azad' (Free) Jammu and Kashmir government. After the Maharaja's forces embarked on 'systematic savageries'[13] against unarmed Kashmiris, tribesmen from Pakistan went in to their rescue. Pouncing on the opportunity, the Indian Government flew its troops to Srinagar on 27 October 1947.

In an attempt to camouflage its usurpation, the Indian Government erected a smokescreen of promises to the people of Kashmir, Pakistan and the world. In the letter of acceptance of the Maharaja's offer of accession, India's Governor-General stated that it was his government's 'policy that, in the case of any state where the issue of accession has been the subject of dispute, the question of accession should be decided in accordance with the wishes of the people of that state'. Jawaharlal Nehru informed Liaquat Ali Khan that the Indian intervention was 'not designed in any way to influence the state to accede to India'.[14] The Pakistani Prime Minister called the accession 'fraudulent'.[15]

Meeting stiff resistance from the people of Kashmir, India lodged a complaint with the UN Security Council. Pakistan filed a counter complaint. After listening to both sides, the Security Council established in January 1948 the UN Commission for India and Pakistan (UNCIP) to mediate in the dispute. At UNCIP's initiative, the Council adopted a resolution on 21 April 1948 recommending measures 'appropriate to bring about cessation of the fighting and to create proper conditions for a free and impartial plebiscite to decide whether the State of Jammu and Kashmir is to accede to India or Pakistan'. On 13 August 1948, UNCIP adopted a more elaborate three-part resolution providing for a cease-fire, a truce agreement, and a plebiscite. Both India and Pakistan reaffirmed 'their wish that the future status of the State of Jammu and Kashmir shall be determined in accordance with the will of the people'. On 5 January 1949, UNCIP adopted another resolution incorporating supplementary principles about the truce, the appointment of a Plebiscite Administrator and arrangements for 'a free and impartial plebiscite'.

When India made baseless accusations of non-compliance by Pakistan to justify its refusal to implement UN resolutions, Washington suggested flexibility on legal points. Nehru, in rage, said that he 'would not give an inch. He would hold his ground if Kashmir, India, and the whole world would go to pieces'.[16] A joint appeal by President Harry S. Truman and Prime Minister Clement Attlee on 31 August 1949 for arbitration on differences of interpretation of the UNCIP plan elicited a similarly truculent response. Proposals made in December 1949 by the Security Council President, General A. G. L. McNaughton of Canada, for reduction of forces on both sides of the cease-fire line prior to the plebiscite were rejected by India.[17] Owen Dixon of Australia, the next UN representative, tried to secure India's agreement to alternative proposals, but came to the conclusion that India's agreement 'would never be obtained to demilitarization'. He then canvassed personal suggestions for either four 'regional plebiscites' or for limiting the plebiscite to the Valley of Kashmir. No progress was made. India now called for condemnation of Pakistani 'aggression'. As this had 'nothing to do' with the plebiscite, Dixon concluded that there was nothing further that he could do.[18]

Pakistan's decision to enter into an alliance with the United States in 1953 was used by India as a pretext to renounce the pledge of plebiscite, refusing to explain how Pakistan's relations with another country could either absolve India of its obligations or prejudice the Kashmiri right of self-determination.[19] Soon, India received Soviet backing and its use of the veto made India increasingly defiant of the Security Council.

In 1957, New Delhi asked the 'Constituent Assembly' in Srinagar to ratify the Maharaja's accession. Pakistan brought the matter to the attention of the UN Security Council which adopted a resolution on 24 January 1957, reminding 'the Governments and Authorities concerned of the principle...that the final disposition of the State of Jammu and Kashmir will be made in accordance with the will of the people expressed through the democratic method of a free and impartial plebiscite conducted under the auspices of the United Nations' and reaffirming that any action taken by this assembly 'would not constitute a disposition of the State in accordance with the above principle'.

Relations with the USA, USSR and China

It was in this crucible of objective realities that the core of Pakistan's foreign policy was shaped. Confronted with threats to its existence and the tyranny of imbalance of power, Pakistan responded just as states have throughout history—it sought to ameliorate the disparity of power by cultivating the sympathy and support of other states, near and far. Among these, Britain lacked the power, and the Soviet Union the inclination, to play an effective role for peace, and both were too debilitated by war to provide economic assistance. The United States alone had the resources to provide assistance. Moreover, its foreign policy clashed with Pakistan's on relatively few issues other than the Palestine question. Pakistan started courting the US from the start.

The United States paid little attention to the Pakistan Movement. President Franklin D. Roosevelt tried to goad Winston Churchill in favour of decolonization but was apparently unaware of Muslim support for the Allies in the Second World

War. The US Commissioner in New Delhi, William Philips, disliked the proposal 'to break India into two'.[20] The demand for a state in the name of Islam was difficult for secular America to comprehend.[21] It was significant, however, that after Pakistan was established the United States immediately began to show understanding. President Truman sent a warm message on Pakistan's Independence, assuring 'firm friendship and goodwill'.[22] The US was among the first countries to establish an embassy in Karachi. Truman gave a 'sympathetic' ear when Pakistan's Ambassador spoke about the need 'to balance our economy, to industrialize our country, to improve health and education and raise the standard of living'.[23] Pakistan hurriedly approached the United States in October 1947 for a loan of approximately $2 billion over five years for economic development and defence purchases in order to 'attain a reasonably independent position and...to make a fair contribution to the stability of the world order'.[24] Taken by surprise, Washington politely turned down the request saying it did not have funds of that magnitude.

In order to attract sympathy and support, Pakistani leaders emphasized the country's strategic location, on the one hand, and compatibility of Pakistan-US interests on the other. While conveying the next request for US assistance, Mir Laik Ali referred to 'the proximity and vulnerability of Western Pakistan to Russia'.[25] Speaking to the visiting Assistant Secretary of State George McGhee in October 1949, Finance Minister Ghulam Mohammed stressed the importance of establishing a bloc of Islamic nations 'as a check to any ambitions of USSR'.[26] During his visit to the United States in May 1950, Prime Minister Liaquat Ali Khan underlined Pakistan's strategic location 'in relation to communications to and from the oil-bearing areas of the Middle East'. Emphasizing the commonality of interests between Pakistan and the United States, he described the two countries as 'comrades' in quest of peace and democracy.

Washington was still unenthusiastic about assistance to Pakistan because of fear of antagonizing a politically and economically more important India.[27] American analysts, however, recognized the value of Pakistan's location. In March 1949 the US Joint Chiefs of Staff noted the strategic importance of the Karachi-Lahore area 'as a base for air operations' against the Soviet Union and 'as a staging area for forces engaged in the defence or recapture of Middle East oil areas'.[28] Assistant Secretary McGhee was impressed by the willingness of Pakistani leaders to support US-backed efforts to prevent communist encroachments in South Asia.[29] Pakistan's prompt support for UN action in Korea in 1950, and for the conclusion of the peace treaty with Japan in 1951, further embellished its image in the United States. It came to be perceived .as America's 'one sure friend in South Asia'.[30]

Pakistan-USSR relations got off to an inauspicious start.[31] Moscow did not care to send a message on Pakistan's Independence. Even after Foreign Minister Zafrulla Khan took the initiative in a meeting with Foreign Minister Andrei Gromyko in April 1948 to suggest an exchange of ambassadors, Moscow did not react in a hurry. Pakistan opened its embassy in Moscow in December 1949. The Soviet Ambassador did not arrive in Karachi until March 1950.

The Pakistani administrative elite looked at Soviet policies with suspicion. The Soviet Union was perceived as heir to the Czarist urge to carve out an outlet to the warm waters of the Arabian Sea, and its communist ideology as a conspiratorial and revolutionary movement subversive of law and order. Pakistan did not, however, dismiss the positive aspects of Soviet policies, the rapid economic progress achieved by the Soviet Union, and its opposition to colonialism. Lacking knowledge of Soviet repression, progressive poets and writers sang praises of communist ideals of equality and freedom.

Liaquat Ali Khan took the initiative in a talk with the Soviet chargé d'affaires in Tehran in mid-May 1949 to indicate his desire to visit the USSR. On 4 June he received an invitation from Josef Stalin which he promptly accepted.[32] He intended to visit the Soviet Union but neither side attached urgency to the matter. When, six months later, it was announced that Liaquat

Ali Khan would visit the United States, Moscow showed no further interest in his visit to the Soviet Union. Perhaps, its initial decision to invite him was prompted by the announcement of Truman's invitation to Nehru. It is possible, too, that Liaquat Ali's decision to seek an invitation from Moscow was designed to show his pique at being ignored by Truman, who had invited Nehru. However, no evidence is known to corroborate either assumption, although Liaquat Ali's acceptance of Stalin's invitation did serve to awaken Washington to the consideration of inviting him. The cooling of Moscow's interest in Pakistan was due also to Pakistani leaders' harsh anti-communist rhetoric and official discouragement of contacts with the Soviet Union.

Pakistan had few contacts with the countries of East Asia in the early years after Independence. After the establishment of the People's Republic of China on 1 October 1949, Pakistan was among the first countries to extend recognition to the new government on 4 January 1950. A year later, Pakistan established an embassy in Beijing, recognizing China's importance. Providentially, prospects of Pakistan's relations with China escaped serious damage during the Korean crisis. Although the Pakistan Government denounced the North Korean attack on South Korea in June 1950 as 'a clear case of aggression'[33] and even considered sending an army brigade, the idea was abandoned because the United States balked at the suggestion of a commitment to support Pakistan in the event of Indian aggression. This decision proved a blessing, as otherwise Pakistani troops could have been involved in fighting against the Chinese forces which came to North Korea's help after the United States extended the war beyond the 38th parallel.

Pakistan's anti-communist rhetoric was largely ignored by China. Evidently it understood Pakistan's motives. Pakistan, too, became sensitive to Chinese reactions. In 1954, Prime Minister Mohammad Ali Bogra started making a distinction between Chinese and Soviet policies. Premier Zhou Enlai followed a sagacious policy, avoiding criticism of Pakistan during his visit to India at the height of the *'Hindi-Chini bhai bhai'* (Indians and Chinese are brothers) phase in June 1954. Beijing also showed forbearance for Pakistan's policy on the issue of China's representation in the UN General Assembly. Though Pakistan recognized the Chinese Government *de jure,* it supported the US-sponsored manœuvre by which the Nationalist regime in Taiwan continued to occupy the Chinese seat. Not until 1961 did Pakistan rectify this aberration.

China criticized the South-East Asia Treaty Organization (SEATO) but not Pakistan. Premier Zhou Enlai felt hurt, he told the Pakistani Ambassador, because he regarded Pakistan as a friend. Still, he 'fully understood' Pakistan's circumstances.[34] At the Bandung Conference in April 1955, Mohammad Ali wanted the communiqué to refer to Soviet imperialism, but clarified that China 'is by no means an imperialist nation'. He specially praised Zhou who 'has shown a great deal of conciliation'. When the Pakistani proposal was opposed by some participants including India, Zhou, statesman that he was, helped to reconcile the difference by suggesting that the communiqué refer to 'colonialism in all its manifestations'.[35] Zhou publicly declared at Bandung that he and Mohammad Ali 'achieved a mutual understanding'[36] after the latter explained that Pakistan was not against China, had no fear that China would commit aggression and, further, that if the United States took aggressive action under SEATO, Pakistan would not be involved. In the joint communiqué issued after Zhou's visit to Pakistan in December 1956, the two Prime Ministers were 'happy to place on record that there is no real conflict of interests between the two countries'.[37]

Yet, to appease its allies, Pakistan occasionally relapsed into an improvident mode. In October 1959, Pakistan voted for a UN General Assembly resolution on Tibet which was critical of China. In April 1959, Ayub Khan made the extraordinary proposal of joint defence with India. Even after Nehru ridiculed the offer by rhetorically asking 'Joint defence against whom?', Ayub Khan persisted, forecasting that South Asia would become militarily vulnerable in five years to major invasions from the north,[38] gratuitously offending both China and the Soviet Union.[39] It is a tribute to the wisdom and foresight of the Chinese leaders that they continued to show forbearance, overlooking Pakistan's aberrations. Fortunately, these have lapsed into history; since 1959, friendship and cooperation between the two countries has followed a steady and unswerving path, and has become a crucial´factor for peace in South Asia. No other country has been as comprehending of Pakistan's constraints as China.

Alliances: 1954-55[40]

Fear of upheavals in the strategic Middle East, and a decline in British power and prestige, moved the United States toward direct involvement in the defence of the region. Pakistan came to be looked upon as a potential partner in arrangements aimed at completing the ring of containment around the Soviet Union.[41] The task of launching this major initiative was taken up by President Dwight D. Eisenhower and Secretary of State John Foster Dulles. The new administration manifested its goodwill toward Pakistan immediately. In response to Pakistan's appeal for supplies of wheat to avert a food crisis in 1953, the United States acted with unusual speed. Eisenhower asked Congress to approve the supply of one million tons of wheat. Dulles testified in support, calling Pakistan 'a real bulwark'.[42] Within two weeks Congress gave bipartisan approval and Eisenhower signed the bill. Following a tour of the region, Dulles found that Pakistan alone had 'genuine feeling of friendship' for the United States and the 'moral courage' to stand up. He suggested an alliance of the 'northern-tier' countries—Turkey, Pakistan, Iraq and Iran.

Still, the United States did not 'dare' to give military assistance to Pakistan.[43] State Department officials did not want to displease New Delhi: 'India is the power in South Asia. We should seek to make it our ally rather than cause it to be hostile to us. Pakistan is distressingly weak.' Nehru spoke of dire consequences if the US gave Pakistan aid. The American Ambassador in India, Chester Bowles, warned of 'catastrophe'. Neither Eisenhower nor Dulles was dismissive of these views, but the strategic objectives in the vital Middle East claimed precedence.

Washington's half-hearted policy, manifest in the US offer in March 1954 of only $29 million in assistance, caused deep disappointment in Pakistan. Ayub was 'heart-broken' and Mohammad Ali was most unhappy. The amount was not commensurate, they argued, with the additional risks Pakistan assumed by openly allying itself with the United States. The vehemence of the Pakistani leaders' protest surprised Washington. Having first pressed the United States for an alliance, these leaders now seemed to imply that it was being forced on them. Analogies were cited of a man leading a girl up the primrose path and then abandoning her. Mohammad Ali gave, in reply, the apt example of a man asking for a gun to shoot a mad dog and being given a needle and thread to repair a hole in the trouser.[44] In the event, Pakistan signed a Mutual Defence Assistance Agreement on 19 May 1954 under which the US undertook to provide defence equipment to Pakistan 'exclusively to maintain its internal security, its legitimate self-defence, or to permit it to participate in defence of the area'. The assistance was governed by the US Mutual Defence Assistance Act of 1949 and the Mutual Security Act of 1951 which related to the defence of the free world.

Disappointment with the amount of US assistance also cooled Pakistan's initial enthusiasm toward the American idea of a South-East Asia Treaty Organization for the purpose of deterring communism in general and Vietnam in particular. Upset by Pakistan's 'self-stimulated' expectations, Dulles asked the US Embassy to inform Pakistan that it should not join SEATO to oblige the United States. Pakistan decided not only to attend the Manila Conference in September 1954 but also to sign the Treaty. It succeeded in eliminating any reference to China or communism and extending the scope of the Treaty to cover 'the entire territories of the Asian parties'. But, on other issues, Pakistan yielded to US preferences. The United States entered a reservation to restrict its commitment to consultation among Treaty members only in the event of communist aggression.

Zafrulla Khan decided to sign the Treaty even though his brief required the delegation to first consult the government; if his judgement were not upheld, he offered to resign. The Cabinet acquiesced in his view. Pakistani concerns about the amount of US assistance had some effect. It did not get an immediate increase in arms assistance but the allocation for economic aid was raised to $114 million as against $15 million in 1954.

The proposal for a defence arrangement in the Middle East bristled with problems. Pakistan did not see eye to eye with Washington on the equities of the issues in the Middle East. It was historically supportive of the Palestinian cause, friendly with Iran no less under Prime Minister Mohammed Mossadeq than under the Shah, and sympathetic toward Egyptian aspirations, despite reservations about the Neguib-Nasser Government's emphasis on Arab nationalism, seemingly downgrading solidarity with non-Arab Muslim countries. Pakistan enjoyed especially close relations with Saudi Arabia, Jordan and Iraq. There could be no question of Pakistan joining the West against the interests of Muslim nations in the Middle East.

The foundation of the Baghdad Pact was laid by Turkey and Iraq in the Pact of Mutual Cooperation for 'security and defence' signed in February 1955 in the Iraqi capital. In April they invited Pakistan to join the Baghdad Pact. Initially sceptical, Ayub Khan, then Defence Minister as well as Commander-in-Chief of the Army, was persuaded by Prime Ministers Nuri Said of Iraq and Adnan Menderes of Turkey about the advantages of joining the pact. His opinion was decisive in security matters. Within days the Cabinet approved accession to the Baghdad Pact. President Jamal Abdel Nasser denounced the Baghdad Pact in general and the Iraqi Government in particular for breaking rank with the Arab world. Not popular to begin with, the royal regime in Iraq was overthrown in a bloody *coup* in 1958. Iraq pulled out of the pact which was renamed the Central Treaty Organization (CENTO) in 1959.

Second Thoughts on Alliances

A mismatch between the motivations of Pakistan and its Western allies was apparent from the outset. The US object was to bolster security in the Middle East; that of Pakistan was to strengthen itself in order to contain the Indian threat. The alliance lacked the bond of a common adversary. Still, current imperatives prevailed over seemingly remote risks, though the seeds of disaffection were inherent in the ambiguous bargain.

In Pakistan, the value and wisdom of the policy of alliances came under question immediately. The country was isolated in the kindred community of African-Asian nations which were suspicious of the West and looked upon the Soviet Union as an ally in the struggle for emancipation from Western domination and exploitation. India used Pakistani alignment as a pretext to renounce its obligation for a plebiscite in Kashmir. The Soviet reaction was furious. Discarding its neutral stance in Pakistan-India disputes, it threw its powerful weight behind India. During their visit to India in December 1955, Nikolai Bulganin and Nikita Khrushchev spited Pakistan by declaring they were 'grieved that imperialist forces succeeded in dividing India into two parts'. The *'Hindi-Roosi bhai bhai'* (Indians and Russians are brothers) relationship was reflected also in their reference to Kashmir as 'one of the states of India'. They also visited Afghanistan and spoke in support of the Afghan demand for Pakhtoonistan. Egypt too was quick to denounce the Turco-Pakistan alliance as 'a catastrophe for Islam'.[45] The Saudi radio echoed the influential Arab Voice from Cairo, calling the Baghdad Pact 'a stab in the heart of the Arab and Muslim states'.[46] Coming from a country that is the cradle of Islam, Saudi criticism hurt. Estranged from its fraternity, the nation felt humbled. The alliance was seen to be at the cost of honour.

Opposition to alliances built up over the years because the policy cut across other aims and aspirations of Pakistan. Foremost among these was the deep-seated desire for solidarity with the *ummah*, the global Muslim community. Nowhere was the clash more glaring than in the Suez Crisis. President Nasser's decision to nationalize the Suez Canal Company in July 1956 precipitated a crisis. The Western countries apprehended that Egypt's exclusive control over this maritime highway would jeopardize their vital trade interests. Pakistan joined them, placing emphasis on interests of nations 'vitally concerned with the maintenance of the freedom of navigation'.[47] The policy undervalued the politics of the situation. Ceylon, India and Indonesia too depended on the Suez Canal for trade, but they did not oppose its nationalization. The policy did not meet with popular approval. Worse, Pakistan's diplomacy lost balance as it came under the pressure of allies.

At the first London Conference in mid-August, Foreign Minister Hamidul Haq Chowdhury succumbed to pressures and decided, apparently without clearance from his Prime Minister, to join eighteen (out of twenty-two) countries in supporting the suggestion for an international board to supervise the canal. Pakistan's vote not only provoked a charge of betrayal from Egypt, it also raised a political storm in Pakistan. Pained by the obloquy Pakistan incurred in the Muslim World, political parties including the ruling Muslim League censured government policy. The masses, the media and veterans of the Pakistan Movement of the stature of Fatima Jinnah and Sardar Abdur Rab Nishtar wanted unqualified support for Egypt.

Huseyn Shaheed Suhrawardy, who became Prime Minister at this stage, steered the government out of the storm. At the second London Conference in September, Pakistan made amends. Foreign Minister Firoz Khan Noon spoke against the proposal to set up a Users' Association. Egypt was delighted by 'the return of the prodigal'. Suhrawardy retrieved Pakistan's honour. He would have been more kindly remembered had he not given gratuitous offense by venting unpopular views, however logical they might have appeared to him. Asked by a journalist in December 1956 as to why Muslim countries did not band together instead of getting tied to the West, he said: 'My answer is that zero plus zero plus zero is after all equal to zero!'[48]

Declining popular support for the alliances contrasted with Pakistan's growing dependence on American economic and military assistance. Allocations increased substantially so that over twelve years, from 1954 to 1965, Pakistan received $4 billion in economic assistance and $1.372 billion in defence support.[49] Modern armour and artillery for the army and aircraft for the air force raised Pakistani confidence in defence capability. Speaking in the National Assembly in February 1957, Prime Minister Suhrawardy expressed satisfaction over the 'dividends' of the country's foreign policy. But if Pakistan was satisfied with the quantum of American aid, its 'great disappointment' was due to the American failure to throw its weight behind a just settlement of the Kashmir dispute.[50] Washington was too even-handed, downgrading an ally to the same level as a neutral state with a pro-Soviet tilt. At the popular level, Pakistani criticism was articulated in a cultural context that expects a friend to be sacrificing and supportive, as Pakistan was.

Pakistan was not alone in having second thoughts about the alliances; opinion in the United States also began to swing within a few years. At first allies were admired and favoured, and neutral states criticized and penalized in the allocation of economic assistance. In 1954, influential Republican Senator William Knowland opposed the policy of 'rewarding neutralism', and in 1956 Dulles denounced neutralism as 'an immoral and shortsighted conception'.[51] By 1957, however, Eisenhower endorsed India's neutrality and became critical of the American 'tendency to rush out and seek allies'. He called the alliance with Pakistan 'a terrible error'.[52]

Opinion in Pakistan was deeply agitated. While Pakistan was 'taken for granted' by its allies and penalized by the Soviet Union, neutral India was courted by both the US and USSR.[53] Pakistan seemed to have made a bad bargain both politically and materially. While alliances cost Pakistan more than self-esteem, neutralism enhanced India's prestige. Under pressure of criticism in the National Assembly, Firoz Khan Noon, now Prime Minister, exploded in frustration on 8 March 1958: 'Our people, if they find their freedom threatened by Bharat, will break all pacts and shake hands with people whom we have made enemies because of others.'[54] When General Ayub voiced Pakistani grievances during his visit to the United States in April 1958, Dulles tried to mollify him by explaining that the American relationship with India was on an intellectual level whereas that with Pakistan was 'more from the heart'.[55]

In the midst of changing attitudes in both countries, the United States asked for facilities for a communication base at Badaber near Peshawar for electronic monitoring of Soviet missile tests in Central Asia, and permission for its high-flying U-2 aircraft to use the Peshawar air base for illegal reconnaissance flights over the Soviet Union, assuring Pakistan that, if the flights were ever exposed, 'the United States would declare it had waged the incursion without their approval'.[56] Ayub Khan decided to accede to the American request in a secret agreement. In March 1959 the two countries also signed the Agreement of Cooperation by which the US pledged, in case of aggression against Pakistan, to 'take such appropriate action, including the use of armed forces, as may be mutually agreed upon and as is envisaged in the Joint Resolution to Promote Peace and Stability in the Middle East'.

The US administration expressed appreciation for Pakistan as a 'wholehearted ally' which undertook 'real responsibilities and risks' by providing facilities 'highly important to [US] national security'.[57] It agreed to provide F-104 fighter aircraft, and, despite changes in American opinion in favour of India, Washington continued to give substantial economic and military assistance to Pakistan. The provision of the base facility, however, did not stem the tide of opinion in America.

India flaunted itself as a counter-model to China. The world was supposed to be watching 'who would win—India under democracy or China under communism'.[58] Senator John F. Kennedy warned of apocalypse: 'If India collapses, so may all of Asia.' The Eisenhower administration increased aid to India from $93 million in 1956 to $365 million in 1957[59] and a record $822 million in 1960. Deterioration in India's relations with China over Tibet in 1959 provided a further fillip to burgeoning US support. In 1960 the US decided to provide an additional

$1,276 million for the export of twelve million tons of wheat to India over the next four years. The wooing of India was more pronounced after Kennedy became President. Although he had no illusions about 'Nehru's talent for international self-righteousness',[60] he regarded India as 'the key area' in Asia. In his inaugural address he paid tribute to 'the soaring idealism of Nehru'. Viewing India as 'a potential brake on Chinese aggression',[61] Kennedy's first budget provided $500 million for economic aid to India as against $150 million for Pakistan. Soon, the United States also decided to provide a 400 megawatt nuclear power plant to India.

Pakistan continued to hope for a balanced American approach. During his visit to the US in July 1961, President Ayub Khan emphasized the mutuality of benefits of Pakistan-US cooperation. He received a sympathetic response in Congress and 'charmed everybody' in Washington.[62] At his suggestion, Kennedy promised to speak to Nehru in favour of a Kashmir settlement and, if unsuccessful, to support Pakistan at the United Nations. Also, when Ayub Khan expressed concern about US military assistance to India, Kennedy replied that 'if a Sino-Indian conflict ever erupted, and India asked the United States for military aid, he would first consult with Ayub before making a commitment'.[63]

When Nehru came to Washington in November 1961, Kennedy raised the Kashmir question with him. The Indian leader ruled out any solution other than one based on the cease-fire line. Kennedy was disappointed generally; talking to Nehru, he said, was 'like trying to grab something in your hand, only to have it turn out to be just fog'.[64] Their meeting was a 'disaster'. Nehru's visit was 'the worst' by a foreign leader.[65] When Nehru decided to invade and occupy defenseless Goa, Diu and Daman in December 1961, Kennedy professed shock.[66] 'The contrast between Nehru's incessant sanctimony on the subject of non-aggression and his brisk exercise in *machtpolitik* was too comic not to cause comment. It was a little like catching the preacher in the hen-house.'[67] Adlai Stevenson, the US representative to the UN, eloquently declaimed that 'if the United Nations was not to die as ignoble a death as the League of Nations, we cannot condone the use of force in this instance and thus pave the way for forceful solutions of other disputes'.[68] But the rhetoric was soon forgotten. Neither disappointment with Nehru nor admiration for Ayub Khan had much influence on American policy of support for India, or hostility toward Pakistan, in the context of relations with China.

Indus Waters Treaty 1960

One significant outcome of this period was the Indus Waters Treaty of 1960. Agriculture in the dry lands of the Indus river basin has for centuries depended on irrigation. Of the total irrigated area of 37 million acres in 1947, 31 million acres were on the Pakistan side. India's claim to the waters of the rivers that rose or passed through its territory was untenable in law, and, realizing this, Nehru refused Liaquat Ali Khan's proposal for arbitration in 1950. India's proclivity to resort to unilateral action posed a grave threat to Pakistan's economic survival. As David Lilienthal, former chairman of the Tennessee Valley Authority, stated, 'No armies with bombs and shellfire could devastate a land so thoroughly as Pakistan could be devastated by the simple expedient of India's permanently shutting off the source of waters that keep the fields and people of Pakistan green.'[69]

The World Bank decided to mediate in the negotiations between Pakistan and India to find a solution of the dispute that would provide India additional supplies of water without damage to Pakistan. The highly technical issues took almost a decade to resolve but the Bank's efforts fructified in the Indus Waters Treaty which was signed in September 1960. The Treaty allocated the waters of the three eastern rivers (Ravi, Beas and Sutlej) for use by India, and the waters of the western rivers (Indus, Jhelum and Chenab) for use in Pakistan. It also bound India not to interfere in the flow of all the waters of the western rivers, except for domestic and non-consumptive uses, generation of power and for agriculture subject to specified limits.

In effect, the compromise conceded to India what it wanted, but the World Bank, Australia, Britain, Canada, Germany, New Zealand and the United States provided funds for the construction of reservoirs and link canals in Pakistan to replace water which previously flowed from the eastern rivers to irrigate land in Pakistan. Of the estimated expenditure of $1 billion, the United States contributed about a half. Also, the Treaty secured a transitional period of ten years during which India undertook not to shut off the flow of waters in irrigation canals.

Pakistan-China Cooperation: 1959-65

As early as 1959, Ayub Khan suggested the idea of settling the undemarcated border between China's Xinjiang province and the Northern Areas of Kashmir which were under Pakistan's control. Encouraged by China's reasonable attitude in boundary agreements with Nepal and Myanmar, Pakistan sent a formal note to China in March 1961, proposing demarcation of the common boundary. The Chinese response was favourable and, in May 1962, the two countries announced their decision to enter into negotiations which started on 12 October 1962, nine days before the first Sino-Indian border clash. Conducted in a friendly spirit of mutual accommodation, the talks succeeded within two months.[70] It is worth recalling that after the countries agreed on the watershed principle, the Pakistan Government discovered that grazing lands historically used by people of Hunza fell to the north of the boundary. To save them hardship, Pakistan appealed to Premier Zhou for allocation of that area of 750 square miles to Pakistan, which he accepted.

Relations between the two countries continued to deepen especially after Pakistan, defying American pressure, established air links with China, breaching the US strategy of containment and isolation of China. A windfall of the use of the Pakistani corridor by Chinese leaders in transit to and from countries of the Middle East, Africa and Europe was an increase in the frequency of their contacts with their Pakistani counterparts, facilitating a sympathetic understanding of each other's concerns. Pakistan was thus in a position to explain the Chinese viewpoint in forums from which China was then excluded.[71] During his visit to China in March 1965, Ayub Khan was accorded an effusive welcome. Chairman Mao Zedong expressed warm appreciation for Pakistan's support. The joint communiqué denounced the 'two Chinas' policy. Also, the two sides 'noted with concern that the Kashmir dispute remains unresolved and consider its continued existence a threat to peace and security in the region. They reaffirmed that this dispute should be resolved in accordance with the wishes of the people of Kashmir as pledged to them by India and Pakistan.'

A unique characteristic of China's policy over the years has been to observe implicit respect for Pakistan's sovereignty. The Chinese leaders seldom proffered unsolicited advice. During exchanges of views with their Pakistani counterparts, they would describe their own experiences and let Pakistanis draw appropriate conclusions. Even when Pakistan embarked on the improvement of relations with the Soviet Union in 1960, the Chinese leaders did not try to restrain Pakistan, expressing instead understanding of this policy.

Deterioration in Relations with the USA: 1962-63

In the early 1960s China was under multiple pressures. The United States naval and air power was operating close to its seaboard. The Soviet Union turned hostile as an ideological rift opened between the two countries. Obliged to resist both superpowers, China was concerned also about Indian encouragement to separatist elements in Tibet and its imperious attitude on the boundary issue. Beijing now understood even better than before the difficulties Pakistan confronted at the hands of inimical India backed by the Soviet Union. Sharing adversity, China and Pakistan drew closer.[72] Pakistan demonstrated courage in resisting the political and economic pressures of its American ally, and grasped China's hand of friendship across the Karakorum Range.

Oblivious to the Sino-Soviet split, Washington viewed China as part of a monolithic communist bloc which needed to be contained and isolated. It looked askance at 'Pakistan's drift toward Communist China'[73] and tried to apply pressure to bring Pakistan into line. At the same time pulling India into the American orbit was a dominant passion. It was not surprising, therefore, that Washington saw the Sino-Indian border clash as a defining moment in the history of democracy's crusade against communism.

After the first serious border clash on 20 October 1962 in which the Indian forces were worsted, Washington saw in this situation an opportunity to pull India into alignment. Kennedy's Ambassador in New Delhi, John Kenneth Galbraith, embarked on efforts, more pathetic than comic, to coax a personal request for military aid from Nehru himself, playing on his vanity by telling him that he 'is loved in the US as no one else in India'. Forgetting his non-aligned professions, Nehru 'reversed policy 180 degrees to seek military assistance from the United States'.[74] Galbraith gleefully reported that Indian officials were 'pleading for military association'.[75] On 3 November the United States began an airlift of military equipment. Britain, too, sent plane loads of weapons without any payment. Israel as well responded to Nehru's request by sending a shipload of heavy mortar.[76]

Emboldened by the West's support and assistance, India decided to mount a division-strength attack on 14 November in the north-east, leading to large-scale hostilities in which the Indian force was routed. Although the fighting was still limited to the border, a frightened Nehru, in panic, projected that the Chinese forces would descend into the plains of Assam, and broadcast a goodbye to its people. 'In this mood of crisis, the Prime Minister sent off two startling letters to President Kennedy'.[77] The first letter of 19 November, 'describing India's predicament as desperate', requested the 'dispatch of US fighter aircraft and a supporting radar network, with US pilots and technicians'.[78] The second letter has not yet been declassified, apparently to spare embarrassment to the memory of 'the father of non-alignment'.[79] An official then working in the Kennedy administration described one of the two as 'a hysterical letter, a silly letter asking us to bomb China'.[80] Nehru wanted Kennedy to send a dozen squadrons of fighter aircraft to protect India's major cities and two squadrons of B-47 bombers with US pilots to attack Chinese positions.[81] Kennedy decided to dispatch an aircraft carrier—the USS *Enterprise*—to the Bay of Bengal.[82] But before he could reply, to his and to India's utter surprise, China unilaterally announced a cease-fire on 21 November and the withdrawal of its forces to pre-war positions, twenty kilometers behind their claimed boundary, vacating 'practically all the territory their army gained in the east'.[83] Nevertheless, Kennedy decided to provide further military assistance to India. Britain's response was even more enthusiastic.

The people of Pakistan felt betrayed by the American decision to rush arms to India. Foreign Minister Mohammad Ali denounced the US decision as 'an act of gross unfriendliness'. India, he pointed out, 'was making a mountain of a molehill'. Keeping the bulk of its forces poised on Pakistan's border was 'a strange method of resisting the Chinese'. If friends of Pakistan and India wanted to see good relations between the two countries and settlement of disputes between them, he said, 'Time for reliance on words and assurances has gone.'[84]

Though unhappy with Pakistan's China policy, Washington valued the base facilities it had at Badaber. Recognizing that the unresolved Kashmir question obstructed their aim of pushing Pakistan and India into a joint front against China, America and Britain decided to send Assistant Secretary of State Averell Harriman and Commonwealth Secretary Duncan Sandys to explain to Nehru the need for negotiations to resolve the Kashmir dispute. In a separate meeting Harriman told Nehru that, unless tensions over Kashmir eased, the US could not continue to provide military assistance. Nehru reluctantly agreed to join Ayub in a statement on 29 November 1962 for 'a renewed effort to resolve the outstanding differences...on Kashmir and other related matters'.[85]

Negotiations on Kashmir: 1962-63

The first of the six rounds of Pakistan-India meetings was held in Rawalpindi from 24-27 December. The Pakistan side, led by Z. A. Bhutto, suggested that the two sides build on the existing foundation of the Security Council resolutions and reports of the UN mediators. It recalled also the proposals put forward by McNaughton and Dixon regarding regional plebiscites. The Indian side, headed by Swaran Singh, did not accept the idea. At the second round of meetings in New Delhi in January 1963, India again opposed any reference to the people of Kashmir, arguing that if the Muslim people of the State voted for Pakistan, the Hindus of India would consider that as proof of disloyalty of all Muslims in India and their safety and security would be endangered. Instead, India proposed a 'political settlement', hinting at the partition of the State. That idea was further discussed at the third and fourth rounds. The Indian side suggested division of the State along a boundary broadly corresponding to the cease-fire line with minor adjustments and modifications. The Pakistan team probed the idea of division along the Pir Panjal watershed in northern Jammu, linking it to ascertainment of the wishes of the people six months after withdrawal of Indian forces, while placing the Valley under international control in the interim period. A similar suggestion was made earlier by Ayub Khan through Duncan Sandys, which was turned down by Nehru.[86] No progress was achieved at the fifth and sixth rounds in April and May. Instead of narrowing differences, the positions of the two countries became divergent. Before breakdown, the two sides reverted to their original positions.

American and British envoys tried to persuade Pakistan and India to agree to a compromise, but they were not prepared to expend influence to promote a just settlement. Obsessed with enlisting India to contain China, they ruled out Pakistan's suggestion for making the supply of arms to India contingent on a Kashmir settlement. As the danger of a further flare-up on the border with China receded, India lost the incentive for a settlement with Pakistan, and the negotiations fizzled out.

RCD and IPECC

Bound by ties of history and culture, Iran, Pakistan and Turkey felt that CENTO was too one-dimensional, and they needed to supplement it by another organization to enlarge their contacts and cooperation in economic and cultural fields. To that end the heads of the three States decided at Istanbul on 22 July 1964 to establish the Regional Cooperation for Development (RCD). Over the following years, agreements were reached in the RCD to establish a number of industrial projects, with two or all three States agreeing to share in investment and production. Although the projects were relatively small, RCD symbolized the aspiration of the people of the three countries for closer cooperation.

A similar sentiment grew between Pakistan and Indonesia. They both looked upon the African-Asian solidarity movement as a better alternative to the formation of the non-aligned group which excluded not only such countries as Iran, Pakistan, Philippines and Thailand, but also China, the largest and most important developing country. India's motivation in keeping China out was clear. As Soekarno well remembered, Zhou Enlai had out-shone Nehru as a statesman and leader of acumen and sagacity at the Bandung Afro-Asian Summit in 1955. By keeping China out, India wanted to retain the limelight for itself. Pakistan and Indonesia also understood India's hegemonic ambitions. They cooperated closely in preparations for the second Afro-Asian Summit in Algeria, which was aborted because of the overthrow of President Ben Bella of the host country in April 1965. Such commonalities of interest led the two countries to decide on the formation of the Indonesia-Pakistan Economic and Cultural Cooperation (IPECC) in August 1965. Although IPECC, like RCD, made slow progress in building cooperation, it provided a useful forum for consultation.

Withering of Alliance with the USA

Instead of using what he had himself described as a 'one-time opportunity'[87] for Pakistan-India reconciliation, Kennedy decided in May 1963 to delink aid to India from a Kashmir settlement, and approved a programme of enhanced military assistance to India. Relations between Pakistan and the United States came under renewed strain. The slide accelerated after Lyndon B. Johnson succeeded Kennedy. Taking a tough line with Pakistan, he sternly warned Foreign Minister Z. A. Bhutto, who was in Washington to attend Kennedy's funeral, that 'Pakistan's flirtation with China was rapidly approaching the limits of American tolerance'[88] and that Premier Zhou Enlai's coming visit to Pakistan would jeopardize US economic and military aid to Pakistan.[89] In 1964 when the Johnson administration allocated $500 million for a five-year programme of military aid to India, Ayub protested that the decision would oblige Pakistan to reappraise CENTO and SEATO. Johnson's response was even more curt, threatening that the US too would be obliged to re-examine its relations with Pakistan if it continued to develop its relations with China. When Pakistan signed an air agreement with China in April 1965, Johnson cut off a loan for the upgradation of Dhaka Airport, disinvited Ayub Khan and suspended further economic assistance. He might have been even more incensed were he aware that Ayub Khan, then on a visit to the Soviet Union, was promising the Soviet leaders that Pakistan would not renew the lease for the US base at Badaber if they adopted a salutary policy on Kashmir.

Ironically, Secretary of State Dean Rusk was to ask Foreign Minister Bhutto in April 1966 for Pakistan's help to arrange a meeting with the Chinese Foreign Minister for discussions on Vietnam.[90] A few years later President Nixon used Pakistan as a channel of communication with China and for Henry Kissinger's secret visit to Beijing in 1971. But quite apart from lack of foresight regarding China, the breakdown of the Pakistan-US alliance came about as a result of American refusal of assistance to Pakistan after the outbreak of the Pakistan-India war in 1965.

Drift to the 1965 War

The Pakistan-India war over Kashmir in 1965 was the culmination of a process of hopes of peaceful settlement first raised and then betrayed, desperation born of frustration, jingoism triggered by an unconnected clash over a disputed boundary, and unintended escalation. Leaders on both sides lost control over actions decided under pressure, provoking like reactions and allowing the build-up of momentum that pushed them into an unwanted war.

The fundamental cause of tension lay in India's refusal to honour its obligation under UN resolutions to allow the holding of a plebiscite in Kashmir, and pursuing instead a strategy to perpetuate its occupation of two-thirds of that State. Unjustified in law, it was unacceptable to Pakistan and the Kashmiri people. After the border crisis with China, India reverted to its rigid position. Opinion in Pakistan blamed Ayub Khan for having missed the opportunity to press for a breakthrough. In October 1963, New Delhi again embarked on legal manœuvres to integrate the disputed territory with India. For Nehru, a 'gradual erosion' of the special status of Kashmir was in progress. Pakistan denounced the proposed changes as 'clearly illegal' and a 'flagrant violation of India's commitments'. Its protests were in vain and only intensified its sense of frustration.

Disturbed by the Indian design, the agitation launched by the Kashmiri people assumed massive proportions following the theft of *Moo-e-Muqaddis*—hair of the Holy Prophet (PBUH)—from the Hazratbal shrine. They poured out in a spontaneous eruption in cities and towns across the Valley. Even after the recovery of the holy relic, the agitation did not cease. The people demanded an opportunity to exercise their right of self-determination. Kashmir was in the grip of a crisis, with India resorting once again to repression against unarmed people. Pakistan appealed to the UN Security Council which held lengthy debates in February and May 1964, but the Soviet veto prevented any effective action. This failure on the part of the apex organ of the United Nations was yet another blow to prospects of peace between Pakistan and India.

Tension was temporarily relieved in April 1964 when Nehru released Sheikh Mohammad Abdullah, the dismissed former Prime Minister of Indian-occupied Kashmir. Abdullah believed that Nehru wanted a resolution of the Kashmir question, an assessment encouraged by Jayaprakash Narayan, a leader respected in India for his advocacy of morality in politics. In a courageous article,[91] Narayan exploded some of the myths India had fostered; elections held by India in Kashmir, he argued, did not represent a vote for integration with India. He ridiculed the argument that self-determination by the people of Kashmir would trigger country-wide communal rioting and prove a prelude to the disintegration of India. He advocated that India should rethink its position in the light not only of its own interests but also those of Pakistan, and of cooperation between the two.

In this hopeful atmosphere, Sheikh Abdullah came to Pakistan in May, and, at his suggestion, Ayub Khan agreed to visit New Delhi for a meeting with Nehru. The next day, 27 May, Nehru died. With him perished the tenuous hope raised by Abdullah. The new Indian Prime Minister, Lal Bahadur Shastri, did not invite Ayub Khan. In December 1964, New Delhi resumed moves for a unilateral solution through the merger of Kashmir with India. This was further proof of India speaking of negotiations but acting unilaterally.

Momentum towards war between the two countries built up as a result of incidents in the Rann of Kutch in early 1965. The boundary in this flood-basin of the Arabian Sea, which separates the Indian State of Gujarat from the Pakistani Province of Sindh, was a subject of dispute since before Independence. While India laid claim to the whole of thé marshy waste to the northern edge of the Rann, Pakistan held that the boundary ran along the 24th parallel. An area of 3,500 square miles was thus disputed. India tried to enforce its claim by establishing military posts and obstructing Pakistani patrols in the area claimed by Pakistan. A serious incident ensued in April in which the Indian force suffered heavy casualties. Shastri threatened general war, declaring that 'the army will decide its own strategy and deploy its manpower and equipment in the way it deems fit'.[92]

The danger of escalation was averted by the approaching monsoon, and by the efforts undertaken by Prime Minister Harold Wilson and the British High Commissioners in Islamabad and New Delhi. They promoted the conclusion of an agreement on 30 June 1965 which provided not only for a cease-fire but also a time-bound, self-executing mechanism for peaceful settlement of the dispute through (1) negotiation and, if that failed, after two months (2) arbitration by an international tribunal to be constituted within four months with the UN Secretary General designating its chairman. The agreement further provided for (3) acceptance of the award as final, and (4) the tribunal to remain in office until the implementation of the award. Predictably, the bilateral talks failed. The arbitration tribunal was established in 1966 and its award, announced in February 1969, was duly implemented.

The tribunal awarded 350 square miles to Pakistan,[93] allowing India 90 per cent of the disputed territory. Still India was indignant; speeches in its Parliament were 'extremely bellicose'.[94] Only Jayaprakash Narayan, who later came to be revered in India for his advocacy of truth in politics, had the courage and wisdom to commend the Kutch agreement 'as an object lesson in peace-keeping' which should be applied to all disputes 'including that of Kashmir'.[95] Given the Indian desire to settle disputes solely on its own terms, negotiations between Pakistan and India have been usually sterile. Even the dividing line in the Sir Creek at the western terminus of the agreed boundary in the Rann, which the Kutch tribunal thought was a minor issue, has remained undemarcated, entailing endless suffering for poor fishermen from both sides in recurrent cases of alleged trespass.

The perceived reverse in Kutch gave India a grudge to nourish and a score to settle. It proved to be another stumble towards war, which came within five months as the Kashmir cauldron once again boiled. International restraints were meanwhile weakened. US diplomacy was placed on the defensive during the Kutch crisis, appearing penitent in the face of India's vehement protests over the use of American weapons by Pakistan during the clash. Washington announced an embargo over further supply of arms or spare parts to both countries. The decision was injurious to Pakistan because its equipment was almost entirely of US origin, while the restriction had little effect on India which imported arms largely from the Soviet Union. Similarly one-sided was the impact of Johnson's order to discontinue additional aid or loans because the World Bank Consortium for India had already met and pledged aid, but the meeting of the Consortium for Pakistan had to be postponed. In a mood of desperation, Ayub Khan exploded saying that America was 'power drunk'; and on another occasion he said Pakistan was seeking 'new friends, not new masters'.[96]

Tension between India and Pakistan grew as New Delhi embarked on further steps to integrate occupied Kashmir, and Abdullah and his colleague, Mirza Afzal Beg, leader of the Plebiscite Front, were arrested in May 1965 on their return after meetings with leaders of Muslim countries during Hajj, and with Premier Zhou Enlai in Cairo. These Indian moves triggered another popular upsurge in Kashmir. Although the Gandhi-style disobedience movement was non-violent, India unleashed its forces to crush the struggle in the State.

The 1965 War

Recurrent popular uprisings in occupied Kashmir, their brutal repression by India, and the rise and fall of hopes for a settlement through peaceful means, fostered mounting frustration in

Pakistan. Official thought turned to what else might be done to pressure India and jolt the world community to recognize the need of fulfilling the pledge given by India to Pakistan and the United Nations to let the Kashmiri people themselves determine their future. A high level group of civil and military officials recommended that armed volunteers should be sent across the cease-fire line.[97] Although limited in scope, the plan was first rejected by Ayub Khan. Later, as the situation in Kashmir deteriorated, he approved an even riskier course in May 1965, himself suggesting that the plan should 'go for the jugular' by including a possible attack on Akhnur, a nodal point on the transport and supply link for the Indian forces in Kashmir. The decision was to trigger a chain of reactions that spiraled into a war that President Ayub did not want.

Controversy surrounds the question of why Ayub Khan changed his mind, jettisoning caution and authorizing a plan that involved obvious risks. He himself realized that any armed engagement in Kashmir would lead to a general war but, according to his apologists, he was pushed into the decision by his adventurous advisers. Foreign affairs experts were said to have misled Ayub Khan by giving the confident assessment, even assurances, that in the obtaining global and regional situation the conflict would remain confined to the disputed State.[98] Few decision makers readily accept blame. The whole truth has to include the deepening sense of desperation shared not only by the President but also his advisers and indeed the entire nation. All felt it was morally incumbent on them to do something to secure self-determination for the Kashmiri people. Knowledgeable experts believed that, if Pakistan did not act then, India's burgeoning military expansion would aggravate the power disparity so as to exclude an initiative later. Another factor, fostered by the Kutch affair, was hubris: policy makers concluded that neither the Indian leadership was bold enough to pick up the gauntlet nor the armed forces courageous enough to fight.[99] Incredibly, in retrospect, it was not considered necessary to prepare for the contingency of war. A proposal for raising another army division was turned down on economic grounds.

The chiefs of the air force and navy were not even informed of the plan. The army leadership, though it was fully in the picture, remained oblivious to the danger of war. Even mines laid along the Punjab border during the Kutch crisis were removed.

The volunteers entered Kashmir in August. Poorly equipped for survival in the cold and desolate conditions in the high mountains on the way, they were even less prepared to mobilize cooperation among the unarmed villagers of the areas they entered. The Indian forces reacted aggressively, crossing the cease-fire line and occupying large territory in the Kargil area in the north and Haji Pir Pass between Uri and Poonch in the west, posing a threat to Muzaffarabad, the capital of Azad Kashmir. India further raised the stakes by shelling Awan Sharif village in Pakistan, killing 20 persons. The unforeseen losses necessitated a response, and Pakistan decided to launch an attack in Chhamb at the southern end of the cease-fire line. The Pakistani force made rapid progress, bringing the other side under pressure. Fearing the worst, India decided to unleash a general war. Its forces crossed the international boundary before dawn on 6 September, aiming at the capture of Lahore, Pakistan's second largest city. Legendary acts of valour and sacrifice saved the day for Pakistan, halting the Indian thrust. A few days later Pakistan launched a counter-offensive towards Amritsar. It too failed, getting bogged down literally, with Pakistani tanks trapped in agricultural fields flooded by India breaching an irrigation canal.

The two armies fought large pitched battles with armoured divisions and heavy artillery. Their air forces and navies also came into action. The small but highly professional Pakistan Air Force shot down 75 Indian aircraft for the loss of 19 of its own. Even the outnumbered air contingent in East Pakistan took the battle into enemy airspace. The tiny navy audaciously attacked Dwarka, an Indian naval base 200 miles from Karachi. Although the war ended in a stalemate, Pakistani armed forces made marginally larger gains, despite their smaller size.[100]

The UN Security Council adopted its first resolution on 4 September, calling for a cease-fire and the withdrawal of all armed personnel to the positions held before 5 August, the date on which, according to the UN's information, armed men began to cross the cease-fire line. Neither this nor the resolution of 6 September was acceptable to Pakistan. In reply to Secretary General U Thant's letter asking for implementation of a cease-fire, Ayub Khan said that a 'purposeful' resolution must provide for a self-executing arrangement for settlement of the Kashmir dispute.

China extended valuable support to Pakistan, both directly and implicitly. In transit through Karachi on 4 September, Foreign Minister Chen Yi expressed support for 'the just action taken by Pakistan to repel Indian armed provocations'. On 7 September the Chinese Foreign Ministry condemned India's 'criminal aggression', charging that it was trying to 'bully its neighbours, defy public opinion and do whatever it likes'.[101] China further declared on 12 September that its non-involvement in the Kashmir dispute 'absolutely does not mean that China can approve of depriving the Kashmiri people of their right of self-determination or that she can approve of Indian aggression against Pakistan'. Having earlier protested against Indian 'acts of aggression and provocation' along China's border, China gave an ultimatum to India on 16 September to dismantle its military structures on the Chinese side of the border, stop incursions and return livestock and kidnapped civilians 'within three days' or it would bear 'full responsibility for all consequences'.[102]

The threat of expansion of the war served to inject a sense of urgency in the deliberations of the Security Council. Its resolution of 20 September demanded cessation of hostilities as 'a first step towards a peaceful settlement of the outstanding differences between the two countries on Kashmir and other matters', and 'decided' to consider as soon as the cease-fire took effect 'what steps should be taken to assist towards a settlement of the political problem underlying the present conflict'.[103] Pakistan accepted the resolution on 22 September.

Few countries blamed Pakistan for its attempt to defreeze the festering Kashmir dispute; many criticized India for aggression, and several provided memorable assistance to Pakistan.[104]

Indonesia dispatched six naval vessels, Iran provided jet fuel, Turkey guns and ammunition, and Saudi Arabia gave financial support. President Nasser echoed sympathy for Pakistan and endorsed the Arab summit's communiqué which called for a settlement of the Kashmir dispute 'in accordance with the principles and resolutions of the United Nations'. Premier Kosygin 'took exception to India's crossing the international border'. Prime Minister Harold Wilson was 'deeply concerned' when the Indian forces 'attacked Pakistan territory across the international frontier', though the UK backtracked after India raised a storm over his remarks. Only Yugoslavia sided with India, apart from the Malaysian representative in the Security Council, a person of Indian origin. His remarks, impugning Pakistan's right to existence, provoked Pakistan to sever diplomatic relations with Malaysia.

The alliances proved unavailing. The SEATO council did not meet even for consultations; and CENTO could not be activated. Washington did not consider the Defence Agreement of March 1959 applicable. It also ignored the pledge given in the context of US arms assistance to India in 1962, by which it reaffirmed 'previous assurances that it will come to Pakistan's assistance in the event of aggression from India against Pakistan'.[105] Finding its policy in South Asia in a shambles with the two countries using US arms to fight each other, rather than against its enemies, the US adopted a hands-off stance, and decided to stop the supply of arms to both countries, which hurt Pakistan more because its arms were of American origin. Pakistani opinion regarded the American decision as yet another betrayal.

Tashkent Declaration

While both Washington and London were reluctant to get involved, Moscow took the initiative for peace. It had a stake in ensuring disengagement between Pakistan and India and, thus, preventing a dangerous polarization between China and the Soviet Union, one backing Pakistan and the other India. In inviting Pakistan and India to Tashkent, it also hoped for gain in the 'USSR's stature among non-communist Afro-Asian states as a responsible and constructive superpower'.[106]

The Pakistan delegation to the Tashkent conference, held from 4-10 January 1966, was internally divided on how far to push for linking a peace agreement to a settlement in Kashmir. Some, calculating that the Soviet Union could not allow the conference to fail, argued for insistence on establishing a mechanism for resolution of the Kashmir issue. Shastri modestly explained to Ayub Khan that, as a pygmy succeeding a giant in Nehru, his position did not permit him to change India's stance. The Soviets considered the Kashmir question too 'complicated'. When Bhutto pressed harder, Gromyko peremptorily told him that he was trying to 'win at the conference table what Pakistan had been unable to win at the battlefield'.[107] Clear about the priority need for disengagement, Ayub Khan overruled his more ambitious advisers and accepted Kosygin's compromise draft. The Tashkent Declaration provided for the withdrawal of forces, and envisaged further meetings 'on matters of direct concern to both countries', but made no direct mention of Kashmir. Ayub Khan's acceptance of this ambiguous formulation, though eminently rational, was exploited by his opponents who unjustly accused him of squandering at the negotiating table what the armed forces had won on the battlefield. Bhutto later exploited this myth to considerable political advantage. For the people, the agreement was an anticlimax because official propaganda had misled them to believe that Pakistani forces had gained great advantage if not victory over India.

Relations with the Great Powers: 1965-70

Pakistan's acceptance of the Security Council's demand for a cease-fire surprised Chinese leaders but, after Ayub Khan explained Pakistan's constraints,[108] they, as usual, showed understanding of Pakistan's decision even though their own view was different. An engaging characteristic which has

distinguished Chinese leaders has been their respect for
Pakistan's right to determine what is best for itself. China's
support to Pakistan at a moment of crisis made a deep impression
on the Pakistani people. President Liu Shao Chi's visit to
Pakistan in March 1966 was a memorable occasion. In Lahore,
Karachi and Dhaka, his welcome by enthusiastic multitudes was
on a scale rarely seen since Independence. His description of
Sino-Pakistan relations as *mujahidana dosti* (friendship in
righteous struggle) aptly translated the sentiments of the
Pakistani people and boosted their morale. Here was a friend
the nation could trust and rely on. The friendship forged in the
heat of the war developed in succeeding years.

To help Pakistan's defence capability at a time when the
United States had told Pakistan that the alliance was over and
embargoed military sales, in 1966 China provided equipment
for two divisions of the army as well as MIG aircraft for the air
force. It also gave $60 million for development assistance in
1965, a further $40 million in 1969 and $200 million for the
next five-year plan. With China itself a low income developing
country, this assistance was generous and placed emphasis on
the transfer of technology to help Pakistan achieve self-reliance.
The Heavy Mechanical Complex, the Heavy Rebuild Factory,
the Kamra Aeronautical Complex and several other industrial
plants were later undertaken with Chinese assistance. To provide
a land link, the two countries decided in 1969 to build a road
across the Karakorum.[109] China played a major part in the
construction of the spectacular Karakorum Highway linking
Gilgit in the Northern Areas with Kashgar in Xinjiang over the
second highest mountain range in the world through the 15,800
foot high Khunjerab Pass. Speaking at the UN General Assembly
in October 1970, President Yahya Khan described friendly
cooperation with China as the 'cornerstone' of Pakistan's policy.
In the communiqué issued after his visit to China the following
month, the Chinese reiterated support on Kashmir; and Pakistan
reaffirmed that 'Taiwan was an inalienable part of China'.

Starting in 1960, and accelerated as a result of the Anglo-
American neglect of Pakistan's interests following the Sino-

Indian border clash in 1962, Pakistan's policy of normalization of relations with the Soviet Union gathered momentum after the 1965 War. Ayub Khan visited the USSR in October 1967 and Kosygin came to Pakistan in April 1968 when he announced Soviet assistance for building a steel plant. Moscow appreciated Pakistan's decision not to renew the lease for the American base at Badaber. Kosygin visited Pakistan again in May 1969 for a meeting with Yahya Khan, the new military ruler. The Soviet Union also agreed to sell a small quantity of defence equipment to Pakistan. Although military supplies were discontinued after India protested to Moscow, illustrating the limits of Pakistan-Soviet cooperation, the Soviet Union committed over a billion dollars in soft loans for thirty-one development projects[110] in Pakistan up to 1971, when Yahya Khan's inept diplomacy during the East Pakistan crisis provoked a breakdown of the developing *détente* with the Soviet Union.

Special relations with the United States were further eroded after 1965. Johnson told Ayub Khan that the alliance phase was over; any further economic aid was made conditional on Pakistan curtailing its close ties with China. Although Washington resumed development assistance to Pakistan (and India) in June 1966, the ban on military sales continued, excepting only spare parts for previously supplied equipment. The termination of the Badaber lease ended the special relationship in 1968.

The situation improved after President Richard Nixon took office in 1969; he had advocated close relations with Pakistan in the 1950s and appreciated its role as an ally. He did not view Pakistan-China relations in a frozen inimical perspective. Cognizant of the sea change in China's position following the Sino-Soviet split and the border tensions between them, he was among the first leaders in America to detect a 'dimly perceived community of interests between the United States and China'.[111] To that end, the Nixon administration considered Pakistan an asset. The upbeat tone of Pakistan-US relations was soon manifest in the strong US support for aid to Pakistan at the Consortium meeting in May 1969. In August, Nixon visited

Pakistan, and, in October 1970, the US allowed the sale of a limited number of B-57 and F-104 aircraft to Pakistan.

Nixon and his National Security Council Assistant, Henry Kissinger, calculated that China, confronted with the 'nightmare of hostile encirclement', might welcome 'strategic reassurance' from improved relations with the United States. Soon after taking office, they made cautious moves towards 'a new beginning'.[112] The Chinese response to the tentative probes was affirmative. Kissinger, well known for his preference for secret diplomacy, first used personal friends for confidential contacts with the Chinese Embassy in Paris. Later, in October 1970, Nixon raised the level by asking Yahya Khan to inform the Chinese leaders that he considered *rapprochement* with China 'essential'. After talks with Chinese leaders in November, Yahya Khan conveyed their response in an elaborately confidential manner; Kissinger was fascinated by Ambassador Agha Hilaly's insistence on dictating the message at slow speed which he had to take in longhand. For four months messages were passed through this channel in utter confidentiality. Pakistan was equally helpful in providing a plane for Kissinger's secret visit to Beijing on 9-11 July 1971. Nixon personally disclosed the news to a stunned world, simultaneously announcing Beijing's invitation to him to visit China.

Moscow's reaction to the development was both angry and quick. Taking advantage of the spiralling crisis in East Pakistan, it concluded a Treaty of Peace, Friendship and Cooperation with India. Its Article IX committed the two countries to mutual consultation in the event of an attack or threat of attack and to take 'appropriate effective measures' in order to remove such threat. The Soviet Union in effect provided India an umbrella against intervention by China, allowing India to execute its design with impunity. The Soviet object was 'to humiliate China and to punish Pakistan for having served as an intermediary'.[113]

OIC: 1969

Israeli aggression against Egypt, Jordan and Syria in 1967 had evoked strong condemnation in the world. The Muslim peoples were stirred as never before because of the Israeli occupation of Jerusalem, the first *qibla* of Islam. Mammoth demonstrations were held in Pakistan. Ardent solidarity with the victims of aggression was manifested not only in words but also in concrete ways; Pakistani military trainers in those countries volunteered their services and participated in action. Pakistan's Representative at the United Nations, Agha Shahi, vigorously supported resolutions in the General Assembly calling for respect for international law and the rights of the people of occupied territories pending Israeli withdrawal. He piloted the resolution by which Israeli measures to change the status of Jerusalem were declared invalid.

The formation of the Organization of the Islamic Conference (OIC) followed the arson inflicting extensive damage to Al Aqsa Mosque on 21 August 1969, triggering a tidal wave of outrage among Muslims throughout the world who revere the mosque, which is associated with the Prophet's Ascension (PBUH). Arab and non-Arab Muslim States joined at the first Islamic Summit conference held in Rabat, on 22-24 September 1969; they adopted a moving declaration reflecting the profound distress of Muslim peoples, agreed to coordinate action to secure Israeli withdrawal from all Arab territories occupied in 1967 and affirmed full support to the Palestinian people in their struggle for national liberation. Recognizing that a common creed constituted a powerful bond between Muslim peoples, the leaders decided to institutionalize the conference and established the OIC with a permanent secretariat in Jedda, pending the liberation of Jerusalem.

Criteria for membership of the OIC were defined against the background of India's 'pathetic importuning'[114] for an invitation to attend the Islamic Summit, on the ground of its large Muslim population. Cognizant of the abiding concern of the Muslim community in South Asia for the welfare of their co-religionists throughout the world, Pakistan—itself being an heir to that legacy—agreed to accord representation to the Muslims of India at the conference. But when India tried to participate as a State and sent a non-Muslim envoy to the conference, it was excluded on Pakistani initiative. If size of the Muslim population were the criterion for membership, many other States, such as USSR and China, should have been invited to participate, their Muslim minorities being larger than the population of most Muslim States.

The Disaster of 1971

Bengal played a key role in the rise of Muslim nationalism in British India. The Muslim League which led the struggle for Pakistan was founded in Dhaka. The Pakistan Resolution of 1940 was moved by A. K. Fazlul Haq while Khawaja Nazimuddin and Huseyn Shaheed Suhrawardy, all three from Bengal, were in the forefront of the Pakistan Movement. The sense of solidarity among the people of East and West Pakistan was strengthened by shared pride in the success of their common political struggle. But the Government of Pakistan failed to take timely cognizance of the problems inherent in the distance, economic disparity and difference of languages between the two Wings of the country.

East Pakistani dissatisfaction was first heard in early 1948. The Quaid-i-Azam's statement in Dhaka that Urdu alone would be the national language met with a negative reception. Few of the administrative officials inherited by Pakistan were Bengalis.[115] East Pakistan did not have a sense of participation in the government in distant Karachi. In 1950 the East Pakistan Muslim League asked for 'maximum autonomy'. Delay in constitution-making and holding national elections widened the gulf between government and people. The Muslim League was eclipsed in the provincial election held in East Pakistan in 1954. The United Front which won 223 out of 237 seats asked for 'complete autonomy according to the Lahore Resolution',[116] ignoring the more accepted 1946 resolution of the elected Muslim League legislators which was unambiguous in the demand for Pakistan as 'a sovereign independent State'. The grab of power, first by bureaucrats and then in 1958 by the army, largely from West Pakistan, accelerated alienation between the two Wings.

East Pakistan's isolation during the 1965 War and, with the bulk of the armed forces stationed in West Pakistan, its lack of self-defence capability, gave a fillip to the existing demand for autonomy. In March 1966, the Awami League leader Sheikh Mujibur Rahman put forward Six Points[117] calling for a new constitution under which the federal government would be responsible 'only for defence and foreign affairs', for which purpose it would be 'provided with requisite revenue resources' by the federating units. Ayub Khan's highly centralized government equated the demand for autonomy with secessionism. A process of polarization set in with West Pakistani opinion looking at East Pakistanis as dupes of Indian propaganda, and Bengali elites ascribing motives of domination and exploitation to West Pakistanis. Ayub Khan said, 'They are not going to remain with us.'[118]

Alert to the storm brewing in East Pakistan, India encouraged Bengali separatism. Operatives of its secret service agency— Research and Analysis Wing (RAW)—intensified subversion. They met with a group of extremists in 1966 in Agartala to plan sabotage.[119] A raid on an armoury led to the arrest of twenty-eight persons in January 1969. The case against a few civilian officials and low-level armed forces personnel was not without substance but the government also implicated Mujibur Rahman, though he was in custody during the Agartala Conspiracy period. Trial by a special tribunal robbed the proceedings of credibility. Opinion in East Pakistan concluded that the case was concocted for political persecution.

Later, in the general elections, nature too seemed to collude in the tragedy. A cyclone of ferocious intensity in November 1970 left death and devastation in its trail. The federal government was charged with not only incompetence but indifference to the plight of the people of East Pakistan. In the ensuing election, the Awami League swept the polls winning 160 out of 162 seats from East Pakistan, sufficient for an absolute majority in the National Assembly. Its position on Six Points became even more rigid. Yahya Khan, encouraged by Z. A. Bhutto, leader of the Pakistan People's Party, which emerged as the largest party in the West Wing, declined to transfer power unless an understanding was first reached on an acceptable constitutional formula. Even if Mujibur Rehman wanted to compromise, he was now a prisoner of his party and his own extremist rhetoric.

· 'Almost all nations will fight for their unity, even if sentiment in the disaffected area is overwhelmingly for secession', observed Henry Kissinger, adding, 'So it was during our Civil War, with Nigeria toward Biafra and with Congo toward Katanga.'[120] But Yahya Khan's decision to use force was a gamble with the dice loaded against Pakistan. It was foolish to hope that 42,320[121] West Pakistani troops could suppress 75 million people in East Pakistan, with India determined to obstruct and prevent the effort through instigation, abetment and military intervention. RAW stepped up efforts to cultivate retired Bengali army officers for armed resistance.[122] The Indian agency also laid a trap to sever direct air links between the West and East Wings, thus adding to the central government's mounting difficulties in East Pakistan.

On 30 January 1971 an Indian Airlines plane named *Ganga*, on a Srinagar-Delhi flight, was hijacked to Lahore by two Kashmiri youths. They were lionized as freedom fighters on arrival at Lahore airport. Let alone popular opinion, even the usually calculating Z. A. Bhutto applauded the 'brave freedom fighters'.[123] Their leader set the plane on fire. New Delhi made furious protests, demanding compensation and immediate surrender of the criminals. Struck by this bolt from the blue, Islamabad was paralysed, too proud to concede peremptory Indian demands and too weak to control the emotional outburst of popular opinion. Before it knew what was happening, India suspended overflight rights of Pakistan's planes. Subsequently, a Pakistani inquiry tribunal discovered the facts: the leader of the 'hijackers' was a recruit of Indian intelligence, trained and coached for the mission; the 'weapons' given to him and his innocent accomplice were toy pistols and wooden grenades; and the *Ganga* was the oldest plane in the airline's fleet. Pakistan had walked into a well-laid trap.

After Yahya Khan ordered the crackdown in East Pakistan in March 1971, the Indian Government moved into higher gear. India saw in the crisis an 'opportunity of the century' to cut Pakistan into two.[124] RAW operatives smuggled out Tajuddin Ahmad, an Awami League leader, escorted him to a border village to proclaim the independence of Bangladesh and installed him as head of the provisional Bangladesh government in Mujibnagar, a house in Calcutta rented by RAW.[125] On 31 March the Indian Parliament adopted a resolution assuring Bangladeshis that 'their struggle and sacrifices will receive the wholehearted support of the people of India'.[126] Indira Gandhi reassured Parliament that she would make timely decisions about the developing situation. Within days, the Indian Border Police started operating inside East Pakistan. India began building up a rebel force called Mukti Bahini, setting up, first secretly and later openly, 84 training camps; an estimated 100,000 men were taught guerrilla skills.[127]

Public opinion and the media in the US and Western Europe were outraged by the Pakistani military action. The excesses committed by Pakistani forces were reported at great length, and the number of refugees that entered India was wildly exaggerated. Few bothered to take notice of Indian interference or its rejection of proposals for impartial international inspection. To ease India's burden on account of refugees, the United States provided $350 million in aid. It did not dissuade Indira Gandhi from her preconceived purpose. 'The opportunity to settle scores with a rival that had isolated itself by its own short-sightedness was simply too tempting'; all efforts by the international community to promote a political solution were resisted as India 'insisted on terms that escalated by the week'.[128] President Nixon read the Indian design clearly, but the official establishment was swept off its feet by popular reaction. He acquiesced in the State Department's decision to embargo delivery of arms to Pakistan.

India soon decided to take military action in East Pakistan. Only its implementation had to be deferred in the light of Chief of Staff General Manekshaw's view that the army needed six to seven months to prepare for war.[129] The monsoon season was too wet for operations; besides, the defence establishment suggested precautions to exclude the risk of China coming to Pakistan's rescue, and delay an attack till the winter when snow would block the high Himalayan passes. For reassurance against China, India signed a Treaty of Friendship with the Soviet Union in August. With the Soviet veto in its pocket to stymie the UN Security Council, orders were issued to the armed forces to prepare for operations.[130] Other preparations, too, were 'excellent'.[131] A Policy Planning Committee was established to ensure political and military coordination at home and the build-up of international opinion through propaganda and high level visits.

In contrast, conditions in Islamabad were confused and chaotic. Yahya Khan 'was oblivious to his perils'; Pakistan's military leaders were 'caught up in a process beyond their comprehension'.[132] Yahya Khan did not inform others in government of his role in providing a secret channel between Washington and Beijing, and few grasped the strong reaction it provoked in Moscow. The importance of the Indo-Soviet Treaty was not correctly assessed; some thought the Soviet objective was to restrain India.

The US underwrote most of the expense on relief of refugees from East Pakistan, and India took the assistance without showing any gratitude to the administration. Indira Gandhi, bent upon humiliating Pakistan, was dismissive of American efforts to promote a political settlement. She rejected Washington's suggestion for UN monitoring of the border in order to curb guerrilla activities from its territory. By October, Yahya Khan informed Washington that he was willing to grant full autonomy to East Pakistan. A month later he was even agreeable to a unilateral withdrawal of forces. Any such decision would have been better than the fate which befell the country. Unaccountably, Yahya did not act on these ideas.

Before moving in for the 'kill', Indira Gandhi undertook an international tour. She visited Washington on 4-5 November, mainly for the purpose of influencing public opinion. President Nixon detested the condescension Indira Gandhi exuded, like her sermonizing father,[133] and he was opposed to her designs against Pakistan, but he was not unsympathetic to India. During the two years of his administration, the United States had given $1.5 billion in aid to India.[134] His conversation with Indira Gandhi was 'a classic dialogue of the deaf' and he 'was disturbed by the fact that although Mrs Gandhi professed her devotion to peace, she would not make any concrete offers for de-escalating the tensions'.[135] She protested that she was not opposed to Pakistan's existence but 'her analysis did little to sustain her disclaimer'.[136] In fact, she argued that Pakistan should not have come into being. As Nixon later recorded in his diary, Indira Gandhi 'purposely deceived me in our meeting',[137] having 'made up her mind to attack Pakistan at the time she saw me in Washington and assured me she would not'.[138] In retrospect, Nixon further lamented: 'how hypocritical the present Indian leaders are' and how 'duplicitous' Indira Gandhi.

The Indian Army commenced cross-border operations in November: 'From 21 to 25 November several Indian Army divisions, divided into smaller tactical units, launched simultaneous military actions.'[139] Troops, tanks and aircraft were used to assist the Mukti Bahini occupy 'liberated' territory. Nixon sent another letter to Indira Gandhi informing her of Yahya Khan's offer of unilateral withdrawal, and he also wrote to Kosygin to intercede with her. She was implacable. On 29 November she told the US Ambassador, 'We can't afford to listen to advice which weakens us.'

On 2 December, Yahya Khan invoked the 1959 Agreement asking for US assistance. The State Department argued that the Agreement did not oblige the US Government to give a positive response. According to Kissinger,[140] it 'ignored all other commu nications between our government and Pakistan'. Their 'plain import was that the United States would come to Pakistan's assistance if she was attacked by India'. He thought: 'The image of a great nation conducting itself like a shyster looking for legalistic loopholes was not likely to inspire other allies who had signed treaties with us or relied on our expressions in the belief the words meant approximately what they said.' In the event, the White House was stalled by the State Department. Not even a statement was issued. Meanwhile, the military situation in East Pakistan grew desperate by the day. 'Yahya chose what he considered the path of honour', and on 3 December ordered attack across the border from West Pakistan. This decision, like others Yahya Khan made, proved disastrous.

A resolution introduced by the United States in the Security Council on 4 December calling for a cease-fire and withdrawal of forces received eleven votes in favour but was vetoed by the USSR. In the General Assembly a resolution was adopted on 7 December by a vote of 104 to eleven but it too failed to deflect India from its ruthless course.

China was supportive of Pakistan, and Premier Zhou recognized that India was guilty of 'gross interference' in Pakistan's internal affairs. China continued to supply military equipment under existing agreements and extended political support to the Pakistani position in the United Nations. At the same time, it was circumspect and did not make any promises to Pakistan that it could not fulfil.

On 7 December Washington learned that Indira Gandhi was determined to continue fighting 'until the Pakistani army and air force were wiped out'.[141] Moscow encouraged New Delhi in its design, promising that it would initiate military moves against Xinjiang if China threatened India. The crisis now involved high stakes, and the threat of great power confrontation loomed on the horizon. Washington decided it could not allow Moscow to intimidate Beijing if it wanted its China policy to retain credibility. On 9 December, Nixon authorized the dispatch of a task force of eight ships, including the aircraft carrier *Enterprise* from the Pacific to the Bay of Bengal; the 'objective was to scare off an attack on West Pakistan...[and] to have forces in place in case the Soviet Union pressured China'.[142] He stressed upon the Soviets, who had 'proceeded to equip India with great amounts of sophisticated armaments', to restrain India. On 12 December, he sent a hot line message to Leonid Brezhnev saying, 'I cannot emphasize too much that time is of the essence to avoid consequences neither of us wants.'[143] To make the point more concretely, the Soviet authorities were also informed of fleet movements.

Evasive at first, Moscow finally responded on 13 December to say that they were conducting 'a clarification of all the circumstance in India'. Kuznetsov was sent to New Delhi to work for a cease-fire. On 14 December at 3 a.m. the Soviet Ambassador in Washington delivered a message reporting 'firm assurances by New Delhi that India has no intention of seizing West Pakistani territory'.

At this stage, Poland proposed a resolution in the Security Council which called for the immediate transfer of power to the elected representatives in East Pakistan, and a cease-fire and troop withdrawals by both sides. Presumably it had Soviet support and could have even at this eleventh hour saved Pakistan from further humiliation. But, as often happens in a crisis, the rush of events overtakes human capacity to make timely decisions. To India's relief, the resolution was not pressed to a vote. Under mounting US and Soviet pressure, Indira Gandhi offered an unconditional cease-fire on 16 December, the day Indira Gandhi told the Indian Parliament that she had 'liberated' East Pakistan. Over 90,000 Pakistani soldiers and civilians had surrendered. West Pakistan had capitulated. She had avenged several centuries of Hindu humiliation at the hands of Muslim sultans and emperors; 'Delirious with joy' the members of Parliament gave her a 'thunderous ovation'.[144]

Nixon's account lends credibility to his claim that, 'By using diplomatic signals and behind the scenes pressures we had been able to save West Pakistan from imminent threat of Indian aggression and domination.' It also raises the question that, if the United States had taken an equally tough line in regard to Indian aggression on East Pakistan, it would not have been so easy. Nixon 'wanted to let the Soviets know that we would strongly oppose the dismemberment of Pakistan by a Soviet ally using Soviet arms'. But, given the nature of the American system and absence of support in Congress, he could hardly follow a policy of intervention to aid a brutal and hated regime in Pakistan. According to Nixon, 'the State Department felt that independence for East Pakistan was inevitable and desirable'. However, even he 'recognized that political autonomy for East Pakistan would be the probable outcome of a political solution, and we were willing to work in that direction. The main point was that the fighting should stop and the danger of a great power confrontation should be removed.'

Neither of the pacts proved useful in 1965 and 1971. SEATO members did not consider Indian aggression against Pakistan to come under the purview of the Treaty, nor did CENTO members. Pakistan withdrew from SEATO in November 1972. CENTO was still found marginally useful and Pakistan continued its membership until March 1979, when it joined the Non-Aligned Movement.

Residual Pakistan

The 1971 disaster divided and diminished Pakistan, betrayed the dream of the founding fathers, and demoralized the nation. A dark shadow hovered over the prospects of the people. With their pride in the armed forces destroyed, their leadership exposed as self-centred and incompetent, the people were bewildered and distraught. Over 90,000 soldiers and civilians were taken prisoner after the Pakistani contingent in East Pakistan was overwhelmed, and some 5,000 square miles of its territory in West Pakistan was under Indian occupation. One million inhabitants were dislocated from these areas of residual Pakistan. In this tortured and turbulent situation, Z. A. Bhutto assumed office as President of residual Pakistan. His government had to 'pick up the pieces', bring the nation to grips with the new reality, and rebuild morale and confidence. Above all, it needed to rehabilitate Pakistan in the world polity and reorientate failed policies both at home and abroad.

For sympathy and support Pakistan turned to friends. The new President visited China in January 1972, and received diplomatic support and economic and military assistance. Bhutto also undertook a whirlwind tour of Islamic countries in the Middle East and Africa, first in January and again in May-June. They upheld the principles of law for the unconditional release of Pakistani prisoners and the withdrawal of Indian forces from occupied territories. President Nixon continued to extend a helpful hand: 'The cohesion and stability of Pakistan are of critical importance to the structure of peace in South Asia.'[145] Britain was unsympathetic, not only recognizing Bangladesh precipitately but persuading several countries of Western Europe, Australia and New Zealand to do so simultaneously. In disgust, Bhutto quit the Commonwealth. Little was expected of the Soviet Union. When Bhutto visited Moscow in March 1972 in the hope of moderating its hostility, Soviet leaders suggested recognition of Bangladesh and negotiations with India for a 'realistic' solution of the post-war problems.

Simla Agreement

Pakistan had to sue for peace with India from a position of utter weakness. India was intent on dictating its terms. Holding 90,000 Pakistani soldiers and civilians prisoner, and with Pakistani territory under its possession, New Delhi set itself three major goals: legalization of the Indian position in Jammu and Kashmir, recognition of Bangladesh and limitation of Pakistan's rights as a sovereign State. The task of Pakistani diplomacy was to minimize the price it had to pay. The limited extent of its success is manifest in the agreement signed at Simla.[146]

In its first draft at the Simla conference which began on 28 June, India proposed that relations between the two countries should be governed in future by a set of principles selected by India. The list was remarkable less for what it included than for what it left out. Particularly glaring was the total omission of any mention of the Charter of the United Nations, the universally agreed framework for the maintenance of international peace and security. Unable to defend the omission, the Indian side agreed to the addition of a sub-paragraph to provide that 'the principles and purposes of the Charter of the United Nations shall govern the relations between the two countries'.

India was adamant in its insistence that the two countries 'undertake to settle all issues between them bilaterally and exclusively by peaceful means'. In effect it meant that differences could be settled on terms acceptable to the more powerful party, and all other means of peaceful settlement envisaged in the UN Charter would be inapplicable as between the two countries. The Indian suggestion was an obvious attempt to reverse the progress of civilization which has been connected with the exclusion of the use or threat of force and, instead, the settlement of differences on the basis of law and justice through impartial determination. In the end, Pakistan acquiesced in the formulation which provided for settlement of differences 'by peaceful means through bilateral negotiations or by any other peaceful means agreed upon between them'. Pakistan would not have accepted this extraordinary provision were it not for the circumstances under which negotiations were conducted at Simla. It, however, drew comfort from the fact that this sub-paragraph could not be read without regard to the primacy of the United Nations Charter acknowledged by both sides in the preceding sub-paragraph. All members of the United Nations have assumed the obligation under Chapter VI on Pacific Settlement of Disputes to 'seek a solution by negotiation, enquiry, mediation, conciliation, arbitration, judicial settlement, resort to regional agencies or arrangements, or other peaceful means'.

With regard to Jammu and Kashmir, India asked that the dispute should be settled 'here and now' by making the cease-fire line an international boundary. The proposal ignored the principles Pakistan and India had accepted in the UN Security Council resolutions and attempted to deprive the Kashmiri people of their right of self-determination. That was unacceptable to Pakistan even in its terrible straits. Similarly, Pakistan acquiesced in the Indian refusal to return to the 1949 cease-fire line, but insisted on the insertion of the 'without prejudice' clause in the paragraph requiring that 'the line of control resulting from the cease-fire of 17 December 1971 shall be respected by both sides without prejudice to the recognized position of either side'. Significantly, the last paragraph recognized a link between a final settlement of Jammu and Kashmir and the establishment of durable peace and normalization of relations between Pakistan and India. Speculation about a verbal understanding between Z.A. Bhutto and Indira Gandhi regarding acceptance of the *status quo* in Kashmir is not only uncorroborated, but is entirely pointless, as obligations of States arise only from agreements.

Normalization of Relations with Bangladesh

The separation of East Pakistan was a tragic fact for Pakistan to contend with. Bangladesh had to be recognized but the Pakistan Government could not ignore the feelings of a traumatized nation. Dhaka did not make the task easier. Miscalculation led it to believe that Pakistani prisoners of war could be used as a lever of pressure to secure acceptance of its claim to a share of Pakistan's assets, disregarding the liabilities. It took nearly two years for New Delhi and Dhaka to realize that Pakistani prisoners were an asset of declining value. World opinion became critical of their prolonged detention. Finally, in September 1973, India itself obtained the concurrence of Bangladesh to the release of all Pakistani prisoners excepting 195, which issue was not resolved till the next year. On humanitarian grounds, Pakistan accepted the transfer of a substantial number of non-Bengalis. Over 250,000 persons who had served in government in East Pakistan, or had family connections, were allowed to move to Pakistan. As many others had wanted to come after they were thrown out of their jobs. Tragically, they have remained stranded.

Nothing did more to convince Dhaka about the inadvisability of blocking the release of all the Pakistani prisoners than China's decision, in response to Pakistan's request, to use its veto to bar the admission of Bangladesh to the United Nations. In retrospect, China did a great favour to Bangladesh as well. Had Dhaka gone ahead with the trials, prospects of normalization of relations would have retreated for even longer. Also, fortunately for the two countries, the Islamic Summit Conference in Lahore in 1974 provided an opportunity for common friends to persuade Bangladesh to abandon the idea of trying Pakistani captives. Pakistan promptly extended recognition, and Prime Minister Mujibur Rahman came to attend the Islamic Summit.

Beginning of the Nuclear Programme[147]

The 1971 disaster demonstrated once again the relentless Indian threat to Pakistan's security and survival, its inability due to disparity of resources to maintain force levels adequate to safeguard territorial integrity, and the undependability of alliances and the United Nations for the maintenance of its peace and security. The alternative Pakistan began to ponder was the acquisition of nuclear weapons capability. In 1972 Bhutto met with Pakistani scientists to discuss the possibility.

The decision was easier made than implemented. Pakistan possessed neither fissile material nor explosion technology. Nor was it easy to import after the 1974 Indian atomic explosion, using equipment and materials obtained from Canada and the United States on the pretext of peaceful purposes. Industrialized countries formed a cartel which imposed stringent restraints on export of equipment and technology. France, which first agreed to supply to Pakistan a nuclear fuel reprocessing plant for the separation of plutonium, later succumbed to American pressure and reneged on the agreement. Meanwhile, Pakistan embarked upon an alternative route for the indigenous production of fissile material. It began to build a plant for the enrichment of uranium.

While continuing efforts to acquire nuclear technology, Pakistan pursued the aim of establishing a non-discriminatory non-proliferation regime in South Asia. Even after India conducted a nuclear explosion test, pretending it was 'peaceful', Pakistan took India on its word that it had no intention to produce nuclear weapons, and proposed the creation of a nuclear weapon-free zone in South Asia. The UN General Assembly endorsed the proposal in 1974 and has continued since to adopt the resolution annually with an overwhelming majority. Only India, Bhutan and Mauritius have usually voted against the proposal. Determined to retain the nuclear weapons option, India likewise rejected several other proposals to join Pakistan in renouncing nuclear weapons.

The question is often raised whether Pakistan's efforts to promote non-proliferation was consistent with the rationale of its policy of developing nuclear capability. Would not mutual renunciation deprive Pakistan of the deterrence necessary to ward off the perennial threat by a more powerful and inimical India? Though manifestly logical, the question is based on the assumption that India might be prepared to renounce the nuclear weapons option which, experience has confirmed, is quite unlikely. Moreover, were India to renounce the option, it would in effect abandon also its aim of hegemony over South Asia, which drives its pursuit of nuclear weapons. It would then become unnecessary for Pakistan to develop the nuclear option.

Relations with the USA: 1972-79

One of the factors that contributed to Pakistan's cautious policy up to 1980 was its strained relations with the United States. From equable even friendly treatment of Pakistan until the mid-1970s, the United States had turned to a policy of discrimination and sanctions largely due to differences on the nuclear issue.

After India conducted its nuclear explosion test in 1974, Washington accepted the *fait accompli*, but decided to target Pakistan to demonstrate its non-proliferation zeal. Kissinger warned Pakistan of the risks of opposing the American objective. Prime Minister Z. A. Bhutto was not intimidated, though his attribution of the domestic agitation against him following the rigged election in 1977 to American instigation was rather self-serving. His public charge that 'political bloodhounds were after him because of his opposition to US policies on a number of international issues'[148] only added strain to Pakistan-US relations.

The United States supported efforts for a non-discriminatory non-proliferation regime in South Asia in words, but in practice it singled out Pakistan for sanctions. The Symington and Glenn Amendments, which provide for aid cut-off to countries that embark on plutonium separation or uranium enrichment outside international inspection and control, built in a loophole to exempt India and Israel from their purview. When Washington applied this law to Pakistan in 1979, Islamabad protested against this 'act of discrimination...[applying] different standards to different states',[149] but evoked no sympathy at the time.

The slide in Pakistan-US relations accelerated after the United States blocked the Pakistan-France agreement for a reprocessing plant in 1978, and cut off economic assistance in April 1979. Relations took a nosedive in November 1979 when a mob of young people, infuriated by a false report broadcast by an unidentified radio alleging US occupation of the Holy Kaaba, sacked the American Embassy in Islamabad in which four staff members perished.[150] President Carter was furious, until the situation abruptly changed a month later with the Soviet intervention in Afghanistan.

Afghanistan Crisis

Few countries are closer to Pakistan in culture and history than Afghanistan. The hope for friendly cooperation was, however, vitiated at the start. On the eve of the establishment of Pakistan, the Afghan Government denounced the 1893 treaty establishing the Durand Line as the boundary with British India, and launched an irredenta in the guise of support for 'Pushtoonistan'. Afghanistan was the only country to vote against Pakistan's admission to the United Nations. In the decades that followed, relations between the two neighbours remained strained though, fortunately, tensions usually remained under control. Pakistan appreciated King Zahir Shah's restraining influence; the Afghan Government refrained from exploiting Pakistan's vulnerability during the wars with India in 1965 and 1971.

Apprehensions of deterioration of bilateral relations rose in Islamabad when Sardar Mohammad Daoud, a known Pakistan-baiter, overthrew Zahir Shah on 17 July 1973 and designated himself President. Aiming to use foreign support to consolidate his power at home and pursue confrontation with Pakistan, Daoud cultivated close relations with the Soviet Union. However, the embrace soon turned into a bear-hug. The Soviets penetrated internal politics, providing support and assistance to the revolutionary People's Democratic Party of Afghanistan (PDPA). By 1976, Daoud appeared to have realized that the Soviets had an agenda of their own. To counterbalance Soviet influence, he embarked on efforts to improve relations with Pakistan, Iran and other Muslim countries. He and Prime Minister Z. A. Bhutto exchanged visits in 1976. Bilateral relations continued to improve after General Ziaul Haq assumed power in Pakistan in July 1977. Daoud's talks with Zia were 'extremely useful' and he told Zia that he intended 'to mould public opinion in my country...to normalize relations with Pakistan'.[151] This policy did not, however, please Moscow or the PDPA. The contest culminated in the 'Saur Revolution' on 27 April 1978. Daoud and members of his family were murdered and Nur Muhammad Taraki was installed as President. Not only was Pakistan disappointed that the hope of improved relations with Afghanistan eluded its grasp, it was also concerned that the PDPA might act as a cat's paw of the Soviet Union which had an agenda of its own. However, there was little Pakistan could do as the country was in disarray. It had been bled white by the three-month long agitation against Bhutto for rigging the elections in March 1977 and Zia's military government had become unpopular after he reneged on his promise to hold elections within 90 days of the take-over. Making the best of a bad situation, Pakistan decided to extend prompt recognition to the PDPA regime.[152] Zia went to Kabul to meet President Taraki in the hope of mutual accommodation.

A party of intellectuals without a popular base, the PDPA embarked on a suicidal policy of radical reforms which outraged the conservative people of Afghanistan. It was also riven with rivalry between its predominantly rural and Pushto speaking Khalq and urban-based Persian speaking Parcham factions. Infighting led to Taraki's murder in September 1979. His successor, Hafizullah Amin, was both headstrong and defiant of Soviet guidance. His rivals in the party and the Soviets considered him a danger to the stability of the revolution. On 26 December 1979, Soviet forces rolled across Amu Darya, Amin was executed and Babrak Karmal, leader of the Parcham faction, was installed as President. It was a clear case of blatant military intervention. When asked by a Pakistani foreign ministry official at whose invitation the Soviet forces were sent to Afghanistan, the Soviet Ambassador in Islamabad replied 'Babrak Karmal',[153] who was then in exile and obviously in no position to speak for the Afghan Government.

The fateful decision for military intervention was made, it was later revealed, by the aged and sick Leonid Brezhnev under pressure of hard-liners in the Politburo of the Communist Party. Ideological solidarity with the revolution in Afghanistan and a perception of threat from Islamic resurgence in Iran and other countries to its south to Soviet control over Central Asia were, probably, factors in their calculation. The Soviet intervention provoked a deep sense of alarm in Pakistan. Suddenly the buffer disappeared, and if, after the aggressive advance to Pakistan's border, the Soviets consolidated control in Afghanistan, they could use it as a springboard for a leap down the Bolan and Khyber Passes to fulfill the historical Czarist ambition for access to the warm waters of the Arabian Sea. Pakistan therefore felt it could not acquiesce in the Soviet intervention, but it could, even less, afford confrontation with a superpower. At the time, Pakistan was internally weak and internationally isolated. Bhutto's execution in April 1979, upon conviction on a charge of murder, had polarized opinion at home as never before. Zia's decision to ignore appeals for clemency by foreign leaders and media antagonised almost the whole world. Also, relations with the United States, already strained by discriminatory American sanctions imposed in 1979 to penalize Pakistan for defying American law against uranium enrichment, had nosedived in November 1979, following the destruction of the American Embassy in Islamabad.

Islamabad decided on a middle course,[154] avoiding confrontation but raising a low-pitched voice of concern and protest. Its statement, issued two days later, criticized the intervention but without mentioning the Soviet Union by name. The 'induction of foreign troops' was described as a 'serious violation' of the norms of peaceful coexistence and the principles of the UN Charter. Rather defensively, the statement explained Pakistan's 'gravest concern' in the context of its links of Islam, geography and non-aligned policy with Afghanistan, and concluded by expressing the hope that foreign troops would be removed from Afghan soil 'forthwith'.

The United States, which had earlier treated Afghanistan with neglect, suddenly woke up to the dangers of Soviet power to 'within striking distance of the Indian Ocean and, even the Persian Gulf...an area of vital strategic and economic significance to the survival of Western Europe, the Far East, and ultimately the United States'.[155] Washington issued a strong condemnation of the 'blatant' Soviet intervention.[156] Calling it a 'grave threat to peace', President Carter proclaimed a boycott of the Moscow Olympics and suspended arms limitation talks. The US depended on this region for a quarter of its oil imports, and West European countries for two-thirds of their oil requirements. Most Muslim countries condemned the Soviet intervention and many of the non-aligned nations joined in calling for the withdrawal of Soviet troops.

Still apprehensive of the dangerous implications of involvement in the Cold War, Pakistan sought a political settlement of the crisis through the United Nations. At its request, the genuinely non-aligned countries, critical of Soviet violation of the principles of law, took the lead in drafting a balanced resolution. When it was vetoed by the USSR in the Security Council, a special session of the General Assembly promptly adopted the same resolution on 14 January 1980, with a majority of 104 countries voting in favour, only 18—mostly satellite states—against, with 18 abstentions. The resolution strongly deplored 'the recent armed intervention in Afghanistan' and called for 'immediate, unconditional and total withdrawal of the foreign troops in order to enable its people to determine their own form of government and choose their own economic, political and social systems free from outside intervention, subversion, coercion or constraint of any kind whatever.'

An extraordinary session of the OIC Foreign Ministers held in Islamabad later in January took a much tougher position in a strong indictment of the Soviet intervention. The meeting decided to suspend Afghanistan's membership of the OIC, and affirmed solidarity with the struggle of the Afghan people to safeguard 'their faith, national independence and territorial integrity'. A great majority of the members of the Non-Aligned Movement (NAM), were also critical of Soviet intervention and, out of 92 members, 56 voted for the General Assembly resolution. India joined a coterie of Soviet friends and apologists in the NAM Coordinating Bureau to prevent the adoption of a resolution on Afghanistan. It did not, however, damage the Afghan cause so much as it did the credibility of NAM itself.[157]

More critical to the outcome of the crisis was the opposition to the Soviet intervention inside Afghanistan. The invasion by foreign troops to protect a regime with an alien ideology transformed the resistance into a popular *jihad*. Despite Soviet warnings and threats, Pakistan decided to provide clandestine assistance to the *mujahideen*. This decision, made without foreign prompting, had complex motivations. Self-interest and solidarity with the fraternal Afghan people were certainly weighty considerations. In fighting for their own cause, the *mujahideen* kept the Soviets at bay from Pakistan. Also, President Zia liked the limelight in which he now basked internationally.

Still, Pakistan sought to save the issue from being sucked into the orbit of the Cold War. The main thrust of its policy was diplomatic and, to that end, the resolution proposed at the regular session of the UN General Assembly in 1980 was toned down. It emphasized uncontroversial principles as the basis for a political solution: (1) immediate withdrawal of foreign forces, (2) preservation of the sovereignty, territorial integrity, independence and non-aligned status of Afghanistan, (3) respect for the right of its people to determine their own form of government and economic system free from outside intervention, subversion, coercion or constraint, and (4) creation of conditions for the voluntary return of Afghan refugees to their homes in safety and honour. It further suggested international guarantees of non-use of force against the security of 'all neighbouring countries' and efforts by the UN Secretary General to promote a political solution. This resolution, which was retained in substance for the next seven years, attracted ever greater support which increased from 111 votes in favour in 1980, to 123 in 1987. During the same period, negative votes and abstentions combined declined from 36 in 1980 to 30 in 1987.[158] Every year the Soviet Union suffered a stinging blow to its prestige.

Revival of Pakistan-US Alliance

Washington encouraged Pakistan to support and assist the Afghan resistance. Within days of the Soviet intervention, and without even consulting Pakistan, President Jimmy Carter announced an offer of $400 million in economic and military assistance. Ziaul Haq's scornful if undiplomatic rejection of Carter's offer as 'peanuts' gave the wrong impression that Islamabad only wanted a higher amount in aid. Actually, it sought, even more, a guarantee of American assistance in the event of a Soviet or Soviet-backed Indian attack on Pakistan. It asked for the upgradation of the 1959 executive Agreement on Defence Cooperation into a binding treaty. The 'credibility and durability'[159] of American assurances was low, founded in the widely held belief that at critical junctures, especially in 1965, the United States betrayed a friend and ally. Besides, the aid package was 'wrapped up in onerous conditions' which, Pakistan felt, 'could affect the pursuit of our nuclear research and development'.[160] As for the amount, Pakistan was prepared to accept $200 million in economic aid, but not $200 million for defence. Not only was it incommensurate with the enhanced risks of reinvolvement in the Cold War, Pakistan resented the fact that the proffered aid level was determined by fear of Indian reaction, thus 'denuding it of relevance to our defensive capacity'. The US refused to delink economic assistance from the defence component.

Non-acceptance of US aid in 1980 reduced the risk of again involving Pakistan in the Cold War. It also helped in projecting the Afghan cause in its genuine perspective of a liberation struggle. Moreover, it saved Pakistan's relations with Iran from further strain. Iranian media perception of Pakistan as a proxy for US interests in the region was painful to Pakistanis who value Iran as a friend and a fraternal neighbour. The sincerity of Pakistan's solidarity with Iran was illustrated again in April 1980 when it expressed 'shock and dismay' at the US assault on Iran in an attempt forcibly to take out American Embassy staff, and 'deplored this impermissible act which constitutes a serious violation of Iran's sovereignty'.[161]

After President Ronald Reagan succeeded Carter in 1981, the United States offered a new package of loans and grants amounting to $3 billion over five years.[162] The amount of $600 million a year for development and defence was a significant improvement over the Carter offer of $400 million for 18 months. The five-year programme provided durability to the US commitment, though it still did not provide a satisfactory answer to Pakistan's security concerns as Reagan, too, found Congressional opinion reluctant to support a formal security guarantee to Pakistan. However, the Reagan administration evinced a reassuring understanding of Pakistan's vulnerabilities as a front-line state, and the clearance given for the sale of forty F-16 aircraft was seen as earnest US concern for Pakistan's security.

On the nuclear issue, the two countries maintained their formal positions, Pakistan reiterating its intention to continue research, and the US proclaiming its non-proliferation concern. But Washington turned the pressure off. Acknowledging past discrimination and expressing understanding of Pakistan's rationale,[163] it accepted Zia's assurance that Pakistan would not develop nuclear weapons or transfer sensitive technology.[164] The US administration had little difficulty in securing Congress' approval for waiver of the Symington prohibition. Senators and Congressmen who had earlier targeted Pakistan for discriminatory strictures no longer commanded decisive influence.

Pakistan chose not to accept concessional loans for military sales, and instead opted to pay the market rate of interest, so as to safeguard its non-aligned credentials. Pakistan wanted also to retain its credibility as an independent actor in the hope of persuading the Soviet Union to agree to a political solution of the Afghanistan question outside the Cold War context. In the event, the sacrifice won no appreciation from either Moscow or New Delhi. They denounced Pakistan even though a year earlier India had signed a deal with the USSR covering the acquisition of the latest MIG aircraft, T-72 tanks and warships, for a give-away price of $1.6 billion on soft terms though the market value was estimated at $6 billion. In retrospect, Pakistan's more-pious-than-the-Pope posture proved to be costly.[165]

1988 Geneva Accords

UN efforts to promote a political solution began in earnest with the appointment in 1981 of Diego Cordovez, a senior UN official from Ecuador, as the personal representative of the Secretary

General. Before he could convene the first Geneva meeting, Iran declined to participate arguing that the Soviet withdrawal should be unconditional, and Pakistan was unwilling to meet with the Afghan regime which it did not recognize. Cordovez had to persuade Kabul to agree to indirect talks. The Soviet Union refused to join the talks, taking the position that its forces entered Afghanistan at Kabul's invitation and would be withdrawn when Kabul no longer wanted their presence, but it sent high level officials to Geneva to be available for consultation.

Negotiations began in Geneva in June 1982 by exploring the structure of a settlement that would integrate the components of the UN General Assembly resolution. An energetic and persuasive diplomat of high calibre, Cordovez sidetracked past controversy by proposing an agreement on mutual non-interference and non-intervention between Afghanistan and its neighbours as a means of obtaining a Soviet commitment to the withdrawal of forces. To satisfy the Soviet demand for American non-interference, he conceived the idea of guarantees to be provided by both superpowers. Negotiations were not, however, serious at first. The Soviet Union was confident that its mighty forces equipped with the latest weapons would rout the ragtag *mujahideen* armed with antiquated rifles. It misjudged the situation as it could not pin down these guerrillas who were supported by the Afghan populace.

Hopes for a political settlement arose when Yuri Andropov succeeded Brezhnev as the leader of the Soviet Union. In a meeting with Zia after Brezhnev's funeral in November 1982, he gave a 'hint of flexibility'. UN Secretary General Pérez de Cuellar and Diego Cordovez who met Andropov in March received 'new encouragement' for pursuing UN mediation. Andropov counted to them the reasons why the Soviet Union wanted a solution: raising his fingers one by one, he mentioned costs in lives and money, regional tensions, setback to *détente* and loss of Soviet prestige in the Third World.[166]

Buoyed by these positive signals, Cordovez successfully pressed the two sides at meetings in April and June to agree on the components of a comprehensive settlement, including an agreement on non-interference and non-intervention, guarantees by third states, and arrangements for the voluntary return of refugees. Discussions made good progress. The Kabul side objected to the phrase 'existing internationally recognized boundaries'[167] and suggested its substitution by the words 'international borders'. Cordovez was optimistic that the Soviet forces would leave, and envisaged their 'gradual withdrawal' within a reasonable time frame. But the Soviet-Kabul side dragged their feet, indicating that the hard-liners marked time as Andropov was ailing. After he died, they reverted to the policy of a military solution, which continued under Konstantin Chernenko and also under Mikhail Gorbachev till the end of the summer in 1987.

The struggle in Afghanistan was unequal but the *mujahideen* demonstrated courage and resourcefulness in resistance; their sacrifices and stamina drew deserved praise and tribute. Assistance to them increased in order to neutralize the Soviet induction of more lethal artillery, helicopter gunships and bombers for savage and indiscriminate destruction of villages to interdict *mujahideen* activities. The US raised covert allocations for the supply of arms from $250 million in 1985, to $470 million in 1986 and $630 million in 1987.[168] The American contribution was reportedly matched by Saudi Arabia; also, China, Iran and several other countries provided substantial assistance. Pakistan calibrated the flow of assistance to the *mujahideen* cautiously so as to minimize the risk of spillover of the conflict, but it became bolder with time and experience. It realized that a superpower's forces could not be defeated militarily, but attrition inside Afghanistan, combined with blows to its prestige internationally, offered the only hope of wearing down Moscow. Negotiations in Geneva and resolutions in the OIC, NAM and the United Nations were a part of the strategy for increasing political pressure.

In the Geneva talks, twelve sessions were held over six years. Cordovez and the Pakistani side occasionally discussed the question of a compromise between the Kabul regime and the *mujahideen,* although this subject was not on the agenda. UN resolutions only referred to the principle of respect for the right of the Afghan people to determine their own form of government and economic system. Kabul and Moscow at first refused even to recognize the reality of internal resistance: 'everything comes from outside'.[169] Foreign Minister Gromyko dismissed the idea of a broad-based government in Kabul as 'unrealistic phantasies'. Cordovez himself realized the need for a compromise among the Afghans but, as he correctly said, 'The UN is not in the business of establishing governments.'[170] In 1983, when Andropov indicated a desire for settlement, Cordovez was inclined to favour a role for former King Zahir Shah, who offered to work for uniting the Afghans. The idea received enthusiastic support from Afghan exiles. A poll organized by Professor Syed Bahauddin Majrooh, a prominent Afghan scholar who was editing a paper from Peshawar, found that 70 per cent of the Afghan refugees in Pakistan favoured Zahir Shah's return. But this view was rejected by the more powerful *mujahideen* parties. When Majrooh was later assassinated, opponents of the king were suspected of having organized the crime.

By late 1986 all issues were settled except two: the time frame for the withdrawal of Soviet forces and the wording of the reference to the boundary between Pakistan and Afghanistan. The texts of the agreements having been all but finalized, Cordovez remarked, 'It [is] now true for the first time that the only issue remaining [is] the question of the time frame'.[171] That, however, was the crucial issue. In 1986 the Soviet Union said that its forces would be withdrawn four years after the conclusion of the Geneva Accords. Pakistan asked for withdrawals to be completed in three months. This was narrowed down by mid-1987: the Soviets wanted eighteen months for withdrawal while Pakistan went up to seven months. The issue was not to be settled until after the failure of the Soviet military offensive in the summer of 1987. Mikhail Gorbachev then finally decided to abandon the misadventure; by then the imperatives of democratic and economic reforms at home also necessitated an end to confrontation with the West.

In July 1987 Najibullah proposed a coalition offering twelve ministries and the office of vice president to the *mujahideen* Alliance. Gorbachev endorsed the idea of national reconciliation to facilitate the process of 'constructing a new Afghanistan'. The Alliance leaders were, however, unanimous in rejecting a coalition with the PDPA. In September 1987 Cordovez put forward a 'Scenario Paper' envisaging a representative assembly comprising seven Alliance parties, the PDPA and select Afghan personalities to decide a transitional arrangement. Aware of the Alliance's views, Islamabad did not accord the idea much attention. When it was conveyed to them in early 1988, the Alliance leaders ruled out any dialogue with the PDPA. Engineer Gulbuddin Hikmatyar, Professor Burhanuddin Rabbani and Maulvi Yunus Khalis also ruled out any role for the king. Since resistance against the Soviets still commanded priority, Pakistan considered it inadvisable to press the *mujahideen* lest that should divide and weaken the Alliance.

Gorbachev and Foreign Minister Shevardnadze succeeded in winning endorsement of the party Politburo for the policy of terminating military involvement in Afghanistan.[172] The costs of the policy in human and material resources, and the obloquy it entailed even in the Soviet Union's non-aligned backyard, were glaringly disproportionate to any benefits that continued hold over Afghanistan might yield. The new generation of communists no longer shared the ideological fervour of the founders, nor faith in the inevitability of communism's victory. In fact, the Soviet system was faltering, the economy was in decline and the people were alienated. The cost of military confrontation and the arms race with the West, occupation of Eastern Europe, tension with China and, finally, of intervention in Afghanistan had 'ruined' the Soviet Union.

Gorbachev announced at a press conference in Washington on 10 December 1987 that the Soviet forces would withdraw from Afghanistan within twelve months of the conclusion of the Geneva Accords and, further, that during that period the forces would not engage in combat. Gorbachev also delinked the question of withdrawal from an internal settlement in Afghanistan. Though he reaffirmed support for 'a coalition on the basis of national reconciliation and the realities of the situation',[173] Moscow was no longer prepared to allow the Alliance's rejectionist attitude to obstruct its decision to extricate the Soviet Union from the Afghan quagmire. Nor was it willing to undertake the removal of the Kabul regime and hand over the government to the Alliance.

The twelve-month time frame was close to a 'single digit' which was acceptable to Pakistan and other supporters of the struggle in Afghanistan. But just as prospects for the conclusion of the Geneva Accords brightened, President Zia took the position that the conclusion of the Accords should be postponed until after agreement was reached on the formation of a government in Kabul with the participation of the *mujahideen.* This took Prime Minister Muhammad Khan Junejo completely by surprise: heretofore, Pakistan's refrain was that the only outstanding obstacle to the conclusion of the Geneva Accords was a reasonable time frame for the withdrawal of Soviet forces. Besides, making the formation of a coalition government a precondition seemed a recipe for delaying the withdrawal of the Soviet forces because the *mujahideen* Alliance was averse to the idea of a coalition with the PDPA. Now the Soviets were no longer prepared to wait. When, on 9 February, Zia pressed the visiting Soviet First Deputy Foreign Minister Yuli Vorontsov for postponement of the final Geneva round, his comment was withering: 'For eight years you have been asking us to leave Afghanistan. Now you want us to stay. I smell a rat!'[174]

The logic of Zia's eleventh hour volte-face was never explained. Pakistan's foreign friends were as mystified as the Junejo Government. Pakistan could block the Geneva Accords, but could not prevent the Soviets from withdrawing, either unilaterally or pursuant to an agreement with the Kabul regime. Clearly, withdrawal under the Accords was decidedly more advantageous, because the Soviet Union would be internationally bound to withdraw its forces completely within a prescribed time frame and under UN monitoring. It would be legally bound also to refrain from intervention in Afghanistan. Pakistan, too, would receive Soviet and US guarantees of respect for the principles of non-interference and non-intervention. In contrast, unilateral withdrawal would entail no such commitments.

For Moscow, the residual consideration was the manner of disengagement to avoid disgrace to the Soviet Union and danger to the retreating forces. It prized the Geneva Accords because contained in them was a commitment to observe the principle of non-interference and non-intervention. Pakistan and the United States would be under an obligation to discontinue assistance to the *mujahideen,* and that might save Soviet friends from massacre. No less important was their symbolic value, as a UN-sponsored agreement would provide a fig leaf to cover the Soviet defeat. Pakistan could only gain by cooperating in sparing humiliation to the Soviet Union, which would open the possibility to improve relations with this superpower.

The Soviet preference for the Geneva Accords was not unknown. Islamabad used the leverage to obtain significant modifications of the texts. Two of these were suggested by Gulbuddin Hikmatyar, an engineer by training, who grasped points of law better than many diplomats. He pointed out that Pakistan's signature on an agreement with Afghanistan would constitute recognition. Secondly, the agreement would require discontinuation of arms supply to 'rebels'. He was right on both points. When Vorontsov was in Islamabad in February, he was informed that Pakistan would publicly state that the signing of the agreement would not constitute recognition of the Kabul regime. He instantly agreed not to make this matter an issue, and did not contest the logic that peace in Afghanistan required all sides to discontinue arms supply. But, he convincingly explained, Moscow could not go back on its existing commitments to Kabul. 'Negative symmetry' was not feasible but when told that in that event 'positive symmetry' would ensue, and the *mujahideen*, too, could continue to receive supplies, he did not disagree. The discussion served to preclude subsequent misunderstanding between Islamabad and Moscow.

The final Geneva round began on 2 March 1988. The talks proceeded slowly because the Pakistan delegation did not have authorization to finalize the Accords. On their part, the Soviets conveyed agreement to reduce the time frame for withdrawal to nine months. The Kabul representatives tried to create an obstacle by haggling over the wording of the reference to the boundary between the two countries in order to safeguard the Afghan position of non-recognition of the Durand Line. It was an artificial issue: the Geneva talks were not convened to settle the boundary problem. Pakistan had no difficulty in accepting the neutral phrase requiring the two countries 'not to violate the boundaries of each other'.

The replacement of the Kabul regime was never a part of the Geneva agenda but, as Diego Cordovez said in a statement issued on 8 April, 'it has been consistently recognized that the objective of a comprehensive settlement...can best be ensured by a broad-based Afghan Government', and to that end he agreed to provide his good offices. By that time Zia realized that the formation of such a government could not be made a precondition for the conclusion of the Accords.

The Geneva Accords were signed on 14 April 1988 by the Foreign Ministers of Afghanistan, Pakistan and the Soviet Union, and the Secretary of State of the United States. Pakistan and the United States declared on the occasion that their signatures did not imply recognition of the Kabul regime. The US further declared that 'the obligations undertaken by the guarantors are symmetrical' and that it retained the right to provide military assistance to the Afghan parties, and would exercise restraint should the Soviet Union also do so. Pakistan made the same point, and underlined the right of the Afghan people to self-determination.

The Geneva Accords marked the first time the Soviet Union had withdrawn from a 'fraternal' state. Gorbachev acknowledged that the intervention was a 'mistake'. A Soviet journal blamed 'an inner group of a few Politburo members headed by Leonid Brezhnev [who], discounting the likely opposition of the Muslim world, China, the United States and the West, decided to take the fateful decision'.[175] Over 13,000 Soviet soldiers were killed and 35,000 wounded.[176] The financial drain was estimated at 100 billion rubles. A classic example of 'imperial over-stretch',[177] it could well be considered the proverbial last straw that broke the camel's back. To say that, like the United States in Vietnam, the Soviet Union lost the war in Afghanistan due to pressures of domestic and international opinion is by no means to undervalue the courage and heroism of the *mujahideen,* and the fortitude and sacrifices of the Afghan people.

Re-entry into the Commonwealth

Britain's partisan role in the 1971 crisis was disappointing for Pakistan. If media criticism of the excesses committed by Pakistani authorities was understandable on humanitarian grounds, the British failure to censure Indian military intervention was reflective of an expedient and unprincipled policy. As earlier noted, London did not even allow a decent interval to lapse before recognizing Bangladesh. Z. A. Bhutto decided to pull out of the Commonwealth, which did not entail any great loss except inconvenience to Pakistani settlers in Britain. National pride was served by giving a counter-punch to Britain which looked at the Commonwealth as a source of comfort in its time of decline from world power status.

If the precipitate decision to quit the Commonwealth was largely personal, the decision to rejoin was no less so. It was made by President Zia at the suggestion of visiting British leaders, subject to the condition that re-entry be arranged in an honourable way. For several years the proposal was frustrated by Prime Minister Indira Gandhi. She vetoed Pakistan's return at the Melbourne Summit in 1980 despite pleadings by the Australian Prime Minister. Her decision was also quite personal, and surprised even the Indian Foreign Secretary who earlier told the Pakistani Ambassador that India would not stand in the way.[178] Rajiv Gandhi followed his mother's line, justifying the opposition on the pretext that Pakistan was ruled by a dictator.

Actually, democratic rule was not a precondition for membership. In any case, India did not abandon its opposition even after the elections in 1985, the installation of a civilian government and an end to Martial Law. Not until after the 1988 election in Pakistan did India give up its opposition. Neither the manner of leaving the Commonwealth nor that of seeking re-entry reflected credit on the maturity of decision-making in foreign policy.

ECO and its Expansion

The Regional Cooperation for Development, formed in 1964, did not realize its potential in trade and industry due to resource constraints. After the revolution in Iran in 1979 the organization became quiescent even though it was nominally revived in 1983 under a new name—the Economic Cooperation Organization (ECO). In 1992, ECO was expanded to include Afghanistan and the six Central Asian Republics of Azerbaijan, Kazakhstan, Kyrghyzstan, Tajikistan, Turkmenistan and Uzbekistan. It has since held four summit meetings and taken ambitious decisions to enlarge the ambit of regional cooperation, but achieved little progress.

The first summit, held in Tehran in February 1992, endorsed the goal of 'ultimate elimination of all tariffs and non-tariff barriers' among the members and underlined the importance of developing cooperation in transport and communications, energy, industry and agriculture. In February 1993, the ECO Council of Ministers prepared the Quetta Plan of Action elaborating proposals for enlarged cooperation in already agreed fields. The Istanbul Summit, held in July 1993, approved in principle the creation of regional shipping and airline companies, a reinsurance corporation and a trade and development bank. Agreements to implement these proposals, and on transit trade and visa simplification, were signed at the Islamabad Summit in March 1995. The fourth summit in Ashkabad in May 1996 agreed to streamline decision-making and strengthen the secretariat of the organization. Turkmenistan, Afghanistan and Pakistan signed an agreement at Ashkabad for the construction of gas and oil pipelines. Civil war in Afghanistan continues, however, to preclude implementation. Earlier, Iran and Pakistan had agreed to build a gas pipeline.

Meanwhile, Iran has completed the Meshad-Sarakhs-Tagen rail link with Turkmenistan, which will facilitate passenger and freight traffic between Iranian ports and the Central Asian Republics. Iran has also announced a plan to build the Zahidan-Kerman rail link which would connect Pakistan by railway not only to Central Asia but also via Russia to Europe. In addition, Pakistan has decided to upgrade the Karakorum Highway to provide access for the landlocked Central Asian States via China to Pakistani ports, but, passing through high mountains, the economics of this road link seem problematic. Meanwhile, the shortest, 1,600 km. route from Central Asia to the Arabian Sea, via Kabul or Herat, remains blocked because of civil war in Afghanistan.

Economic cooperation among developing countries, even with cultural affinities and friendly relations, has been a difficult goal to realize mainly because their economies are more often competitive than complementary, and the machinery and technology they need for industrialization is obtainable mostly from developed countries. Realization of economies of scale by enlargement of the market requires not only reduction of customs duties on which governments depend for revenues, but also elaborate safeguards to ensure equitable sharing of sacrifices and benefits. Moreover, as developing countries, they lack the resources required for development of rail and road networks.

SAARC: 1985-97

Impulses toward cooperation in South Asia have been weak historically, primarily because of political discord and the existence of bitter disputes among the states of the region. Neither a common threat perception and maturing of nationalisms that actuated states of Western Europe to abandon old patterns of conflicts, nor a shared vision of security through cooperation that motivated countries of South-East Asia, has been obtained in South Asia. In this region conflict has often arisen from within. Consequential tensions and bitterness over a prolonged period have desiccated the region.

Fears founded in the political experiences of the peoples of the region are compounded by asymmetries of resources. India, the largest and most industrialized country in the region with 72 per cent of its land area and 77 per cent of its production, could abuse the regional forum for exploitation, to the detriment of the less developed countries. Even the promoters of the cooperation idea, therefore, recognized the need for a cautious and gradualist approach.

The proposal for a regional association for cooperation was initiated by President Ziaur Rahman of Bangladesh in 1980. Bhutan, Maldives, Nepal and Sri Lanka supported the idea. Pakistan was initially apprehensive lest the forum be used by India to realize its dream of hegemony over the region. Islamabad decided, however, to defer to the preference of these friendly countries. India was quite pleased with the proposal but feigned reluctance.[179] Its only substantive concern was that the smaller countries might 'gang up' to corner it on regional and bilateral issues, and worked to build in safeguards to preclude such a possibility.

The proposal was formally discussed at a meeting of officials of the South Asian countries in Colombo in April 1981. They endorsed the view that regional cooperation in South Asia was 'beneficial, desirable and necessary'. They also 'noted the need to proceed step by step, on the basis of careful and adequate preparations'. It was agreed that decisions should be taken on the basis of unanimity. At India's suggestion it was further agreed that bilateral and contentious issues should be excluded from the scope of the regional forum.[180]

Lengthy preparatory work went into identification of areas for fruitful cooperation. The list was progressively expanded to encompass agriculture, rural development, telecommunications, meteorology, health and population activities, science and technology, education and tourism. Significantly, cooperation in trade and industry was relegated in the early years. Some of the countries of the region wanted to gain experience and study the implications of cooperation in trade so that their economies would not be swamped.

After four years of preparatory work the South Asian Association for Regional Cooperation (SAARC) was formally launched at a summit meeting at Dhaka in December 1985. Its formation, with lofty aims of promoting the welfare of the peoples of the region, accelerating economic and social progress and contributing to mutual trust, was greeted with a mixture of hope and cynicism in and outside the region, given the background of poverty, tensions and suspicion in the area. This prognosis was found to be realistic in the years that followed.

Twelve years later, meeting at Male in the Maldives, the SAARC summit itself evaluated the results of regional cooperation as disappointingly meager. Apart from a plethora of meetings of officials, involving considerable expense, the association had made precious little gain in the economic and social spheres. Some of the leaders appeared to recognize that without a more realistic approach to conflict-resolution, SAARC was unlikely to improve its prospects.

Implementation of a programme for regional cooperation integral to the objective of the well-being of the peoples of the region is 'fraught with very grave and daunting difficulties'.[181] This is particularly true in the field of economic cooperation among developing countries, evident in the light of experience in the Group of 77; ECDC and TCDC (economic and technical cooperation among developing countries) appear to be flawed concepts. The needs of developing countries for capital and modern technology, and for markets for their exports, can be met largely through cooperation with industrialized and affluent states. That was the key to the rapid economic expansion of the countries of East Asia. In South-East Asia, too, countries have largely relied on cooperation with North America and Europe; intra-regional trade has begun to expand lately as a result of product sophistication.

Trade relations among countries of South Asia have not been very significant historically. India, the biggest exporter in intra-regional trade, has followed a restrictive import policy. With its long-time emphasis on autarkic development and the wide range of its products, it has excluded the import of consumer goods generally and primary manufactures produced by the other countries of the region. Whether it was manufactures like textiles, apparel, carpets and leather goods, or primary products like tea, jute and rice, the other countries found that markets outside the region were more accessible and lucrative. In contrast, trade between them and India evinced colonial characteristics of exchange between raw materials and manufactured goods.

In the early 1990s, it was decided to establish the South Asian Preferential Trade Area (SAPTA). It has achieved little progress in substance. So far the lists of items specified by most members, on which reduced rates of duties are allowed on imports, are relatively small. One of the reasons is that developing countries have to protect nascent industries. No less importantly, the grant of preferential duties involves sacrifice of custom revenues, often a mainstay of budgets of developing countries. Unless compensatory mechanisms are evolved, the less developed countries are bound to proceed at a deliberate pace in the light of actual experience.

The momentum of discussions within the forum persuaded SAARC leaders at the 1997 summit to quicken their march toward the establishment of the South Asian Free Trade Area. (SAFTA). It was announced that SAFTA would be created within four years. Representing once again the triumph of hope over experience with SAPTA, this decision will require fundamental changes in ground realities. Perhaps, if cooperation becomes a habit, it may inspire salutary attitudes also toward political disputes. That would yield a valuable 'peace dividend' and make a real contribution to the acceleration of economic development of the countries of the poverty-stricken region.

Pakistan-India Crises: 1984-1990

Pakistan received information in 1984 that India was preparing an air attack on its uranium enrichment plant at Kahuta; the intelligence was immediately shared with Pakistan's friends who were requested to warn India of the consequences. Apparently, Washington received similar information from its own sources.[182] In 1985, another report was received that India was planning an attack on Kahuta in concert with an Afghan or Israeli agency. Pakistani leaders publicly stated that such an attack would be considered an act of war. Concerns on this account subsided after Pakistan and India agreed informally in December 1985 to refrain from attack on each other's nuclear installations. A formal agreement was later signed which entered into force in 1988.

Crisis again erupted when India decided to hold the largest combined military exercise in South Asian history, code-named Brasstacks, in the winter of 1986-87.[183] Comparable in scale to the biggest exercises of NATO or the Warsaw Pact, it envisaged concentration of a quarter million troops, 9 army divisions and 1,300 tanks in western Rajasthan, at places hardly 50 kilometers from the Pakistan border, giving the assembled forces the capability to launch a piercing strike into Pakistan to cut off northern Pakistan from the southern part. Concerned about the situation, Prime Minister Junejo took up the matter with Rajiv Gandhi in their meeting during the SAARC summit in Bangalore in November 1986. He was given to understand that the exercise would be scaled down, which was, however, not done. As a precaution, the Pakistan Army decided to extend its own exercises and placed its armoured divisions in proximity to the Indian border. This was perceived by the Indian side as a pincer posture menacing the security of its Punjab, where the Sikh people were up in arms since the Indian Army's assault on the Golden Temple, their most sacred shrine. Tension reached its peak in the fourth week of January when the Indian side made the unacceptable demand for unilateral withdrawal of Pakistani forces from the border. At this point the leaders of the two countries established direct contact, and an agreement was reached on 4 February 1987 providing for sector by sector disengagement and the return of forces to their normal locations.

The crisis was ascribable partly to inadequate or unreliable intelligence, faulty interpretation and the tendency to make worst-case assumptions. But that was not the whole truth. Some Indian planners hoped for the crisis to spiral into actual confrontation and conflict, giving them an opportunity to exploit the disparity of forces. Scholarly research later concluded, 'Exercise Brasstacks may have had much larger goals than merely to test the preparedness of the Indian Army. These goals appear to have been open-ended.'[184] To preclude the recurrence of unintentional crises, the two sides concluded an agreement in 1991 which specified force thresholds and distances from the border, that required prior notification in the event of exercises or troop movements. Another crisis-prevention agreement, concluded in 1991, required advance communication about aircraft flying in proximity to the other side's airspace.

Still another crisis erupted in 1990. As the situation in Kashmir continued to deteriorate, high military officials in India were reported to have recommended air strikes on targets in Pakistan. Whether their object was to deter Pakistan or intimidate the Kashmiris, the reports triggered anxiety among analysts that Indian adventurism could precipitate war between the two countries which could escalate to the nuclear level. In May 1990 the President of the United States sent Robert Gates, Assistant for National Security, to Islamabad and New Delhi. Although sensational reports[185] depicting an actual nuclear threat were discounted, the United States obviously possessed enough information to consider it necessary to launch an exercise in preventive diplomacy.

Nuclear Capability and Deterrence

The Government of Pakistan has acknowledged possession of nuclear capability but disclaims having produced nuclear weapons.[186] By the early 1990s, Pakistan was credited with the capacity to produce a small number of nuclear weapons in a short time though it maintains it has not actually done so.

The efficacy of nuclear deterrence is supported by empirical evidence, strategic analysis and professional opinion. Nuclear weapons were a critical asset in the prevention of war between the American and Soviet blocs despite the bitter and prolonged ideological and power rivalry between them. No country with nuclear power has been subjected to aggression. Nuclear weapons, as Kenneth N. Waltz said, 'make the cost of war seem frighteningly high and thus discourage states from starting any wars that might lead to the use of such weapons'.[187] What has helped maintain peace and prevented military adventures in the past can do the same in future. No less weighty is the testimony of Pakistani and Indian military officials on the contribution of nuclear capability to security in South Asia:[188] in the Brasstacks crisis in 1986-87 and the Kashmir crisis in May 1990, the risk of escalation to the nuclear level served to stabilize potentially dangerous situations.

Pakistan's nuclear capacity is considered to be both minimal[189] and frozen at the 1989 level, when the further production of highly enriched uranium was unilaterally discontinued, apparently under American pressure. This decision has been criticized in the country as premature and improvident because of its implications for the credibility and sufficiency of its nuclear capability for deterrence.

Although parity of arsenals is not considered necessary for nuclear deterrence, the capacity has to be sufficient to survive preemption and interception, and for penetration to reach targets. A 'minimal deterrence' considered sufficient today can become insufficient if the adversary develops the capability to disable delivery vehicles before launch and to intercept them after take-off. The production of *Prithvi* and other missiles by India could undermine the precarious stability that has obtained between Pakistan and India since the 1980s. The danger has been compounded as a result of the Indian refusal to sign the Comprehensive Test Ban Treaty (CTBT) in 1996, and thus retaining the option to conduct further test explosions. Their purpose would be to enhance the destructive yield of nuclear bombs and to miniaturize the warhead for missiles. Pakistan should review its policy to ensure the credibility of its nuclear deterrence.

Reimposition of US Sanctions: 1990

In 1990, a year after the Soviet Union withdrew its forces from Afghanistan, President George Bush withheld the issuance of the certificate required under the Pressler Amendment, and the United States reimposed the ban on economic and military cooperation with Pakistan. It even declined to transfer the equipment under earlier sales contracts for which Pakistan had paid in cash. In 1995, recognizing the inequity of keeping both the equipment and the cash paid by Pakistan, amounting to over a billion dollars, President Clinton agreed in principle to resolve this issue. Equipment worth $368 million, comprising mostly outdated arms was to be released, twenty-eight F-16 aircraft were to be sold to a third country and the amount of $658 million refunded to Pakistan as also the balance of about $200 million paid for other weapons. Progress in the disposal of the F-16s has remained slow. Meanwhile, the discriminatory ban on economic assistance and military sales to Pakistan alone remains in force.

Afghan Civil War

The Afghan people suffered grievously in the struggle to recover freedom. A million people perished and some six million had to take refuge outside their country. It was devastated on a scale with few parallels. Already one of the least developed countries, it suffered fearful damage to agriculture, irrigation systems, roads, transport, educational institutions—indeed its entire infrastructure. Nor did its travail end with the withdrawal of Soviet forces. The regime the Soviets installed under Najibullah fought on for nearly three more years. When it finally collapsed in April 1992, a struggle for succession began among the *mujahideen* parties. For their epic sacrifices, the Afghan people deserved a better fate than the continued long nightmare of internecine fighting, political disintegration and economic collapse in the wake of victory.

The *mujahideen* started on a hopeful note of unity after Najibullah's fall. At a meeting in Peshawar on 24 April the Alliance leaders reached an agreement. An Islamic Council headed by Sibghatullah Mojaddedi was installed for two months after which Professor Burhanuddin Rabbani become President for four months. A transitional government was then to be formed for two years. Mojaddedi abided by the accord but Rabbani refused to yield power when his term expired. Fighting broke out among the parties. Pakistan, Iran and Saudi Arabia joined to promote another accord among the Afghan leaders. The agreement they signed at a meeting in Islamabad on 7 March 1993 provided for the formation of a government for a period of eighteen months, with Professor Rabbani continuing as President and Gulbadin Hekmatyar to become Prime Minister. Although the Islamabad Accord was signed by the Afghan leaders, it was not implemented. The cabinet to be 'formed by the Prime Minister in consultation with the President' was not agreed upon. Prime Minister Hekmatyar felt too insecure to enter Kabul. The accord soon broke down. Hekmatyar attacked the capital and, though he was repulsed, the attractive city, which had largely escaped destruction during the *jihad,* was severely damaged as a result of intra-*mujahideen* fighting.

In 1994, a group of students of religious schools (Taliban), outraged by the crimes of *mujahideen* rulers in Kandahar, rose to bring quick retribution to the criminals. Their action evoked enthusiastic popular response. The people evidently yearned for release from the warlords who 'brought sufferings on the Afghans and violated Islamic teachings'.[190] To their surprise, the Taliban found themselves in power, and rapidly gained control over the southern provinces, restoring law and order and gaining the support of the war-weary people. In 1995 they were invited to take over Herat, with the veteran *mujahideen* commander, Ismail, fleeing this western city without a fight. They continued to march northward as local commanders either joined them or fled northwards. Even Hekmatyar, who controlled territory south of Kabul, decided to withdraw from his headquarters at Charasiab. The Taliban then attacked Kabul but were stalled by government forces for almost a year.

The Rabbani regime, which had earlier accused Pakistan of supporting Hekmatyar, now lashed out at Pakistan for supporting the Taliban, failing to understand that internecine squabbling amongst the warlords had bred country-wide disgust. It ignored the fact that Pakistan had throughout tried its best to promote unity among the *mujahideen* leaders. On two occasions, in 1992 and 1994, it provided its good offices in collaboration with other friends of Afghanistan to promote consensus among the Afghan leaders. They themselves decided on the composition of the Afghan government; the breakdown of both accords was a product of rivalries amongst them. No foreign-inspired movement could arouse the popular response that greeted the Taliban.

Pakistan's expectations of friendly relations received a shocking setback on 6 September 1995 when its embassy in Kabul was sacked by a government-sponsored mob. One employee was killed, the ambassador and forty officials were injured, requiring hospitalization, the building was burned down and its records destroyed. Despite such a savage attack, Pakistan exercised patience and refrained from retaliation. When Hekmatyar joined Rabbani's government as Prime Minister in early 1996, Pakistan welcomed their reconciliation, expressing the hope that it would be a step towards the promotion of a broader consensus among regional leaders leading to national unity. In May 1996, a visiting delegation of the Kabul

Government acknowledged liability for the reconstruction of the embassy though it pleaded lack of resources to discharge the responsibility.

A certain calm seemed to have descended over most of Afghanistan: the Kabul Government having successfully stalled the Taliban advance, ruled over five of the north-eastern provinces, Abdur Rashid Dostum's Uzbek militia controlled the northern provinces, and a *mujahideen shura* or council governed the eastern provinces from Jalalabad. But this deceptive calm broke suddenly into a storm in September 1996 as the Taliban burst forth again. Rapidly, they penetrated the eastern Pushtoon provinces, the *shura* that ruled Jalalabad melted away and the city fell to the Taliban without any fighting. The triumphant Taliban then pushed toward the capital from the east as well as the south. Government forces, evidently fed up with fighting for self-serving individuals, were by now too demoralized to put up determined resistance. The Rabbani-Hekmatyar-Masood forces abandoned the capital and, with remarkably little bloodshed, the Taliban took control of Kabul on the morning of 27 September. Their hold over the capital remained precarious, however, as Abdur Rashid Dostum and Ahmad Shah Masood formed an alliance to counter the Taliban.

Hopes of restoration of peace and unity in Afghanistan appeared to have receded further as the country became divided along ethnic lines. Most of the non-Pushtoon areas were outside the Taliban grasp though they controlled twenty of the country's thirty-two provinces. Dostum's Uzbek militia was entrenched north of the Hindu Kush mountains, as he ruled over six provinces from his headquarters at Mazar-i-Sharif, and the legendary *mujahideen* commander Ahmad Shah Masood, dug in the fastness of the Panjshir Valley, posed a threat to the Taliban control over Kabul. In effect, Afghanistan stood divided into three zones, largely along ethnic lines.

A simple and idealistic group with only religious education, and lacking sophistication in their understanding of the world, the Taliban evoked global denunciation for imposing stringent restrictions upon women. They antagonized also the inhabitants of the capital, which under the Afghan rulers was an island of modernity in a sea of conservative and tribal countryside. Their rustic interpretation of Islam was castigated even by the Islamic Republic of Iran, though Tehran's opposition to the Taliban was founded also in the misperception that they were a creation of the United States and Saudi Arabia with the object of containment of Iran. Besides, Iran, like other neighbours of Afghanistan, has a vested interest in a composite government in Kabul to ensure the safety of different ethnic and sectarian segments of the population. Moscow joined the opposition to the Taliban, projecting a Taliban threat to the security of the Central Asian Republics.

Efforts by the United Nations and the Islamic Conference in 1995 and 1996 to promote a compromise between the Kabul regime and its opponents achieved little progress. Iran and Pakistan were even less successful, no doubt because they were perceived to be partisan. Rivalry between the *mujahideen* leaders, founded largely in personal ambitions, was progressively polarized along ethnic lines. The process was intensified following the success of the Taliban in September 1996 when they extended their control over the eastern provinces, bringing almost all the Pushtoon areas under their sway.

Jalalabad, the main town on the road from Kabul to Peshawar in Pakistan, fell without a fight. The governor went into exile and local commanders either melted away or joined the Taliban who then continued their triumphant march toward Kabul. On the way they met some resistance from Hekmatyar's forces in Sirobi but, more surprisingly, the government withdrew without a fight. As the Taliban marched into the capital at dawn on 27 September 1996, President Rabbani and other leaders of his government fled to Mazar-i-Sharif while Ahmad Shah Masood and his forces withdrew into the Panjsher Valley.

The resurgence of fighting triggered fresh diplomatic moves for peace. A Pakistani government official embarked on a diplomatic shuttle between Mazar-i-Sharif and Kabul to persuade Dostum and the Taliban to enter into negotiations. The President of Pakistan undertook a visit to Tashkent for a meeting with the

President of Uzbekistan after which the two leaders jointly called for the formation of a broad-based government in Afghanistan, including representatives of all ethnic and religious groups. These efforts did not prove effective.

International reaction to the Taliban take-over of Kabul was generally adverse. The West was appalled by their stringent interpretation of the *Sharia* laws, in particular the closure of schools for girls and the ban on employment for women outside their homes. The Taliban had enforced these laws earlier in the areas under their control, but few had taken notice as there was little popular protest. Outside Kabul, the question of women's rights did not exist in traditional Afghan society. Besides, the people were preoccupied by basic issues of survival and security, restoration of peace and an effective administration that was religious, modest and uncorrupt.

The UN Security Council adopted a resolution on 22 October 1996 condemning discrimination against women and calling for an immediate cessation of hostilities, an end to the supply of arms and ammunition from outside, and the resumption of political dialogue among all Afghan parties. It was sponsored by Russia which was particularly bitter, apparently because it perceived the Taliban as a threat to the security of the old Soviet realm, now termed by this fallen great power as 'near abroad'. Also, Moscow convened a meeting of the Presidents of the Central Asian Republics in Almaty to consider measures to oppose the Taliban.

The UN Resolution was ignored by the Afghan factions. Efforts by the UN Special Envoy, Herbert Holl, to promote an intra-Afghan dialogue made little progress. Afghanistan appeared divided along geographical and ethnic fault lines, with Dostum's Uzbek militia controlling territory north of the Hindukush, Masood's Tajik forces entrenched in the north-east, a faction led by Karim Khalili running parts of the Hazara areas, and the Taliban in control of the remaining two-thirds of the country.

In May 1997 the situation took an unexpected turn following a revolt in the Uzbek militia. Accusing Dostum of misrule,

General Abdul Malik and other powerful Uzbek commanders occupied Mazar-i-Sharif on 24 May with remarkably little resistance. Dostum fled to Turkey and Rabbani, the titular President of the country, to Iran. At first the Uzbek commanders seemed to have joined cause with the Taliban but the allies soon fell apart and, once again, the dream of Afghan unity seemed to vanish.

Meanwhile, the Taliban government was recognized by Pakistan and Saudi Arabia. Pakistan's interest, as indeed that of other neighbours is in the restoration of Afghanistan's unity, which is a highly desirable objective for the Afghan people themselves. Only peace in Afghanistan can relieve Pakistan and Iran of the burden of Afghan refugees. Some two million of them are still in Pakistan, suffering themselves and burdening Pakistan's economy. Peace is a prerequisite, moreover, for the opening of transit facilities without which cooperation with the Central Asian Republics remains blocked.

A more sinister legacy of the Afghan Crisis for Pakistan is the 'Klashnikov culture' and increased production of narcotics. Modern weapons from Afghanistan have proliferated across Pakistan. Dacoits now have more lethal weapons than the police. Hundreds of foreign citizens who came to join the *jihad* stayed behind in Pakistan, and some of them have indulged in acts of terrorism. The bombing of the Egyptian Embassy in Islamabad in December 1995 was attributed to them. Agents of the Rabbani regime were also accused of perpetrating acts of sabotage in Pakistan.

The Russian people are rightly critical of the Soviet invasion of Afghanistan as 'a great mistake'.[191] Afghans can similarly blame their communist leaders for the disaster that befell their country. Pakistanis alone have few scapegoats. They generally endorsed President Zia's policy of support for the Afghans. Few foresaw the consequences of involvement, and the grave problems that emerged in the wake of the conflict. Western supporters of the Afghan struggle, critical of the Afghan warring parties, have walked away. Pakistan, once praised for 'shouldering great responsibilities for mankind...[and its]

courageous and compassionate role',[192] finds itself left saddled with the burden of refugees and the consequences of the strife next door.

Was Pakistan's policy misconceived? In retrospect the answer is easy but, alas, humans are not gifted with prescience, and policies have to be devised—and can be fairly judged—in the context of the time and contemporary knowledge. Given the history of Soviet expansionism, Islamabad's sense of alarm in 1979 was real. Pakistan was neither in a position to challenge the Soviet superpower nor could it ignore the intervention without peril to its security. An alternative to the middle course it pursued seems difficult to conceive even in retrospect. Success and failure can be a measure of policies, but human struggle cannot be appraised in isolation from the nobility of the cause. The Soviet intervention was morally wrong, the Afghan resistance was right. Pakistan's decision in favour of solidarity with the fraternal people of Afghanistan was not only morally right but based on enlightened self-interest.

Could the consequences of the protracted conflict in terms of the Klashnikov culture and narcotics proliferation be anticipated and obviated? Surely, these could have been minimized if not precluded. These problems as well as malfeasance and venality in transactions between the *mujahideen* and their friends surfaced during the struggle in Afghanistan. Priorities and vested interests did not permit timely remedies.

Were not the Geneva Accords flawed in that they did not provide for transition to peace and the formation of a government of unity for Afghanistan? The above account brings out the fact that from the beginning the Geneva negotiations had only the limited aim of getting the Soviets to withdraw from Afghanistan. All the parties agreed that government formation was entirely an internal affair of Afghanistan, to the exclusion of the Soviet Union, Pakistan or any other country. The United Nations was understandably reluctant to undertake this task. Until the end of the Cold War it avoided assumption of a role for the promotion of reconciliation or consensus in any embattled country. Moscow and Kabul were first dismissive of any suggestion of a role for the *mujahideen* in the government of Afghanistan, except on Kabul's terms. When they later offered accommodation, the *mujahideen* rejected the Soviet puppets. Pakistan as well as other friends and supporters backed the *mujahideen* position. President Zia alone changed his view for reasons that remain obscure, though his unjustified and unlawful dismissal of Prime Minister Junejo in May 1988 provides circumstantial evidence of a personal power motivation. However, even Zia was unable to persuade the *mujahideen* to meet Diego Cordovez to promote a government of unity in Afghanistan.

It was probably too much to expect the *mujahideen* leaders to reach an accommodation with the surrogate regime after the Soviets withdrew, though that might have saved the country from fragmentation. More tragic was the rivalry for personal power among these leaders that prolonged the nightmare for the Afghan people. As a result, the *mujahideen* themselves have been sidelined by new forces in the country. Whether the Taliban will succeed in bringing unity and reconciliation to the war-ravaged country remains to be seen. Also to be watched is the effect of the Taliban success on Pakistan's relations with Iran, which believes that Pakistan wields sufficient influence with the Taliban to ensure accommodation for all Afghan ethnic groups in the future government of Afghanistan. What is obvious by now is the futility of a king-maker role on the part of any outsider. Even a superpower failed in its attempt to impose a government on the Afghans.

Kashmir Uprising

Resisting Indian duress at the Simla Conference in 1972, Pakistan neither compromised its own position on the Kashmir dispute nor allowed any prejudice to the Kashmiri right of self-determination. In speeches in the UN General Assembly it continued to draw the attention of the world community to the festering issue. In the period that followed, the Kashmiri people grew restive, demonstrating that they were not prepared to acquiesce in continued Indian occupation. The Valley exploded in protests in 1973, triggered by the discovery of a book in a library in Anantnag with a drawing of the Holy Prophet (PBUH).[193] Strikes, marches and demonstrations continued even after the Indian Government banned the book. With disaffection continuing to grow, Indira Gandhi decided in 1975 to bring back Sheikh Mohammad Abdullah as Chief Minister once again. After a long stint in the political wilderness, he compromised himself by giving up the championship of Kashmiri demands. He was denounced by the people of Kashmir as well as by Prime Minister Z. A. Bhutto for this perfidy.

Almost a decade later, a cricket match in Srinagar between the visiting West Indies team and India in October 1983 provided another occasion for anti-Indian demonstrations. In February 1984 a group of Kashmiris in England kidnapped an Indian consular official and killed him after the Indian Government refused to meet their demand for the release of a popular Kashmiri activist from jail in Delhi. The historically peaceful people opted for an activist approach, apparently drawing inspiration from the success of the revolution in Iran, the *intifada* of the Palestinian people, and the struggle of the people of Afghanistan against a superpower. The Kashmiri agitation gathered momentum as Indira Gandhi tried to suppress it by appointing a proven martinet, Governor Jagmohan, in Srinagar. He demonstrated his ruthlessness and sinister skills by playing Sheikh Abdullah's son-in-law, G. M. Shah, against Farooq Abdullah, the Sheikh's son, in 1984. When that did not work, Jagmohan imposed his own direct rule in March 1986. With unrest becoming chronic, Rajiv Gandhi again tried Farooq Abdullah, as Chief Minister, but to little avail.

In the elections that followed in 1987, a Muslim United Front comprising several parties in Kashmir decided to contest. It attracted mass support and expected to win, but the election was 'as unfree and unfair as any others',[194] and, when the result was announced giving the Front only four seats, those who thought they could gain political control through peaceful means were thoroughly disillusioned. Some among the young considered an alternative form of political struggle for their destiny. Militant groups began to mushroom in the Valley in 1988 and 1989. A local leader of the extremist Bharatiya Janata Party, which advocated sterner repression in Kashmir, was killed in September 1989. The daughter of an Indian minister was kidnapped.

The Indian Government brought back Jagmohan as Governor, by now 'a rabid communalist', who beat 'all previous records of fascist regimes in the world in the matter of unleashing terror and oppression on the innocent people of the state'.[195] He proceeded from the premise that 'Every Muslim in Kashmir is a militant today. All of them are for secession from India... The bullet is the only solution for Kashmir.'[196] He soon 'converted Kashmir into a virtual prison', imposing 'continuous and indefinite curfews'. Volunteers who tried to alleviate suffering were 'arrested and mercilessly beaten'. Even free kitchens were not allowed to be run. He banned the publication of newspapers and the entry of foreign correspondents.[197] Military and para-military forces in that State were reinforced in January 1990 and special powers were given to them along with immunity from prosecution. As they embarked upon arbitrary arrests, searches of homes, rape and looting, and punitive destruction of houses, Indian rule entered a 'terminal colonial situation'.[198]

Predictably, Indian repression in Kashmir evoked strong denunciation. People in Pakistan marched in protest in cities and towns all over the country. The media condemned Indian atrocities, and the government denounced India for its inhuman policy. India attributed the 'unrest' and 'secessionist attitude' in Kashmir to 'elements' coming into the Valley from the Pakistan side to 'fuel the problem',[199] and accused Pakistan of providing training and arms to Kashmiri militants. Pakistan denied these accusations as baseless, while asserting that, as a party to the Kashmir dispute, it had a right to give political, diplomatic and moral support to the Kashmiri struggle for the realization of their recognized right to self-determination.

The Kashmiri freedom struggle faced new obstacles due to the build-up of an imaginary fear of Islam in the West. Perceived as an ally so long as it inspired opposition to Soviet expansion, as in Afghanistan after the collapse of the Soviet Union, Islam was re-invented as a civilizational threat.[200] The word 'fundamentalism' came into vogue to discredit political movements of Muslim peoples even when their aims were freedom from alien occupation, respect for human rights and democracy. Exploiting this new environment of prejudice, India labeled Kashmiri activists as extremists, fundamentalists and terrorists. The United States threatened in 1992 to place Pakistan on its list of terrorist states.

Most non-governmental human rights organizations, however, maintained objectivity. They published numerous reports of massive violations of human rights and crimes committed by Indian forces in Kashmir, and an Amnesty International report in 1992 commented:

> Widespread human rights violations in the State since January 1990 have been attributed to the Indian Army, and the paramilitary Border Security Force (BSF) and Central Reserve Police Force (CRPF). A 145,000 strong force of CRPF was flown into the State at that time. Cordon-and-search operations are frequently conducted in areas of armed opposition activity... Torture is reported to be routinely used during these combing operations as well as in army camps, interrogation centres, police stations and prisons. Indiscriminate beatings are common and rape in particular appears to be routine.
>
> In Jammu and Kashmir, rape is practised as part of a systematic attempt to humiliate and intimidate the local population during counter-insurgency operations.[201]

A 1993 report jointly compiled by Asia Watch and Physicians for Human Rights, New York, stated:

> In their efforts to crush the insurgency, Indian forces in Kashmir have engaged in massive human rights violations including extra-judicial executions, rape, torture and deliberate assaults on health care workers... Such killings are carried out as a matter of policy.

More than any other phenomenon, these deliberate killings reveal the magnitude of the human rights crisis in Kashmir.

Similarly, another human rights organization with its head office in Paris noted that, 'Rape is not uncommon and there is evidence of its employment as an instrument of terror.'[202]

The Organization of the Islamic Conference adopted strong resolutions upholding the Kashmiri right of self-determination and condemning Indian repression. The OIC's attempts to obtain access to Kashmir for investigation of the grim situation were, however, blocked by India. Pakistan's efforts to secure official cognizance of the plight of the Kashmiri people by the United Nations Human Rights Commission did not succeed, as many of the members of the Commission took a restrictive view of its competence, and were opposed to international prying into their own record or were disinclined to displease India. The United States and some other governments issued statements critical of Indian agencies for arbitrary arrests, torture and deaths in custody, but some of them also criticized Kashmiri militants for acts of a terrorist nature. Pakistan, too, came under adverse notice for police excesses at home, undercutting its credentials for mobilization of support for Kashmiris.

Meanwhile, the leaders of more than thirty political organizations in Jammu and Kashmir decided in 1993 to form the All Parties Hurriet Conference (APHC) to represent the collective aspirations of the people of the State. The APHC united parties demanding the right of self-determination pledged to the Kashmiri people by India, Pakistan and the United Nations, and provided guidance to the on-going freedom movement under collective political leadership. APHC leaders have pointed out that the question as to whether Jammu and Kashmir should accede to Pakistan or become independent is premature. So long as India is not prepared to honour its pledge that the people of the State have the right to determine their own destiny, a debate over alternative options can only divide and weaken their struggle.

The optimism aroused by the formation of a new coalition

government in India following the May 1996 elections quickly evaporated. The manifesto of Janata Dal, the lead party in the coalition, envisaged discussions with Pakistan to resolve the Kashmir dispute, 'keeping in mind the sentiments of the people of the State'.[203] Prime Minister Benazir Bhutto suggested talks 'aimed at the settlement of the issue of Jammu and Kashmir and other outstanding matters between the two countries'. In his response, Prime Minister Deve Gowda made no mention of the core issue. He suggested a 'wide-ranging and comprehensive dialogue' aimed at the realization of 'a firm relationship of trust setting aside the difficulties that impede amity and co-operation'.[204] These formulations, relegating the Kashmir dispute, seemed to throw cold water on hopes for a new beginning in Pakistan-India relations. The Indian decision to organize sham elections in the India-held part of the State further corroborated the lack of seriousness of its professions for improved relations with Pakistan.

The Hurriet Conference boycotted the elections for the Indian Parliament in May, and for the State Assembly in September 1996. All past elections in the occupied State were rigged, but this was the most farcical exercise. Independent media reports eloquently depicted scenes of poor villagers driven at gun-point to polling stations. The National Conference, which has historically provided India a political front for its annexationist aim, won the sham elections. The APHC chairman, Mir Waiz Umar Farooq, pointed out that the popular boycott by the Kashmiris made it clear that elections under Indian aegis cannot be a substitute for the free and impartial plebiscite promised under UN auspices. Pakistan recalled UN resolutions underlining this very principle.

Dialogue between Pakistan and India, suspended in 1994 because it proved sterile, was reopened in February 1997 at the level of foreign secretaries. The Indian emphasis was, as usual, on normalization of trade and travel, though it was willing to discuss all issues. Pakistan underlined the centrality of the Kashmir issue. It was difficult to envisage progress in economic and cultural fields between the two countries so long as India continued its policy of repression of the Kashmiri freedom struggle. While these 'talks about talks' went on in New Delhi, the APHC observed a strike to underscore its demand for inclusion in any negotiations on the future of the State. In any event, no such negotiations took place. Pakistan has throughout assigned primacy to the right of the Kashmiri people to self-determination.

The heroic sacrifices given by the Kashmiri Muslims in their protracted struggle for *azaadi* is a guarantee that the cause will endure. By contrast, India's savage repression has exposed the colonial nature of its stranglehold over occupied Kashmir. Civilized opinion in the world, and in India itself, cannot fail to recognize the inevitability of conceding to the Kashmiri people their aspiration for *azaadi*. Translatable as liberation, independence or freedom, their goal transcends differences among some of the parties over the ultimate aim of the struggle.

Security in a Transformed World

The end of the Cold War fundamentally transformed the global security environment. Southern Africa has stabilized, South-East Asia has moved from conflict to cooperation, and even the endemic confrontation in the Middle East has abated. Paradoxically, the situation in South Asia has hardly changed. As if locked in a time-warp, the region has remained rife with tensions, with no surcease to threats of intimidation and use of force for the resolution of conflicts and no progress in sight toward civilized norms as the arbiter of international relations.

The roots of the antagonism between India and Pakistan can be traced to the history of Hindu-Muslim relations and contention between the Indian National Congress and the Muslim League. But the events since Independence are explicable in the secular paradigm of great power-small power relations. Not only Muslim Pakistan has suffered Indian excesses; Hindu Nepal and Buddhist Bhutan remain subject to unequal treaties; Sikkim was forcibly occupied and annexed despite the treaty India had signed recognizing its separate and autonomous status, and Sri Lanka was the victim of Indian interference and intervention.

It is not merely an aspiration to greatness which every nation has a right to cherish. India has pursued the aim of domination over neighbours. Indian leaders have cultivated this dream over a century. A chairman of one of the committees at the All-India Congress session in 1895, Rao Bahadur Bhide, said India was 'destined by Providence to take its rank among the foremost nations of the world'.[205] Jawaharlal Nehru, the mentor of the post-Independence generations of Indian strategic thinkers, considered India as a world power which 'will have to play a very great role in security problems of Asia and the Indian Ocean, more especially in the Middle East and South Asia'. Outright hegemonic in his narrow nationalistic drive, he advocated the proclamation of an Indian Monroe Doctrine with respect to Asian countries.[206] It is this vision that concerns neighbours; even more troubling is the fact of India's build-up of military power, and its capability to project that power across boundaries to the detriment of the rights and interests of its less powerful neighbours.

Pakistan's past policy of seeking security through alliances to ameliorate the power imbalance, whatever its merits or effectiveness, has lapsed into history along with the context of East-West confrontation in which that policy had a relevance. The time is irrevocably past when Dulles called Islamic Pakistan 'a real bulwark'. Islam which was considered an ally against Soviet expansionism has come to be perceived as a threat. Zionist lobbies have played an active role in defining and distorting Islam in terms of a threat to the West's strategic interest in the oil resources of the Middle East. The West has sufficient power to cope with any military threat, but it appears apprehensive of the ideological challenge from Islam. Pakistan and other countries, proud of their Islamic heritage and committed to political and social reform within the fundamentals of their faith, tend to be viewed as part of this problem.

A provocative thesis was advanced in 1993 by a Harvard professor who projected that conflict in the post-Cold War world, and possibly even a world war, would originate in the clash of civilizations, with Islamic and Confucian states as the main challenge to the West. Although this has been refuted by other scholars, and realistic strategic analysts[207] view the future in the objective context of adjustment of relations between the United States and other existing or emergent poles of economic power, such as Japan, Germany, China and Russia, this prejudice against Muslim peoples continues to be reflected in the Western media. Legitimate movements for freedom from alien rule, democracy and an end to corruption, are frequently sought to be discredited by the use of labels such as extremist, fundamentalist and terrorist while similar movements by Buddhist, Christian and Hindu peoples are perceived by the same media in their proper context. Pakistan needs to guard against attempts by India to exploit prejudices in the West against Islam, as it has already done, by labeling Kashmiri freedom fighters as 'extremists' and 'fundamentalists'. Ironically, some politicians even in Muslim countries like to be 'seen fighting the West's imaginary war against "Islamic extremists", in return hoping to be sandbagged by the West against…domestic difficulties'.[208]

Of course, the perception of confrontation between the West and Islam is shared by few Muslim scholars. In advocating a return to fundamentals of faith, their aim has been internal reform of the Muslim community as a means of rectifying centuries of decline and decadence. In South Asia, the most influential social reformer of the nineteenth century, Syed Ahmed Khan, pleaded for modern education. In the first part of the twentieth century, poet-philosopher Muhammad Iqbal's inspiring message emphasized *ijtehad,* that is, innovation consistent with Islam for the reconstruction of religious thought and the realization of progress and prosperity, which was once the hallmark of the Muslim World.

Increasingly, Western countries have tended to define their stakes primarily in terms of trade and investment, a sphere in which Pakistan is at a disadvantage due to inadequate emphasis in the past on modernization of industrial infrastructure, development of human resources and strengthening of institutions that contribute to economic growth. Apart from access to markets and opportunity for profitable investment, American policy in South Asia has been publicly defined mainly in negative terms: capping nuclear capabilities and deployment of missiles, controlling production and trafficking in narcotics, and interdiction of terrorism. Its interest in security in the region is a factor largely of prevention of war that may escalate to the nuclear level. It is now even less disposed to promote peace than it has been in the past.

The structure of great power relations is in a flux. The United States is currently the sole superpower but the world is not unipolar. Other States, alone or in combination, are developing both economic and military power to safeguard their autonomy in world affairs. Asian powers—China and Japan—may seek to play a more active role in determining a new international order. China, in particular, has a natural interest in peace and stability in South Asia, but its friendly relations with countries of the region are' viewed with suspicion by some in the West and resented by India.

Aspiring to reduce South Asia into its exclusive sphere of influence, India has projected rivalry with China to justify its nuclear and missiles programme. The explanation finds favour with American strategists who conceive of India as a potential check to China's rising economic and military power. Also important in their calculation has been the possibility of co-opting India to safeguard their interests in the Persian Gulf region, with petroleum projected to remain vital to the West's prosperity well into the twenty-first century. India has sedulously underlined a commonality of interest with the West in opposing Islamic 'fundamentalism'. In exchange, New Delhi might be expected to bargain for 'a broader strategic acceptance of India's "stabilizing" role in the region at large'.[209] Such a vision of potential strategic partnership with India provides a clue to the inconsistent and discriminatory policy of the United States. While Pakistan continues to be placed under sanctions, India has been treated benignly even though it continues to accumulate fissile materials, has refused to sign the CTBT, and carries on missile tests.

The aim of peace and stability in Asia will not be promoted by the Indian attempt to dominate neighbours. That is a recipe for conflict in the future, as in the past. Preoccupied with the threat of domination, several of India's neighbours welcome China's emergence as a 'proximate actor of consequence with the ability to erode Indian claims to pre-eminence both within South Asia and the Asian continent at large'.[210] China, which has opposed hegemonism globally, is viewed by them as a sympathizer and supporter.

Pakistan has to formulate its own new strategy for peace and progress. More than ever before, it has to rely on its own resources, political will and defence capacity. Generally, it has been well understood since the 1971 disaster that neither foreign policy nor conventional military means were adequate for the defence of national independence and territorial integrity. Pakistan then embarked on efforts to develop the nuclear option. Fortunately, the nation had the scientific talent and the political and economic resilience necessary to overcome technological barriers and cope with external pressures and penalties. The rationale of the nuclear policy was understood even by American officials in 1981.[211]

A comprehensive strategy for defence has to clarify the nuclear doctrine, and accordingly determine nuclear and conventional force levels. Given the apocalyptic consequences of escalation to the nuclear level, the contingency in which this 'weapon of last resort' might be invoked needs to be pushed as far back as possible. Maintenance of strong conventional forces therefore remains necessary for other contingencies. No less important is the issue of the resources for defence that can be afforded within the economic capacity of the State, which is not only limited but constrained by a heavy and increasing debt burden. As a share of GNP, the defence budget has been reduced over the past decade from 6.5 per cent to 5.3 per cent in 1995-96. Continued decline could entail crippling consequences for defence capability unless the size of the economy continues to grow at a rate fast enough to be able to meet the defence requirements of not only today but also of ten, twenty years hence. There is also the issue of apportioning resources in a manner that will ensure both defence and development.

The strategic objectives of Pakistan are clear. National defence and foreign policies have to aim at warding off threats of external aggression and the preservation of its political independence and territorial integrity. At the same time, the State cannot neglect problems of internal stability and national unity which, as the contemporary world illustrates, can pose equally difficult challenges to national security and survival. Almost all recent cases of disintegration of states or their failure have been due to internal problems, as demonstrated by the Soviet Union imploding due to internal political and economic pressures. The breakup of Yugoslavia and the conflict in Bosnia-Herzegovina is ascribable to ethnic and religious fault lines. Czechoslovakia could not cope with the tearing stresses of two nationalisms. Religious, ethnic, linguistic and historical cleavages explain liberation struggles in Chechnya and in Kashmir. States inhabited by diverse peoples aspiring to safeguard their separate identities are inherently vulnerable to fissiparous tendencies. Even long-established states like Britain, Canada and Spain face separatist movements.

Pakistan is almost unique in having come into existence by the exercise of self-determination either through their elected representatives or in direct referenda. At the start, Pakistan stood on a firm foundation. Problems arose due to failure to recognize the fact of regional and linguistic diversity, and to conceive and pursue polices to promote national integration, resulting in the separation of East Pakistan through Indian military intervention. The threat of external exploitation of internal vulnerabilities persists. Adversaries may fuel linguistic and sectarian conflicts in residual Pakistan, but it would be folly to ignore the fact that the roots are within. The State has to conceive and implement effective and far-sighted policies that will not only curb foreign subversion and sectarian militancy but also address genuine grievances of distinct segments of the population.

India's aim of obtaining a permanent seat on the Security Council has raised another danger on the horizon, particularly for South Asian countries. If India succeeds, it would be in a position to veto any decision it does not like on matters involving threats to peace and security, especially those which it poses itself. Election of members of the Security Council requires, under Article 23 of the UN Charter, 'due regard being specially paid, in the first instance, to the contribution of Members of the United Nations to the maintenance of international security and to the other purposes of the Organization'. Were these criteria to be kept in mind, India could hardly qualify on the basis of its record. It has defied Security Council resolutions on the Kashmir question, resorted to military intervention in Pakistan and Sri Lanka, shown contemptuous disregard for General Assembly resolutions in favour of a nuclear weapon-free zone in South Asia and is the sole opponent of the CTBT. Were these criteria to be ignored and India given a permanent seat on the Security Council, this apex organ of the United Nations, charged with primary responsibility for the maintenance of international peace and security, could hardly discharge that responsibility in respect of South Asia.

During its first fifty years, Pakistan has witnessed the end of colonial domination and the rise of newly independent states as a factor in world politics, an intense Cold War that threatened humanity's annihilation, the collapse of a flawed ideology and the disintegration of the last remaining empire. It has lived through internal turmoil and external threat. Its foreign policy, shaped by the constraints imposed upon it, has succeeded but partially. It was able to overcome challenges to its survival and resist hegemonic pressures but failed to preserve its territorial integrity in the face of a combination of internal disaffection and external aggression.

The future can and should be different from the past. History, it has been said, abhors determinism. But the past is surely a guide to the future. It has lessons to offer for dealing with the challenges that continue to hover over Pakistan's security horizon.

NOTES

1. *M. A. Jinnah, Speeches as Governor General, 1947-48,* Ferozsons Ltd., Karachi, p. 32.
2. Ibid., pp. 11, 62, 65, 67.
3. Prime Minister Liaquat Ali Khan, quoted in Sarwar Hasan, *Pakistan Horizon,* Institute of International Affairs, Karachi, 4 December 1951.
4. Abul Kalam Azad, *India Wins Freedom,* Orient Longman, Delhi, pp. 185 and 187.
5. *The Encyclopaedia of the Indian National Congress,* Moin Zaidi and Shaheda Zaidi, S. Chand & Co., New Delhi, Vol. 13, p. 111.
6. For authoritative information on the problems of Partition, the author has heavily relied on Chaudhri Muhammad Ali, *The Emergence of Pakistan,* Columbia University Press, New York, 1967, S. M. Burke and Lawrence Ziring, *Pakistan's Foreign Policy,* Oxford University Press, Karachi, 1990, and G. W. Choudhury, *Pakistan Relations with India, 1947-66,* Pall Mall Press, London, 1967.
7. M. Munir, Member of the Boundary Commission, quoted in G. W. Choudhury, op. cit., p. 55.
8. Ian Stephens, *Horned Moon,* Chatto and Windus, London, 1954, p. 215.
9. John Connell, *Auchinleck,* pp. 915-8.
10. Ibid., pp. 220-22.
11. Alan Campbell-Johnson, *Mission with Mountbatten,* Atheneum, New York, 1966, pp. 51-56.
12. S. M. Burke, op. cit., p. 17, quoting Security Council's Official Records, 250th Meeting, 18 February 1948.
13. Ian Stephens, op. cit., p. 243.
14. Quoted in Chaudhri Muhammad Ali, op. cit., p. 288, from K. Sarwar Hasan, *Documents on the Foreign Relations of Pakistan: The Kashmir Question,* p. 104.
15. Liaquat Ali Khan quoted in S. M. Burke, op. cit., p. 27, from K. Sarwar Hasan, op. cit., p. 100.
16. Quoted in Robert J. McMahon, *The Cold War on the Periphery—The United States, India and Pakistan,* Columbia University Press, New York, 1994, p. 24.
17. US Secretary of State Dean Acheson sent a message to Nehru recommending acceptance of McNaughton's 'realistic approach to the demilitarization issue' and observing that if India did not 'it will be the third consecutive time India will have refused impartial proposals'. Nehru 'exploded' and called the message 'unfriendly'. Quoted in Robert J. McMahon, ibid., p. 60.
18. Quoted in S. M. Burke, op. cit., p. 35.

19. Retired Justice M. V. Tarkunde of India, a respected advocate of human rights, said: 'The offer of plebiscite was not in the nature of a concession made by India to Pakistan, but was a recognition of the right of self-determination of the people of Jammu and Kashmir.' Quoted from *The Radical Humanist,* March 1990, in Bahauddin Farooqi, *Kashmir Holocaust— The Case Against India,* ed., Khalid Hasan, Dotcare, Lahore, 1992, pp. 26-27.

20. Dennis Kux, *India and the United States: Estranged Democracies,* National Defence University Press, Washington, 1993. p. 32.

21. American experts feared that 'the establishment of an independent Muslim state might balkanize the subcontinent'. Robert J. McMahon, op. cit., p. 65.

22. K. Arif, ed., *America-Pakistan Relations—Documents,* Vanguard Books Limited, Lahore, 1984, p. 3.

23. Z. H. Zaidi, *M. A. Jinnah-Ispahani Correspondence,* p. 538.

24. Memorandum given by Mir Laik Ali Khan, *Documents,* op. cit., p. 5.

25. Ibid., p. 5.

26. Ibid., p. 25.

27. This and the following paragraphs have greatly benefited from research done by Ambassador Dennis Kux whose book on Pakistan-US relations is due to be published in 1997.

28. *Documents,* op. cit., p. 15.

29. Robert J.McMahon, op. cit., pp. 60-75.

30. *New York Times,* editorial, 14 September 1951.

31. For a comprehensive factual and analytical treatment of the subject, *see,* Hafeez Malik, *Soviet-Pakistan Relations and Post-Soviet Dynamics, 1947-92,* Macmillan Press, London, 1994.

32. Sajjad Hyder, *Reflections of an Ambassador,* Progressive Publishers, Lahore, 1987, p. 14.

33. *Documents,* op. cit., pp. 33, 35.

34. *The Hindu,* Madras, 27 November 1954.

35. Quoted from George McT. Kahin, *The African Asian Conference,* in S. M. Burke, op. cit., p. 178.

36. Quoted from George McT. Kahin, in S. M. Burke, op. cit., p. 57.

37. S.M. Burke, ibid., p. 215.

38. *Times of India,* 24 October 1959.

39. On 9 November 1959, Reuter reported Ayub Khan to have said Chinese activities in Tibet and road building in Afghanistan posed a serious threat from the north.

40. The sections on Alliances and the Suez Crisis have benefited largely from Farooq Naseem Bajwa's research work, *Pakistan and the West,* Oxford University Press, Karachi, 1996.

41. In May 1952 Paul Nitze, Director of State Department's Policy Planning

Staff, wrote a paper deploring Western fragility in the Middle East and recommending direct US involvement in the defence of the region because British capabilities were 'wholly inadequate'. Quoted in Robert J. McMahon, op. cit., p. 145.

42. John Foster Dulles said: 'With their religious convictions and courageous spirit, the people of Pakistan and their leaders make their country a real bulwark.' *Documents,* op. cit., p. 81.

43. Briefing the Senate Foreign Relations Committee on 3 July 1953 on military aid to Pakistan, Dulles said, 'We don't dare to do it because of repercussions in India.' *Documents,* ibid., p. 78.

44. Farooq Bajwa, op. cit., p. 87.

45. *Dawn,* Karachi, 22 February 1954, quoted in S. M. Burke, op. cit., p. 202.

46. *Dawn,* Karachi, 26 September 1955, quoted in S. M. Burke, ibid., p. 204.

47. Statement issued on 14 August 1956, quoted in S. M. Burke, ibid., p. 185.

48. *Documents,* op. cit., p. 125.

49. *Documents,* ibid., pp. 285-6, statement by James Noyes, Deputy Assistant Secretary for Defence, on 20 March 1973. Part of the aid was used to build Multan and Kharian cantonments and Sargodha air base.

50. Firoz Khan Noon, *Memoirs,* extracts in *Documents,* ibid., p. 163.

51. *New York Times,* 10 June 1956, quoted in Dennis Kux, op. cit., p. 128.

52. Report of National Security Council meeting of 3 January 1957, quoted in Dennis Kux, ibid., p. 154.

53. Article by Ayub Khan in *Foreign Affairs,* January 1964, extracts in *Documents,* op. cit., p. 226.

54. Quoted from *Dawn,* Karachi, 9 March 1958, in Altaf Gauhar, *Ayub Khan—Pakistan's First Military Ruler,* Sang-e-Meel Publications, Lahore, 1994, p. 113-4.

55. Altaf Gauhar, ibid., p. 119.

56. Hafeez Malik, op. cit., p. 198, quoting Michael R. Beschloss, *May Day: Eisenhower, Khrushchev and the U-2 Affair,* p. 145.

57. US Assistant Secretary of State G. Lewis Jones, quoted in Dennis Kux, op cit., p. 169.

58. India's Ambassador Chagla, quoted in Robert J. McMahon, op. cit., p. 260.

59. In contrast, US aid to Pakistan increased marginally from $162.5 million in 1956 to $170 million in 1957.

60. Arthur M. Schlesinger, *A Thousand Days,* Fawcett Publications Inc., Greenwich, Conn., 1965, p. 483.

61. Summary of declassified *US Policy Documents on South Asia,* Vol. 19, quoted in *Dawn,* Karachi, 3 September 1996.

62. Ayub 'charmed everybody', 'ingratiated' himself with Mrs Kennedy with the gift of a spirited stallion, and 'shone' at a gala dinner. Vice President Johnson described Ayub as a 'seasoned' leader and a

'dependable' ally. Quoted in Robert J. McMahon, op. cit., pp. 278-80.

63. Quoted from US documents in Robert J. McMahon, op. cit., p. 280. Also, summary of *US Policy Documents,* Vol. 19.

64. Arthur M. Schlesinger, op. cit., p. 485.

65. Quoted from *Robert Kennedy in His Own Words* and Arthur Schlesinger, *A Thousand Days,* in Robert J. McMahon, op. cit., p. 281.

66. Kennedy's letter of 18 January 1962 to Nehru, quoted in Dennis Kux, op. cit., p. 197.

67. Arthur Schlesinger, op. cit., p. 487.

68. Ibid.

69. The article 'Another Korea in the Making' published in *Colliers,* August 1951, quoted in G. W. Choudhury, op. cit., p. 157.

70. *See,* Altaf Gauhar, op. cit., p. 234.

71. At the Commonwealth summit in 1964, Pakistan opposed a move to pledge joint opposition to the 'Chinese threat'. Maqbool A. Bhatty, *Great Powers and South Asia: Post Cold War Trends,* Institute of Regional Studies, Islamabad, 1996. p. 165.

72. Mohammad Yunus, *Reflections on China,* Wajidalis Ltd., Lahore, 1986, pp. 131-32.

73. US Embassy, Karachi, press release of September 1963, quoted in Altaf Gauhar, op. cit., p. 245.

74. Dennis Kux, op. cit., p. 204.

75. Quoted from John Kenneth Galbraith, *Ambassador's Journal,* in Altaf Gauhar, op. cit., p. 207.

76. Altaf Gauhar, op. cit., p. 504, quoted from Neville Maxwell, *India's China War,* p. 410.

77. Dennis Kux, op. cit., p. 207.

78. Summary of *US Policy Documents,* Vol. 19, quoted in *Dawn,* Karachi, 3 September 1996.

79. Altaf Gauhar, op. cit., p. 500.

80. Carl Kaysen, Special Assistant for National Security Affairs, quoted in Altaf Gauhar, op. cit., pp. 499.

81. Dennis Kux, op. cit., p. 207, based on Steven A. Hoffman, *India and the China Crisis,* op. cit., pp. 206-8.

82. Ironically, the same ship was considered by India as a symbol of US hostility when it was sent by Nixon in 1971, notes Dennis Kux, op. cit., p. 207.

83. Ibid., p. 208.

84. Mohammad Ali's statement of 22 November 1962, *Documents,* op. cit., pp. 213-15.

85. Altaf Gauhar, op. cit., p. 217.

86. *New York Times,* 11 February 1963, quoted in G. W. Choudhury, op. cit., p. 73.

87. Summary of *US Policy Documents,* Vol. 19, quoted in *Dawn,* Karachi, 3 September 1996.
88. Robert J. McMahon, op. cit., p. 314.
89. Z.A. Bhutto was 'deeply upset and disturbed' at the discourtesy shown to him, noted Talbot. A White House aide thought 'Bhutto was asking for it'; Robert J. McMahon, op. cit., p. 307.
90. Z.A. Bhutto's note for Ayub Khan, extract in *Documents,* op. cit., p. 250.
91. *The Hindustan Times,* 20 April 1964, summarized in Alastair Lamb, *Kashmir—A Disputed Legacy,* Oxford Books, UK, 1991, pp. 248-50.
92. Quoted from *Hindu Weekly,* Madras, in S.M. Burke, op. cit., p. 324.
93. The award allocated to Pakistan narrow stretches of land that surface after the monsoon season along the northern edge of the Rann, while India got the rest, mostly marshy areas.
94. Alastair Lamb, op. cit., p. 256.
95. Quoted from *Hindu Weekly* of 26 July 1965 in S. M. Burke, op. cit., p. 326.
96. Statement of 14 July 1965 quoted in Robert J. McMahon, op. cit., p. 326.
97. This account, and much of the information here about official discussions during the period, is based on the work of Ayub Khan's confidant and biographer, Altaf Gauhar, op. cit.
98. Altaf Gauhar holds the view that Ayub Khan was influenced by Foreign Minister Z.A. Bhutto and Foreign Secretary Aziz Ahmed. That is possible but one of the advisers—Aziz Ahmed—told this author in 1965 that he was unaware of the number of the volunteers to be sent to Kashmir.
99. Ayub Khan, though well educated and experienced as a soldier, held the bigoted notion that 'Hindu morale would not stand more than a couple of hard blows at the right time and place.' Altaf Gauhar, op. cit., p. 329.
100. Pakistani forces captured 1,617 square miles of Indian territory and 201 in Kashmir while India gained 446 in Pakistan and 740 square miles in Kashmir.
101. Altaf Gauhar, op. cit., p. 347-8.
102. China demanded the return of four Chinese inhabitants, 800 sheep and 59 yaks India had kidnapped.
103. UN Document S/Res/211 reproduced in *Documents,* Vol. II, op. cit., pp. 115-16.
104. For details and references *see,* S. M. Burke, op. cit., pp. 338-57, and Altaf Gauhar, op. cit., pp. 340-41 and 347-53.
105. *US National Security Archives,* NEA/PAB; RKMcKEE:gn of 23 May 1977, quoted in Altaf Gauhar, op. cit., p. 196.
106. Hafeez Malik, op. cit., p. 188.
107. Ibid., p. 192, quoting Thomas Thornton, *Soviet Mediation at Tashken*

108. Ayub Khan secretly visited Beijing for this purpose on 20 September. Altaf Gauhar, op. cit., pp. 351-53.
109. A jeepable road was completed in 1971, an asphalt road in 1978. The Karakorum Highway, crossing the Khunjerab Pass at 15,800 ft. (4,800 m.) was opened to adventure-travellers in 1986.
110. Hafeez Malik, op. cit., p. 202.
111. Henry Kissinger, *The White House Years,* Little Brown, 1979, p. 685.
112. Ibid., p. 684.
113. Ibid., p. 767.
114. *Statesman Weekly,* 27 September 1969, quoted in S. M. Burke, op. cit., p. 374.
115. Of 101 top civil and police service officers who opted for Pakistan in 1947 only 18 were Bengalis. Though the number of those who belonged to areas of West Pakistan was also relatively small (35), the issue was politicized so that any non-Bengali was dubbed a 'Punjabi'.
116. The Lahore Resolution adopted by the Muslim League on 23 March 1940 demanded that contiguous Muslim majority 'units' in the north-western and eastern zones of British India should be 'grouped to constitute "Independent States" in which the constituent units shall be autonomous and sovereign.' The 1946 convention of the elected legislators left no doubt that Pakistan was to be 'a sovereign independent state'. For the texts of the resolutions *see,* Syed Sharifuddin Pirzada, *The Pakistan Resolution,* Pakistan Publications, Karachi, 1968.
117. Texts of the original and revised formula are reproduced in Siddiq Salik, *Witness to Surrender,* Oxford University Press, Karachi, 1977, pp. 215-17.
118. Altaf Gauhar, op. cit., p. 411.
119. Asoka Raina, *Inside RAW,* Vikas Publishing Co., Delhi, 1981, p. 49.
120. Henry Kissinger, op. cit., p. 852.
121. Siddiq Salik, op. cit., p. 101. This figure did not include local raisings for para-military formations.
122. Asoka Raina, op. cit., p. 57.
123. Alastair Lamb, op. cit., p. 288.
124. K. Subramaniam, Director of the official Indian Institute of Defence Studies and Analyses said on 31 March: 'What India must realize is the fact that the break-up of Pakistan is in our interest, an opportunity the like of which will never come again.' *The Hindustan Times,* New Delhi, 1971, reported him to have also spoken of a 'chance of the century'. Quoted in Siddiq Salik, op. cit., p. 97.
125. Asoka Raina, op. cit., p. 54.
126. *Bangladesh Documents,* Government of India, Vol. I, p. 672, quoted in Siddiq Salik, op. cit., p. 97.
127. Siddiq Salik, ibid., p. 100.
128. Henry Kissinger, op. cit., pp. 857 and 861.

129. Richard Sisson and Leo E. Rose, *War and Secession—Pakistan, India, and the Creation of Bangladesh*, University of California Press, Berkeley, Cal., 1990, p. 209.

130. Ibid., p. 209. Pakistan received this information through its own sources. Washington learnt from 'resources heretofore reliable' that Indira Gandhi had 'ordered plans for a lightening "Israeli-type" attack to take over East Pakistan', Henry Kissinger, op. cit., p. 857.

131. V. Longer, *The Defence and Foreign Policy of India*, Sterling Publishers, New Delhi, 1988, p. 205.

132. Henry Kissinger, op. cit., p. 861.

133. Nixon was not alone in finding Nehru insufferable. Secretary of State Dean Acheson said he was 'One of the most difficult men with whom I have ever had to deal.' Quoted from Acheson, *Present at the Creation*, pp. 439-40 in Robert J. McMahon, op. cit., p. 56. Truman considered Nehru 'disagreeable' and Kennedy who publicly praised Nehru's 'soaring idealism' found his sense of superiority 'rather offensive'.

134. Henry Kissinger, op. cit., p. 848.

135. *The Memoirs of Richard M. Nixon*, Vol. 1, Warner Books, New York, 1978, p. 651.

136. Henry Kissinger, op. cit., p. 880.

137. Richard Nixon, op. cit., p. 652.

138. Ibid., p. 658.

139. Sisson and Rose, op. cit., p. 213.

140. Henry Kissinger, op. cit., p. 895-6. In footnote 7 on p. 1488, he further says: 'Assurances were given by the Kennedy and Johnson administrations, including a letter from President John F. Kennedy to President Mohammad Ayub Khan on Jan. 26, 1962; an aide-mémoire presented by the US ambassador in Nov. 5, 1962 a public statement by the State Department on Nov. 17, 1962; and an oral promise by President Lyndon Johnson to Ayub Khan on Dec. 15, 1965.'

141. Ibid., p. 901.

142. Ibid., p. 905.

143. Ibid., p. 910.

144. V. Longer, op. cit., p. 215.

145. Statement of Policy for the 1970s, issued on 3 May 1973, *Documents*, op. cit., p. 207.

146. For a first hand account and analysis, *see*, the author's 'Simla Agreement: Negotiation Under Duress' in *Regional Studies*, Islamabad, Autumn 1995, pp. 28-45.

147. For a more comprehensive study on the subject, *see*, the author's article 'Reducing Nuclear Dangers in South Asia: A Pakistani Perspective' in *The Non-proliferation Review*, Winter 1995, Center for Non-proliferation Studies, Monterey, California, pp. 40-55, and *Regional Studies*, Islamabad, Autumn 1994.

148. Prime Minister Z. A. Bhutto's statement in Parliament, 28 April 1977, *Documents*, op. cit., p. 329.

149. Statement by Pakistan Foreign Office, 7 April 1979, *Documents,* op. cit., p. 347.

150. Statement by Pakistan Information Ministry, 21 November 1979, *Documents*, op. cit., p. 366. For rebuilding the embassy Pakistan paid $13.94 million. In addition the US claimed $7.245 million for other property lost. Statement by US Statement Department, 12 November 1981, *Documents,* op. cit., p. 366.

151. K. M. Arif, *Working With Zia,* Oxford University Press, Karachi, 1995, p. 203.

152. Agha Shahi, *Pakistan Security and Foreign Policy,* Progressive Publishers, Lahore, 1988, p. 4.

153. Ibid., p. 6.

154. Ibid., p. 8.

155. President Carter's statement, 21 January 1980, *Documents,* op. cit., p. 372.

156. Statement by US Department of State, 26 December 1979, *American Foreign Policy-Basic Documents, 1977-80.*

157. Riaz M. Khan, *Untying the Afghan Knot,* Progressive Publishers, Lahore, 1993, pp. 18-20. This work provides authoritative information on Pakistan's policy in the Afghanistan crisis and, especially, the UN-mediated negotiations leading to the Geneva Accords in April 1988.

158. For detailed table *see*, Riaz M. Khan, ibid., p. 40.

159. President Zia on NBC-TV, 18 May 1980, *Documents,* op. cit., p. 394.

160. Statement by Foreign Affairs Adviser Agha Shahi, 5 March 1980, *Documents,* op. cit., pp. 388-90.

161. Pakistan Foreign Office Statement, 25 April 1980, *Documents,* op. cit., p. 392.

162. The package included $150 million in economic aid for the fiscal year July 1982 to June 1983, and about $3 billion for economic assistance and military sales credits for the fiscal years 1983-87.

163. In testimony before a Congressional committee on 27 April 1981, Deputy Assistant Secretary of State Jane Coon acknowledged the injustice of past US policy, saying that sanctions were 'applied in the case of one country—Pakistan'. A few weeks later, Assistant Secretary of State James Buckley exuded understanding of Pakistan's perception that the threat to its security 'could not be met by conventional and political means'. For texts of statements, *see*, *Documents,* op. cit.

164. US Department of State, 16 September 1981, *Documents,* op. cit., p. 457.

165. The interest differential was initially 8 per cent a year on $300 million. Fortunately, interest rates declined in subsequent years. The follow-up agreement which remained in force only for three years until 1990 at a level of $700 million a year provided for military sales credits at a concessional rate.

166. Riaz M. Khan, op. cit., p. 107.
167. This phrase was derived from the 1981 UN Declaration on the Inadmissibility of Intervention and Interference in the Internal Affairs of States.
168. Selig Harrison, *Inside the Afghan Talks,* p. 31. *See also,* Barnett R. Rubin, *The Search for Peace in Afghanistan—From Buffer State to Failed State,* Yale University Press, New Haven, 1995, pp. 63-65; slightly different figures are given by Riaz M. Khan, op. cit., p. 88.
169. Quoted by Diego Cordovez, Barnett R. Rubin, op. cit., p. 40.
170. Barnett R. Rubin, op. cit., p. 43.
171. Press briefing by Diego Cordovez, 9 December 1986, quoted in Barnett R. Rubin, p. 77.
172. Shevardnadze told Secretary of State George Shultz on 16 September 1987: 'We will leave Afghanistan...I say with all responsibility that a political decision has been made.' Quoted from Shultz, *Turmoil and Triumph,* p. 1090, in Barnett R. Rubin, ibid., p. 83.
173. Riaz M. Khan, op. cit., p. 234.
174. This exchange took place on 9 February 1988 in the author's presence.
175. *Literaturnaya Gazeta,* Moscow, 17 February 1988, quoted in Agha Shahi, op. cit., p. 93.
176. K. M. Arif, op. cit., p. 327, based on statements by General Alexei Lizichev and Prime Minister Nikolai Ryzhkov.
177. Paul Kennedy, *The Rise and Fall of Great Powers*, Random House, New York, 1987.
178. The author was the ambassador.
179. A former foreign secretary of India told the author that their initial reserve was feigned in order to preempt Pakistani apprehensions.
180. *From SARC to SAARC,* Vol. I, SAARC Secretariat, Khatmandu, 1995, p. 9.
181. Vernon L. B. Mendis, *SAARC—Origins, Organisation and Prospects,* Indian Ocean Centre for Peace Studies, Perth, 1991, p. 124.
182. Report in *New York Times* of 15 September 1984 that a Senate Committee was informed about Indira Gandhi considering an attack on Kahuta, recalled in K. Bajpai, et. al., *Brasstacks and Beyond*, Manohar Publishers, New Delhi, 1990.
183. Ibid.
184. Ibid., p. viii.
185. Seymour Hersh, in 'On the Nuclear Edge' in *The New Yorker*, 29 March 1993.
186. A Pakistani spokesman reiterated on 24 August 1994 that Pakistan has the capacity to produce nuclear weapons but has not done so. Nawaz Sharif, who was earlier and is now again Prime Minister, stated that Pakistan actually had a bomb, but at that time this was contradicted by

the Pakistan Government and described by US State Department as having something to do with domestic politics. Reuter/AP dispatches, 23/24 August 1994.

187. References for the quotations here are cited in the author's paper, 'Reducing Nuclear Dangers in South Asia: A Pakistani Perspective' in *The Nonproliferation Review.*

188. General Aslam Beg, the former Pakistan Army Chief of Staff, has said 'it is the nuclear deterrent that has kept wars in South Asia at bay'. Commenting on prospects for the future, former Chief of Staff of the Indian Navy, Admiral Nandkarni, has observed that with nuclear capability, 'Pakistan would be able to establish a deterrent nuclear posture against India, rendering in the process the balance of conventional forces considerably less significant than it is today.' General K. M. Arif, op. cit., has remarked that 'the dismemberment of Pakistan could have been avoided had the country possessed nuclear deterrence in 1971'. General K. Sundarji, former chief of the Indian Army and a respected analyst of strategic issues, went further to remark that none of the past wars would have occurred.

189. Leonard S. Spector with Jacqueline R. Smith, *Nuclear Ambitions: The Spread of Nuclear Weapons,* pp. 68-69, and Peter Gray, *Briefing Book on the Nonproliferation of Nuclear Weapons,* p. 7. Pakistan's weapons capability in 1994 was estimated at five to ten devices.

190. Mulla Mohammad Umar, Taliban leader, quoted by Rahimullah Yusufzai in *The News International,* Islamabad, 4 October 1996.

191. K. M. Arif, op. cit., p. 327, quoting Eduard Sheverdnadze's statement in *Izvestia* of 19 February 1989.

192. President Ronald Reagan, speech welcoming President Zia to Washington, 7 December 1982, *Documents,* op. cit., p. 481.

193. Alastair Lamb., op. cit. 304.

194. Ibid., p. 331.

195. Bahauddin Farooqi, Writ Petition in *Kashmir Holocaust—The Case Against India,* ed., Khalid Hasan, Dotcare, Lahore, 1992, p. 30.

196. Quoted from *The Current,* 26 May to 1 June 1990, in Bahauddin Farooqi, ibid., p. 31.

197. Ibid., pp. 33-41.

198. Alastair Lamb, op. cit., p. 322.

199. Statement by Prime Minister Narasimha Rao, *The Hindustan Times,* New Delhi, 8 June 1992.

200. Samuel P. Huntington, 'Clash of Civilizations,' *Foreign Affairs,* Summer 1993.

201. Amnesty International, *India—Torture, Rape, & Deaths in Custody,* New York, 1992, pp. 20-21.

202. Federation Internationale des Droits d'Homme.

203. Quoted in Prime Minister Benazir Bhutto's letter of 3 June 1996 to Prime Minister Deve Gowda, *The News International*, Islamabad, 4 June 1996.
204. *The News International*, Islamabad, 10 June 1996.
205. A. M. and S. Zaidi, Vol. II, op. cit., p. 506.
206. *Selected Works of Jawaharlal Nehru*, Second Series, distributed by Oxford University Press, New Delhi, 1984, Vol. 3, p. 133.
207. Zalmay Khalilzad does not even mention the Muslim World as one of the important features of the current international environment. *Strategic Appraisal—1996*, Rand, Santa Monica, pp. 13-14.
208. Mohammad Nawaz Sharif, 'Islam and the West—Vast Scope for Coexistence,' *Dawn*, Karachi, 21-22 July 1996.
209. Ashley J. Tellis, *Strategic Appraisal 1996*, p. 294.
210. Ibid., p. 293.
211. *See*, note 174 above.

BIBLIOGRAPHY

Ali, Chaudhri Muhammad, *The Emergence of Pakistan*, Columbia University Press, New York, 1967.

Ambedkar, B.R., *Thoughts on Pakistan*, Thacker & Co., Bombay, 1947.

Arif, K.M., *Working With Zia*, Oxford University Press, Karachi, 1995.

Arif, K., ed., *America-Pakistan Relations—Documents*, Vanguard Books, Lahore, 1984.

Azad, Abul Kalam, *India Wins Freedom*, Orient Longman, New Delhi, 1959.

Bajpai, K., et. al., *Brasstacks and Beyond*, Manohar Publishers, New Delhi, 1995.

Bajwa, Farooq Naseem, *Pakistan and the West*, Oxford University Press, Karachi, 1996.

Bhatty, Maqbool A., *Great Powers and South Asia: Post-Cold War Trends*, Institute of Regional Studies, Islamabad, 1996.

Burke, S.M., and Ziring, Lawrence, *Pakistan's Foreign Policy*, Oxford University Press, Karachi, Second Edition, 1990.

Campbell-Johnson, Alan, *Mission with Mountbatten*, Atheneum, New York, 1966.

Cordovez, Diego, and Harrison, Selig, *Out of Afghanistan—The Inside Story of the Soviet Withdrawal*, Oxford University Press, New York, 1995.

Choudhury, G.W., *Pakistan's Relations with India, 1947-66*, Pall Mall Press, London, 1967.

Farooqi, Bahauddin, 'Writ Petition' in *Kashmir Holocaust—The Case Against India.*, ed., Khalid Hasan, Dotcare, Lahore, 1992.

Gauhar, Altaf, *Ayub Khan—Pakistan's First Military Ruler*, Sang-e-Meel Publications, Lahore, 1994.

Hasan, Khwaja Sarwar, *Documents on the Foreign Policy of Pakistan*, Institute of International Affairs, Karachi, 1986.

Hyder, Sajjad, *The Foreign Policy of Pakistan, Reflections of an Ambassador*, Progressive Publishers, Lahore, 1987.

Mohammad Ali Jinnah—Speeches as Governor General, 1947-48, Ferozsons, Karachi.

Kadeer, A.A., and Tahir, Naveed A., eds., *Pakistan-Europe Ties*, University of Karachi, 1988.

Kennedy, Paul, *The Rise and Fall of Great Powers*, Random House, New York, 1987.

Khalilzad, Zalmay, *Strategic Appraisal 1996*, RAND, Santa Monica, 1996.

Khan, Riaz M., *Untying the Afghan Knot*, Progressive Publishers, Lahore, 1993.

Kissinger, Henry, *The White House Years*, Little Brown, 1979.

Kux, Dennis, *India and the United States: Estranged Democracies*, National Defense University Press, Washington, DC, 1993.

Lamb, Alastair, *Kashmir—A Disputed Legacy*, Oxford Books, UK, 1991, reprinted by Oxford University Press, Karachi, 1992.

Longer, V., *The Defence and Foreign Policy of India*, Sterling Publishers, New Delhi, 1988.

Malik, Hafeez, *Soviet-Pakistan Relations and Post-Soviet Dynamics*, Macmillan Press, London, 1994.

McMahon, Robert J., *The Cold War on the Periphery—The United States, India and and Pakistan*, Columia Uiversity Press, New York, 1994.

Mendis, Vernon L.B., *SAARC—Origins, Organisation and Prospects*, Indian Ocean Centre for Peace Studies, Perth, 1991.

Nehru, Jawaharlal, *Selected Works*, Second Series, distributed by Oxford University Press, New Delhi, 1984.

Nixon, Richard M., *The Memoirs of Richard Nixon*, Warner Books, New York, 1978.

Raina, Asoka, *Inside RAW*, Vikas Publishing Co., New Delhi, 1981.

Roy, Oliver, *Islam and Resistance in Afghanistan*, Cambridge University Press, Cambridge, 1986.

Rubin, Barnett R., *The Search for Peace in Afghanistan—From Buffer State to Failed State*, Yale University Press, New Haven, 1995.

Sattar, Abdul, 'Reducing Nuclear Dangers in South Asia—A Pakistani Perspective' in *The Non-proliferation Review*, Monterey, Winter 1995.

Schlesinger, Arthur M., Jr., *A Thousand Days*, Fawcett Publications, Greenwich, 1965.

SAARC Secretariat, *From SARC to SAARC*, Kathmandu, 1995.

Shahi, Agha, *Pakistan's Security and Foreign Policy*, Progressive Publishers, Lahore, 1988.

Salik, Siddiq, *Witness to Surrender*, Oxford University Press, Karachi, 1977.

Sisson, Richard, and Rose, Leo E., *War and Secession—Pakistan, India, and the Creation of Bangladesh*, University of California Press, Berkeley, 1990.

Spector, Leonard S., and Smith, Jacqueline R., *Nuclear Ambitions*, Westview Press, Boulder, 1990.

Stephens, Ian, *Horned Moon*, Chatto and Windus, London, 1954.

US Policy Documents, US Government Publications, Washington, DC.

Yunus, Mohammad, *Reflections on China*, Wajidalis, Lahore, 1986.

Ziring, Lawrence, et. al., *Pakistan: The Long View*, Duke University Press, Durham, 1977.

Zaidi, A Moin, and Zaidi, Shaheda, eds., *The Encyclopaedia of Indian National Congress*, S. Chand & Co., New Delhi, 1976-1981.

CHAPTER 3

ECONOMIC DEVELOPMENT

Aftab Ahmad Khan

Over the last five decades, considerable discussion has centred on the theme of economic development. In low income countries, development has come to be regarded as the most significant index of a country's progress, and the most important test to judge the performance of governments. The essence of the process of economic development is a general increase in productive efficiency, which is vitally related to an increase in the availability of capital, technological skills, managerial ability and administrative competence. It may be based in varying combinations of these elements.

Faced with economies characterized by deep-seated weaknesses and rigidities too great to be overcome by market forces alone, many newly independent developing countries including Pakistan in the early post Second World War years resorted to multi-annual comprehensive plans as the most effective means for overcoming economic backwardness and bringing about desired social change. Planning emerged as a tool of development in countries differing not only in their stages of economic progress, but also in their social and economic systems. A multi-year national development plan is a body of economic and social policies expressed in quantified targets and defined tasks. Ideally it sets forth (1) overall social and economic objectives, (2) policies and strategies to guide the development process, and (3) a fairly detailed programme for implementation.

Foreign aid agencies have also played a significant role in promoting planning in the developing world. The macro-economic plans that calculated foreign exchange needs, and showed that a country could profitably absorb foreign aid, were used by bilateral and multilateral agencies to justify credits and grants.

This chapter provides an overall picture of Pakistan's economic progress during the past five decades through a succession of multi-year plans. During this fifty-year period the economy has altered significantly. The size of the national product has grown substantially, its structure has become more diversified and developed, and the practices and techniques of production have been significantly modernized. For an economy deficient in crucial natural resources, the transformation has come a long way. It has involved sacrifices for large sections of the people. Although the inflow of foreign assistance helped finance mounting development outlays, the burden was also borne by a sizeable domestic savings effort, especially in relation to the low level of per capita income.

The country's development effort has had its shortcomings. The rate of population growth stepped far above historical rates, and, as a result, much of the gain in output did not lead to improvement in standards of living. Concentration of wealth increased. The expansion in the provision of social services proved insufficient to satisfy the needs and aspirations of the people. There is a growing disenchantment with the inequitable nature of the growth pattern, an acute impression that the development process has discriminated against poorer regions and income groups.

The economic development of Pakistan has not run smoothly on a single course over the past five decades. When the subcontinent of South Asia was partitioned in 1947, the few existing industrialized regions fell to the share of India: the cotton textile industry in the west, the jute industry in the east, steel in central India, and a variety of medium sized industries, most of them established during the Second World War, mainly in the south. Pakistan's share was the least developed part of the subcontinent. East Bengal, which produced jute that it could neither bale nor manufacture, had mainly a large unskilled population. In the West Wing (present Pakistan), the Punjab had a well developed irrigation system and a population which had traditionally contributed in large part to the British Indian Army; a population which, despite the departure of the Sikhs, was recognized for its excellent cultivators and colonists. Pakistani Punjab had a capable, skilled and stalwart peasantry, including those who came from East Punjab. The North-West Frontier Province was populated by virile Pathans and Sindh was rich in agriculture as a result of recently constructed barrages and canals, but had a ruthless system of feudalism, even for this part of the world.

The subcontinent as a whole was industrially backward, industrialization having begun only towards the end of the nineteenth and the beginning of the twentieth centuries. And, it was unevenly distributed, partly by design and partly by neglect. Thus disparities were created in the development of different regions, and the parts which later came to constitute Pakistan lagged behind in industrial development. Industries had grown up largely in and around the ports of Bombay and Calcutta. The Pakistan areas produced 75 per cent of the raw jute and a high proportion of the best varieties of cotton in the subcontinent, but at the time of Independence it had no jute mills and only a few jute baling presses. The jute trade, both manufacturing and exporting, was based in Calcutta. Similarly, the bulk of long staple cotton grown was sent to western India for processing in its textile mills, and the areas which were to become Pakistan imported their requirements of manufactured goods.

Pakistan, however, inherited some of the best irrigation facilities. Nearly the whole cultivated area of Sindh, Bahawalpur and a large part of the Punjab had excellent irrigation systems. Of the total net sown area in West Pakistan, about 76 per cent was under irrigation and the yield per acre of various crops was higher than elsewhere in the subcontinent. The Partition cut across the irrigation system leaving in India many of the headworks of canals which were of fundamental importance to Pakistan's Punjab. The rivers, on whose waters the economic existence of West Pakistan depended, flowed to Pakistan from India via Kashmir and East Punjab. This gave India control over the supply of canal water in Pakistan and kept the two countries in a state of high tension until the intervention of the World Bank brought a settlement.

The areas of Pakistan were predominately agricultural. According to the 1941 census, only 11 per cent of the population in these regions was classed as urban while 89 per cent was rural. At the time of Partition it was expected that West Pakistan would have a self-sufficient food economy and might have a surplus of about 5 lac (1 lac=100,000) tons of wheat for export. East Pakistan on the other hand was deficient in rice production. For its export earnings, Pakistan was mainly dependent on two cash corps, jute and cotton, and for its requirements of capital and consumer goods it was entirely dependent on imports.

At the time of Independence, the railways, a crucial component of infrastructure, were in a deplorable state of under-development. Out of a total of 41,149 route miles in the subcontinent, Pakistan had 6,980 miles, or only 17 per cent. West Pakistan inherited a total of 5,362 miles of the North-Western Railway, including 319 miles of the old Jodhpur (meter gauge) Railway, and 1,618 miles of railways in Bengal and Assam came to East Pakistan. The system in the East Wing was broken into several parts, with broad and meter gauge sections, and was burdened with a large surplus staff in the lower ranks. With Calcutta forming part of independent India, and the consequent change in the pattern of traffic, the port of Chittagong, which had been dismantled during the Second World War, had to be rebuilt. Because of the diversion of traffic from Calcutta and the stoppage of India's cross traffic between Calcutta and Assam, the broad gauge section lost most of its traffic. The North-Western Railway was better placed; its most serious problem arose from the uncertain and reduced supplies of coal from India, solved in part by converting some of its steam engines from coal to furnace oil and purchasing diesel electric locomotives.

The meagre industrial endowment of the areas which constituted Pakistan at the time of Independence was evidenced by the fact that out of the 14,569 industrial units in British India in 1947, only 1,406 were located in the areas included in

Pakistan. Thus, while our population was about 23 per cent of undivided British India, the manufacturing capacity located in Pakistan was barely 10 per cent; and even this comprised, mainly, such relatively small and unimportant units as flour and rice mills and cotton ginning factories. To make the situation worse, Pakistan lacked industrial credit facilities, technical institutes and research laboratories.

The task before the infant State was stupendous. The economy had to be rehabilitated and built on strong foundations with the meagre resources at its disposal for a large number of competing and pressing demands. The government was alive to the crucial role of industry. After careful deliberation, it announced the first industrial policy in 1949. Realizing the pioneering role which private enterprise could play in industrial expansion, the government threw open all fields of industrial activity to it, except three categories, namely, the manufacture of arms and ammunition, the generation of hydroelectric power, and the manufacture of railway wagons, telephones, telegraphic and wireless apparatus.

This industrial policy aimed at providing facilities to process the raw materials for cotton and jute products, leather, sugar, cement and paper. The emphasis was placed on quick growth based on domestic resources, and on creating a new class of industrial entrepreneurs within the country. The policy broadly envisaged expansion of production, specially in the consumer goods industries, maximizing the scope for private enterprise and enhancing export earnings.

The government assured all possible help, including financial credits for the establishment and development of private industry, and stated its willingness to give favourable consideration to claims for measures of protection to new industries. It welcomed the participation of foreign capital provided that the domestic share was 51 per cent in 13 industries, which were regarded as essential, and up to 30 per cent in other industries. The government felt that, if enough indigenous capital was not forthcoming, foreign investors would subscribe the balance. An assurance was also given regarding the remittance of profits. To put the industrial policy into operation, an advisory council for industries and a number of advisory committees were appointed to consider development in specific industries.

Early Attempts at Development Coordination

Despite the magnitude of the problems which faced Pakistan immediately after Independence—the relief and rehabilitation of refugees, the dislocation in trade and commerce, the disruption of the transport system, the imbalance between public revenues and expenditures, the security problems of the new State—the Government of Pakistan decided that high priority must be given to nation building schemes and a Development Board under the chairmanship of the Minister for Finance and Economic Affairs was set up in early 1948 to:

1) coordinate development plans, central and provincial, so that the available resources were put to the best possible use;
2) make recommendations regarding priorities among development plans;
3) prepare, under the orders of the Economic Committee of the Cabinet, memoranda on matters of general policy affecting development as a whole or any special aspect; and
4) monitor the progress of development schemes in order to remove bottlenecks and difficulties in the way of uniform progress in all sectors and to make periodic reports to the Cabinet.

To associate industrialists, bankers, businessmen, merchants and other interests in an advisory capacity in the important task of planning and development, the government established in 1948 a Planning Advisory Board consisting of both officials and non-officials. It had the following functions:

1) to advise government generally on matters relating to planning and development;
2) to review progress made in implementing the plans; and

3) to educate the public about the various development schemes undertaken in order to get their enthusiastic cooperation.

By the end of 1950, the Development Board had approved a number of schemes whose total cost was estimated at Rs 1,125.68 million. Table I shows the distribution of expenditure between the centre and the various provinces. The schemes of the provincial governments were financed largely by loans and grants from the federal government given on the recommendations of the Development Board which specified conditions for these loans.

Table I

Unit-wise cost of development schemes approved by the Development Board up to 31 December 1950 (in Rs 000)		
	Total estimated cost	Estimated cost during 1948-49	Estimated cost during 1949-50
Centre	320,388.5	15,194.0	31,705.5
Balochistan	10,450.0	4,741.0	2,512.5
East Bengal	248,323.5	4,390.0	59,395.5
The Punjab	373,407.0	52,327.0	76,105.0
Sindh	42,383.5	23,009.0	19,374.0
NWFP	130,728.5	6,807.0	14,379.5
Total	1,125,681.0	106,468.0	203,472.0

Source: Planning Commission, Government of Pakistan.

Planning from 1951 to 1998

The Colombo Plan (1951-57)

The Colombo Plan, inaugurated in 1951, represented the first attempt at an integrated approach to development. It was formulated for member countries of the Commonwealth of Nations belonging to South and South-East Asia. Its principal purpose was to bring hope to the people of the area and to save them from being subverted by the seductive philosophy of communism. The plan was prepared in the absence of reliable data on population, as well as essential economic and financial magnitudes. Even a comprehensive list of well prepared projects was hard to come by.

The Colombo Plan covered a six-year period from 1951 to 1957. It was officially described as essentially one of basic development intended to prepare our country for future development. It focused attention on the expansion of overhead facilities in such fields as communications, power and irrigation. It covered a large number of schemes, including many already approved by the Development Board, with some attempts to integrate the projects and to frame certain targets of development in the light of requirements during the period. An outlay of Rs 220 crore (one crore=ten million) was included in the public sector and Rs 40 crore in the private sector. In addition, an outlay of Rs 45 crore was anticipated outside the plan. Of the total investment of Rs 305 crore, Rs 170 crore was expected to be provided from internal resources, with Rs 120 crore from private savings and Rs 50 crore from budget surpluses. The balance of payments deficit of Rs 135 crore was to be financed to the extent of Rs 15 crore from the country's sterling balances with the Bank of England, and the rest was to be met from external aid. The annual size of development expenditure was expected to rise from Rs 33.5 crore to Rs 48 crore. It was hoped that this outlay, while not producing any spectacular results in terms of the current living standards of the people, would represent a beginning in that direction. However, the planning machinery was not equipped at the time to handle development efficiently, so the only outcome of the programme was investment in certain individual projects.

The Colombo Plan did not include such important schemes as the Thal Development and the Rasul Hydel projects, because they had reached an advanced stage of execution. Their exclusion meant, however, that the programme did not provide an integrated framework for development during the period of its operation. Meanwhile, the effects of the Korean War were becoming evident, and created problems not foreseen by the planners. Prices of capital goods increased and supply difficulties appeared. Financial provisions became increasingly inadequate. Consequently, the plan had to be modified. A Two-Year Priority Programme was formulated to focus on the development of certain essential sectors, which included shipping, telecommunications, thermal power and the manufacture of textiles.

The pace of development under the Colombo Plan was somewhat patchy, but the patches were oases in the vast wilderness of underdevelopment. While industry made considerable progress on account of generous fiscal concessions and a heavily protected home market, agriculture remained relatively neglected. The index of industrial production covering 17 major industries rose from 100 in 1950 to 285 in 1954. Production of food grains actually declined during this period—4 per cent in rice and 9 per cent in wheat. The development picture under the Colombo Plan was also a varying one in other fields. Civil aviation, shipping, port facilities, road transport and telephone facilities were rapidly developed from negligible beginnings. Power generation and rehabilitation of the irrigation system registered significant progress. Development in the social sectors was, however, lacklustre. In short, physical infrastructure received the highest and most urgent attention.

First Five–Year Plan (1955-60)

Realizing the need for a separate high-powered body to prepare a comprehensive and coordinated blueprint for development and to raise the living standards of the people by ensuring rapid, equitable and socially responsive growth, the Government of Pakistan set up a Planning Board in July 1953. The First Five-Year Plan (1955-60) was produced by this Planning Board in 1956, with assistance from the Harvard Advisory Group. It had an estimated outlay of Rs 1,080 crore—Rs 750 crore in the public sector and Rs 330 crore in the private sector. The plan aimed at increasing national income by 15 per cent and per capita income by about 7 per cent.

The First Plan was a comprehensive and coordinated attempt to harness human and physical resources to the maximum extent possible and to open opportunities for a richer and more varied life. It was designed to prepare the ground for a rapid building of the infrastructure and the productive potential of the economy. However, for various reasons, mainly political instability, the plan's performance fell below the projected targets. Although the plan commenced from 1955, it did not get government approval until 1958. Adequate attention was not paid to its recommendations and priorities, and there was no proper coordination between planning and budgeting. Against the plan's expectation of a 15 per cent increase in national income, the actual increase was about 11 per cent. The rise in per capita income also did not exceed 3 per cent mainly because of the rapid growth of population.

The financial resources available for development purposes in the public sector during this period also fell short of expectations. The total non-development expenditure exceeded the government revenue receipts by Rs 28 crore, as against the surplus of Rs 100 crore envisaged. The entire excess of non-development expenditure over revenue occurred during the first three years of the plan; in the last two years, public savings were positive. Foreign exchange earnings from exports fell short of projections by about Rs 94.6 crore, because both the volume and the prices of the country's chief exports of primary commodities declined sharply. On the other hand, imports were about Rs 216.5 crore less than expected. Because of the sharp increase in the prices of imports, the shortfall in real terms was larger. Cutbacks were particularly severe in imports of development goods and allocations to the private sector. Serious shortages of imported raw materials and consumer goods were also experienced. Receipts from project and commodity aid (excluding food) were also about Rs 82.3 crore less than expected, due largely to procedural and administrative delays in commitments and utilization of foreign aid.

A disappointing failure of the First Plan was in the key sector of agriculture. The result was that heavy imports of food grains became necessary, and the country spent about Rs 70 crore of its foreign exchange earnings on imported food grains and on the freight for those quantities received as aid, compared with Rs 41 crore provided in the plan. However, industrial production showed good progress, notably in cotton textiles and sugar. In the fuel and mineral sectors, increases in output were low except in the case of natural gas, which showed substantial growth. The increase in installed industrial capacity was close to expectations. The water development programme fell considerably behind schedule, and the acreage reclaimed from waterlogging and salinity was below target. Investment in rail transport, roads, ports, civil aviation, telecommunications and postal services was satisfactory. Performance was, however, poor in the development of inland water transport and roads in East Pakistan. In the field of social development, moderate progress was realized. Housing received a strong stimulus but only during the last two years of the plan; and medical, hospital and social service facilities showed modest improvement. Education made some perceptible progress, though less than expected. Primary school enrolment increased only a little ahead of population growth; secondary school enrolment rose by 25 per cent, and the out-turn of agricultural, engineering and medical personnel increased between 30 and 150 per cent.

In October 1958, Martial Law was declared in the country. From the point of view of the planners, the most important contribution made by the Martial Law regime was the recognition accorded to the planning organization; the status of the Board was raised to that of a Commission; the President of Pakistan because its chairman, and a deputy chairman with the status of a federal minister was appointed to assist him. The Second Five-Year Plan (1960-65) was formulated by the Planning Commission in the light of the experience of the First Plan and with the full support of the new government.

Second Five-Year Plan (1960-65)

The Second Five-Year Plan envisaged an outlay of Rs 2,300 crore—Rs 1,462 crore in the public sector and Rs 838 crore in the private sector. In addition, an amount of Rs 160 crore was provided for the rural works programme which aimed at initiating self-help programmes. The plan sought to speed up the pace of development and overcome the inadequacies of achievement during the First Plan period, and to ensure that the stage of self-generating growth was reached within a measurable time.

The Second Plan was more than successful in fulfilling its major objectives. The increase in national income during this period was over 30 per cent as compared to the target of 24 per cent. The total development expenditure was estimated at Rs 2,745 crore, excluding an expenditure of Rs 64 crore under the rural works programme, as against the planned Rs 2,300 crore.

Economic development was characterized and sustained by a healthy growth rate in the agricultural sector. In fact, the basic change brought about by the Second Plan was the restoration of a balance between agricultural and industrial development. Whereas the annual growth rate during the 1950s was 1.3 per cent in agriculture and 7.4 per cent in industry, the respective growth rates during the 1960-65 period were 3.4 per cent and 10 per cent.

This period also witnessed significant changes in economic policies. The economy was progressively freed from direct administrative controls, and greater reliance was placed on the market mechanism. An important factor in increasing agricultural production was the abandonment of food grain rationing, the establishment of support prices for wheat at a remunerative level, a 50 per cent subsidy on fertilizers and more liberal imports of tube wells, pumps and other farm machinery for the private sector. There was a general relaxation of controls on imports. The main objectives of the import policy during this period were to ensure a fuller utilization of industrial capacity, the strengthening of export industries, a gradual reduction in the import of goods produced locally and a more rapid development of backward areas. The list of items placed on automatic licences was gradually increased. The Export Bonus Scheme covered all industrial products and a few primary commodities, and was extended to remittances from abroad* and to shipping. There were two basic rates of 20 and 30 per cent for purposes of bonus premium. Increased availability of goods and services, as a result of high growth rates as well as import liberalization, were instrumental in maintaining price stability, despite an increase of 48 per cent in money supply during the period.

One of the main successes of the Second Plan period was the stabilization and improvement in the balance of payments position. Export earnings were higher than estimated, import requirements were smaller than originally projected, and the country exceeded the investment targets despite a lower than projected availability of external resources.

The projections for foreign exchange earnings anticipated an increase from Rs 212.7 crore in 1959-60 to Rs 245 crore in 1964-65, yielding a total of Rs 1,125 crore and leaving a gap of Rs 1,095 crore to be covered by foreign assistance. The actual total earnings for the period, however, were Rs 1,322.8 crore, exceeding the target by 18 per cent. At the same time, total imports were Rs 2,068 crore, or 6 per cent less than the original estimates. Consequently, the foreign exchange gap was only Rs 745.9 crore as against the projected Rs 1,095 crore. Actual exports including invisibles reached a level of Rs 302.5 crore in 1964-65, an increase of 44 per cent over the exports in 1959-60. Export earnings improved at an average of about 7 per cent, the total during the period exceeding the target by Rs 197.8 crore. This was helped by an improvement in the institutional framework for exports. The Export Promotion Bureau was established with regional offices at Dhaka and Lahore.

According to projections, Rs 1,095 crore, or about 50 per cent of the total foreign exchange requirement of Rs 2,200 crore, would have to be obtained from external resources in the form of loans and credits, private foreign investment and technical assistance. In fact, external assistance accounted for 36 per cent of the total imports.

It was possible to proceed with a larger investment programme with considerably less by way of foreign exchange loans and investment than projected in the plan because the country's own earnings exceeded the estimated amount by Rs 197.8 crore. The total external aid committed during the period amounted to Rs 1,061 crore. However, the aid actually disbursed amounted to Rs 753 crore, thus increasing aid in the pipeline by Rs 308 crore.

Third Five-Year Plan (1965-70)

The Third Five-Year Plan was formulated within the framework of a Twenty-Year Perspective Plan (1965-85), and in the light of the achievements and shortfalls of the two previous plans. The principal objectives and targets were to:

(1) attain rapid growth in the national economy with a view to ensuring a breakthrough to self-sustained growth in the shortest possible time, by aiming at a minimum increase of 37 per cent in the gross national product at constant prices. The annual rate of increase was projected at 6.5 as against the previous 5.5 per cent;

(2)   reduce the degree of inter-regional and intra-regional disparity in income per head between East and West Pakistan by increasing their regional income by 40 and 35 per cent respectively;

(3)   provide at least 55 lac new job opportunities to absorb increases in the labour force during these five years, as well as to reduce the existing level of unemployment by over one-sixth;

(4)   strengthen the balance of payments by increasing foreign exchange earnings at a rate faster than the GNP, and by accelerating import substitution; foreign exchange earnings were projected to reach Rs 480 crore by 1970 compared with about Rs 301 crore at the end of the Second Plan;

(5)   develop basic industries for the manufacture of producer goods so that the requirements of further industrialization could be met mainly from the country's own capacity;

(6)   accelerate the transformation in agriculture by giving the highest priority to measures designed to increase per acre yields and by maintaining strong farm incentives and subsidies to ensure maximum realization from farmers' resources;

(7)   arrest the menacing growth of population through effective steps;

(8)   provide better housing, more health services, and greater facilities for education, especially for the lower income groups; and

(9)   make substantial progress towards certain specific social objectives such as diminishing inequalities in the distribution of income, wealth and economic power; providing a measure of social security; and promoting social and cultural change conducive to more rapid economic expansion.

The Third Plan envisaged a total outlay of Rs 5,200 crore, Rs 3,000 crore in the public sector and Rs 2,200 crore in the private sector, with a view to maintaining a rising tempo of development and attaining its main objectives and targets. It visualized that, of the public sector outlay, Rs 1,600 crore would be spent in East Pakistan, and Rs 1,400 crore in West Pakistan; the expected private investment of Rs 2,200 crore would be shared equally between the Wings. In determining the size of this plan, due consideration was given to the expected availability of financial resources and the capacity of the country to implement the development projects and programmes effectively.

Soon after the launching of the Third Plan, it had to be reviewed in respect of its resources, priorities and phasing in the light of various adverse circumstances of nature, such as droughts in the West Wing, and floods, tidal bores and cyclones in East Pakistan. In addition, there was a reduced inflow of foreign economic assistance because of the postponement of the Aid-to-Pakistan Consortium meeting in July 1965, and the outbreak of war with India in September that year.

The re-phasing of the annual outlay during the remaining period of the plan, and the revised sectoral priorities and allocations, were directed towards maintaining its size, basic objectives and main targets. This re-phasing was primarily necessitated by a shortfall in the public sector outlay in the first year, from Rs 470 crore to Rs 342 crore. The shortfall was to be made up by accelerating the rate of annual development expenditure which was revised to a higher level of 14 per cent from the original projection of 11 per cent per annum.

The re-phasing and inter-sectoral adjustments announced in March 1967 reflected a new strategy for achieving the planned GNP growth of 6.5 per cent per annum with a lower investment. This was sought to be achieved through (1) greater concentration on agricultue, selected expansion of agriculture-based industries and provision of more incentives to farmers; (2) fuller utilization of installed capacity and subsequent consolidation of the existing units; and (3) improvement in the capital-output ratio by postponing projects with long gestation periods. The highest priority was accorded to the attainment of self-sufficiency in food during the period. The original and the revised phasing of the Third Plan in the public and private sectors is given in Table 2.

Table 2

	Government financed sector		Private sector		Total	
Year	Original phasing	Revised phasing	Original phasing	Revised phasing	Original phasing	Revised phasing
1965-66	470	342	370	370	840	712
1966-67	530	500	405	400	935	900
1967-68	600	600	435	430	1035	1030
1968-69	670	710	470	480	1140	1190
1969-70	730	848	520	520	1250	1368
1965-70	3,000	3,000	2,200	2,200	5,200	5,200
Annual compound growth rate (1965-70)	11.4	16.2	10.4	11.6	11.0	14.2

Original and revised phasing of the Third Plan

(in Rs 0,000,000)

Source: Economy of Pakistan, 1948-68; issued by Economic Adviser to the Government of Pakistan, Ministry of Finance, Islamabad.

The Third Plan, with a Rs 5,200 crore development programme, was the first within the framework of the Twenty-Year Perspective Plan (1965-85). It, however, witnessed a host of adverse circumstances and, as a result, achievements in most sectors fell short of expectations. Some of these factors were: increased expenditure on defence since the war with India in 1965, drastic cuts in foreign aid along with the hardening of the terms of loans and mounting repayment obligations, successive droughts and floods in 1965-66 and 1966-67 leading to a rise in food imports to be paid from the country's own resources, decline in savings and investment, and a rise in the cost of living. Finally, socio-political unrest that gripped the country in the penultimate year of the plan caused widespread dislocation of economic activity, adversely affecting industrial growth and exports.

The actual development expenditure was Rs 4,294.9 crore against the target of Rs 5,200 crore, indicating a shortfall of 17 per cent in the total programme. In the public sector, the development expenditure incurred was Rs 2143.3 crore against the target of Rs 3,000 crore, showing a shortfall of 29 per cent. In the private sector, total expenditure amounted to Rs 2,151.6 crore, a slight decrease from the target of Rs 2,200 crore.

The plan envisaged that 55 per cent of the total expenditure in the public sector would be financed by domestic resources and 45 per cent by external resources. Actually, about 52 per cent of public sector expenditure was financed through domestic mobilization, and as such the projected ratio between domestic and external resources was not fully realized. The expenditure on defence during 1965-70 was estimated at Rs 1,238.4 crore as against the original projection of Rs 689 crore. The shortfall of Rs 757.7 crore in the revenue surplus was mainly accounted for by the unanticipated rise in defence expenditure. The shortfall in revenue surplus was, however, counter-balanced to the extent of about Rs 344.8 crore through additional taxation over and above the target of Rs 300 crore. The total deficit financing during this period amounted to Rs 232.2 crore as against the planned Rs 150 crore.

There was a shortfall of Rs 320 crore in external resources as a result of the postponement of the Aid-to-Pakistan Consortium in the very first year of the plan; the level of aid pledged and committed went down substantially. Though subsequently the aid flow was to some extent restored, this could not counter-balance the earlier shortfall.

GNP increased by 5.7 per cent annually, agricultural production by 4.5 per cent and export earnings by 7 per cent, compared with respective projections of 6.5, 5 and 9.5 per cent. Some other important targets were subject to more severe shortfalls. An annual growth rate of only 6.8 per cent in value added in the manufacturing sector was realized, compared with

10 per cent; prices increased by over 20 per cent during the period.

A major failure of the Third Plan was reflected in a substantial shortfall in savings and investment targets for the economy, which in turn affected employment opportunities and allocations for social sectors. On the whole, investment in real terms barely showed any improvement. In nominal terms, the public sector development outlay of Rs 620 crore in 1969-70 was 27 per cent higher than the level of Rs 489 crore reached in 1964-65. Allowing, however, for the abnormal increase in prices of investment goods, and a larger element of non-development expenditure on subsidies in later years, public investment in real prices remained at best constant. There was, also, no acceleration in private investment, which actually declined in real terms. As a proportion of GNP, gross investment declined from 18.3 per cent in 1964-65 to 13.5 per cent in 1969-70. If depreciation and replacement requirements on large investments of the past were deducted from a declining gross investment level, net investment ratios were, in fact, even more severely affected.

Gross domestic savings increased from Rs 570 crore in 1964-65 to the Third Plan annual average of Rs 679 crore, but the average rate of savings declined from 11.7 per cent in 1964-65 to 9.7 per cent in 1969-70. The marginal rate of savings over this period was a little more than 6 per cent compared with the target of 20 per cent. The value and structure of imports, the poor performance of the manufacturing sector and the increase in government current expenditure were major factors depressing the rate of savings.

Foreign exchange earnings increased at an annual compound rate of 7 per cent as opposed to the estimated 9.5 per cent, reaching Rs 425 crore in 1969-70. Total payments during the period were about 14 per cent lower than original projections. The availability as well as utilization of external assistance fell short of expectations. The gross inflow was Rs 1,177.9 crore as against the target of Rs 1,550 crore. The plan estimated a requirement of $2,850 million in fresh pledges, that is, $2,700 million from the consortium and $150 million from other sources. Total pledges made during the period were instead $2,339 million, a shortfall of 18 per cent. The commitments and disbursements were estimated to be 16 and 25 per cent respectively less than planned expectations.

In the public sector, the total development expenditure in East Pakistan was estimated at Rs 1,130 crore, and Rs 1,023.3 crore in West Pakistan, with the private sector providing Rs 551.6 crore in East Pakistan compared to Rs 1,600 crore in West Pakistan.

At the end of the Third Plan in 1970, twenty-three years of Pakistan's existence had passed. Doubts about the country's stability and continued existence had been allayed. It had even fought a war, which was a stand-off, with its powerful neighbour, India. The US made Pakistan the show window of its success in economic aid. The West believed Pakistan to be a country which knew how beneficial it was to be a Western protégé and not play with hazardous political and economic theories—not even with democracy, except in the very restrained manner of Basic Democracy invented by President Ayub Khan's advisers. And yet, Hecate, Greek goddess of ill omen and the harbinger of all evil tidings, could hear then the rumblings of storms that began to gather in Pakistan's political and economic life.

The Separation of East Pakistan

Income disparities between East and West Pakistan, and a deep consciousness of being deprived of political participation in the governance of the country, increased in East Pakistan. Bitterness deepened and soon the ties which bound it to West Pakistan disappeared. In December 1971, East Pakistan separated after a tragic war and became Bangladesh.

The issue of economic disparity between West and East Pakistan became politically explosive in the 1950s and 1960s. For a fuller appreciation of the factors involved in this imbalance, it is necessary to bear in mind that, at the time of Independence, East Pakistan inherited an economy which was completely dependent on West Bengal (in India) for processing of its agricultural produce, export of surplus commodities, and supply of essential consumer goods. Modern industrial capacity was very small and infrastructural facilities were extremely inadequate. This, however, was not the case in West Pakistan which had received the benefits of improvements undertaken by the British India Government primarily for strategic reasons. It was generally better developed than East Pakistan, having present all the characteristics of a higher stage of development.

East Pakistan inherited a poor and inadequate system of communications particularly in respect of roads. In 1947, the only seaport, Chittagong, had a limited handling capacity of 5 lac tons per annum. The major portion of the exportable produce of the province was routed through Calcutta. On the other hand, West Pakistan possessed one of the major seaports of the subcontinent, Karachi, with a handling capacity of 28 lac tons per annum.

At the time of Independence, both Wings were industrially underdeveloped, but large scale industry was more extensive in West Pakistan. The Central Statistical Office has estimated that gross value added by large scale industry was Rs 20 crore in West Pakistan as compared to Rs 5 crore in East Pakistan in 1949-50. While there can be some controversy as regards the extent of disparity at the time of Independence, there can be little doubt that West Pakistan started with a larger industrial base. Moreover, in 1948, the generating capacity of public electricity supply undertakings in East Pakistan was merely 7,673 kilowatts, compared to that in West Pakistan of 68,610 kilowatts.

Shortage of private capital was more acute in East Pakistan. There was little indigenous Muslim participation in trade and industry at the time of Independence. In West Pakistan, capital had been more freely available, and the major portion of industrial development was undertaken by private enterprise. West Pakistan also had experience of large scale development and, as such, data and skills were available for launching new projects, whereas there was a lack of these in East Pakistan.

Due to these factors, economic development in East Pakistan did not take place at the rate and to the extent that was necessary. Unfortunately, in the first decade after Independence the central government did not give serious consideration to the vital problem of accelerating the pace of development in East Pakistan with a view to reducing inter-Wing disparity in per capita income. From 1958 onwards, however, the government adopted a series of measures to quicken the pace of economic growth in East Pakistan.

East Pakistan's share in central taxes and duties increased from Rs 15.08 crore in 1958-59 to Rs 80.42 crore in 1970-71, or by 423 per cent. During the same period, the share of the West Pakistan Government increased from Rs 20.1 crore to Rs 74.26 crore, or by 269 per cent. There was also a more rapid growth of public development expenditure in East Pakistan which rose from Rs 45.6 crore in 1960-61 to Rs 256.24 crore in 1969-70, a rise of 462 per cent; in 1970-71 it further increased to Rs 367 crore. With regard to the total development programme, both public and private, expenditure rose from Rs 126 crore in 1960-61 to Rs 376.24 crore in 1969-70, and an estimated Rs 528 crore in 1970-71. In West Pakistan, this rose from about Rs 200 crore in 1960-61 to Rs 557 crore in 1969-70, an increase of 179 per cent. The pace of development in East Pakistan was particularly fast under the Second and Third Plans.

Despite these measures, the disparity in per capita income in terms of the all-Pakistan average was estimated at 30 per cent at the end of the Third Plan. This was exploited for political ends during the 1970 elections with tragic consequences for the unity of the country.

Fourth Five-Year Plan (1970-75)

The Fourth Plan, for the years 1970-75, was drawn up against the background of this deepening crisis. Its strategy was fashioned keeping in view the following objectives, namely, to maintain the tempo of development in the country; reduce inter-regional and intra-regional disparity in per capita income; and move towards a viable synthesis between the claims of rapid economic growth necessary, *inter alia*, for our existence as an independent nation, for social justice in terms of our Islamic ideals, and for the need to remove our internicine conflicts.

Some of the important targets of the Fourth Plan were to:

(1)   attain an annual growth rate of 6.5 per cent of the GNP, which would permit the average per capita income to increase to at least Rs 660 in 1974-75; the target for East Pakistan in this respect was 7.5 per cent per annum as against 5.5 per cent in West Pakistan;

(2)   reduce the disparity in per capita income between various regions at the fastest possible rate;

(3)   provide 75 lac job opportunities compared to the 65 lac new entrants in the labour force;

(4)   increase exports by at least 8.5 per cent annually;

(5)   reduce the country's dependence on foreign loans, with net foreign assistance expected to finance only 15 per cent of total development expenditure;

(6)   move towards a more equitable distribution of income and wealth by increased taxation of upper income groups, by fixing a minimum wage, by reducing the differences in the salary structure, and by greater emphasis on social security schemes;

(7)   increase the outlay on education 2 1/2 times the level of the Third Plan, and enrolment in primary schools by five million, in secondary schools by one million and in institutes for technical education by 280 per cent;

(8)   protect the entire population from malaria and small pox and to bring about a major improvement in curative health facilities by providing 24,000 additional hospital beds and matching requirements of equipment and medical personnel;

(9)   construct approximately half a million housing units for low income groups; and

(10) launch a major urban works programme to improve the environmental conditions in big cities and to cater to the community needs of the neglected areas.

The total size of the Fourth Plan development programme was fixed at Rs 7,500 crore—an increase of 44 per cent over the previous plan. 65 per cent of the proposed plan outlay (Rs 4,900 crore) was earmarked for the public sector while the remaining 35 per cent was allocated to the private sector.

Unfortunately the Fourth Plan soon become irrelevant. It had been fashioned in the framework of a united country with emphasis on East Pakistan. The separation of Bangladesh in December 1971 rendered it infructuous and inapplicable, and it was given up. Instead, the new government introduced a system of annual plans as the principal instrument for economic development.

The Economy from 1970 to 1978

The political convulsions of the late 1960s and the separation of East Pakistan produced adverse consequences for the economy. The growth rate of domestic product was 0.30 per cent in 1970-71 and 1.17 per cent in 1971-72. It registered a sharp jump to 7.21 per cent in 1972-73 and to 7.74 per cent in 1973-74, which stemmed primarily from the export boom caused by the world-wide rise in raw material prices, as well as the 56.8 per cent devaluation of the rupee on 11 May 1972, which was accompanied by a radical simplification of external trade regulations.

The loss of the captive East Pakistan market for its manufactured goods was no doubt a handicap for West Pakistan, but despite that the outlook for its economy was much brighter than that of its eastern counterpart. West Pakistan was better endowed in basic natural resources; the density of population was 200 per square mile as compared to 1,365 in Bangladesh; West Pakistan's share in GNP was around 60 per cent, it had a well developed infrastructure and was industrially considerably ahead of Bangladesh. At the time of the separation of the East Wing, West Pakistan seemed to be on the threshold of an economic take off.

On 20 December 1971, the Pakistan People's Party (PPP) government assumed power in present-day Pakistan. This government had articulated a radical programme of economic and social reforms in its manifesto. Zulfikar Ali Bhutto had described the economic strategy pursued during the Ayub era as a 'monstrous economic system of loot and plunder which the regime lauded as free enterprise'.

Z.A. Bhutto's Government, under the cover of Martial Law in its first four months, introduced far-reaching reforms in terms of its election manifesto to provide a greater share to the common man and to ensure social justice. These reforms were subsequently elaborated and extended, and covered most facets of socio-economic relationships in our society. The principal ones are described here.

Land reforms were introduced in March 1972 to, *inter alia,* resume land from big landlords and ameliorate the conditions of tenants by re-ordering the tenant-landlord relationship. The land reforms slashed down the ceiling of an individual holding from 36,000 to 12,000 Produce Index Units (PIUs). The balance, with marginal adjustments, was resumed by the State without compensation. The number of owners who filed declarations of land holdings was 11,990 for a total area of 17.55 lac acres. The area allowed to be retained by the owners was 9.05 lac acres while 8.50 lac acres were resumed by government without compensation up to March 1974. Out of this, over 40,194 small farmers and tenants were allotted 2.68 lac acres free of cost, each getting an area equal to a subsistence holding. In addition, for the first time, the tenant was given the right of pre-emption in respect of land in his tenancy.

Labour reforms were introduced in February 1972. These were elaborated and enlarged in August 1973 after detailed discussion at the first Tripartite Conference of Government, Labour and Employees. These reforms sought to guarantee the workers their fundamental rights of association and collective bargaining, provided for greater security of service, and included representation in management and a number of financial benefits such as payment of bonus, enhanced rate of compensation for injuries, group insurance and old age pensions. The law pertaining to trade unions was made more progressive and ensured their speedy registration. As a result, the formation of trade unions showed a healthy growth.

Industrial and corporate reforms were introduced in the broad area of industrial management and the organization of the corporate sector, though the PPP accepted the principle of a mixed economy for the country. Under the Economic Reforms Order of 1 January 1972, the government took over the management of 32 industrial units under 10 basic categories, namely, iron and steel industries, basic metal industries, heavy engineering industries, heavy electrical industries, the assembly and manufacture of motor vehicles, the assembly and manufacture of tractors, heavy and basic chemicals, petro-chemical industries, cement industries, and public utilities, that is, electricity generation, transmission and distribution, and oil refineries.

No compensation was paid on the acquisition of management of these 32 units. However, in November 1973, orders were issued acquiring majority ownership in the public limited companies and the entire equity of the private limited companies of the taken-over units. An amendment was made in the rules in March 1974 to provide for payment of compensation for the acquired shares at market value instead of the break-up value as originally envisaged.

The process of nationalization continued. On 18 March 1972, life insurance businesses in the country were taken over by government, and, for an interim period, the Life Insurance Management Board served as the chief policy making and supervisory body. Then the State Life Insurance Corporation of Pakistan started operation with effect from 1 November 1972. The principal objectives of this nationalization were to run the life insurance business on sound and economic lines; provide a more efficient service to policy holders; maximize the return to policy holders by economizing on expenses and increasing the yield on investments; make life insurance a more effective means of mobilizing national savings; and widen the area of operation of life insurance and make it available to as large a section of the population as possible.

Thereafter, in September 1973, the PPP Government nationalized 26 industrial units producing vegetable ghee under a special Ordinance. On 1 January 1974, the shipping industry was nationalized. The fleet strength of the nationalized companies comprised 27 ships with a total tonnage of 329,306. At the same time the petroleum marketing and distribution companies were nationalized, and so were all Pakistani banks.

The nationalization of banks in January 1974 was of great significance. Its objectives were to direct banking activities towards national socio-economic goals; to distribute equitably bank credit to different classes, sectors and regions; to coordinate banking policy in various areas of feasible joint activity without eliminating healthy competition among banks; and to secure the safety and security of the deposits of account holders.

The nationalized commercial banks were reorganized into five constituent units. A Banking Council consisting of a chairman, a deputy governor of the State Bank, an official of the Finance Ministry and three other government appointed members was established to make policy recommendations to the Federal Government with a view to directing banking activities towards national socio-economic objectives, including formulating policy guidelines for banks, laying down performance criteria, evaluating their performance in the light of these criteria and determining the areas of coordination among banks.

In 1976, the government took over flour milling, cotton ginning and rice husking mills. As against earlier nationalizations which had affected large scale manufacturing and monopoly houses, the nationalization of these small agricultural processing units dealt a blow to small industrialists and traders. Their antagonism manifested itself in the anti-government protests that convulsed the country in March 1977, and led to the imposition of Martial Law in July 1977.

Unfortunately, state owned enterprises during the PPP regime, and particularly thereafter, became an instrument for political patronage or a device for accumulating power. The nationalization programme did not contribute to higher efficiency in the corporatist sense nor could it be viewed as an element of a serious commitment to socialism. In many cases state take-overs were the result of political pressures irrespective of economic logic. Jobs in the public sector were also used as a reward mechanism to political favourites. Over-manning coupled with inefficient management had an adverse impact on financial performance.

The over-all performance of the economy during the first eight years of the 1970s is shown in Table 3.

Table 3

Economic performance from 1970 to 1978			
Year	Growth rate of real GDP	Growth rate of commodity producing sectors	Annual rate of change in consumer price index (CPI)
1970-71	0.30	− 1.42	5.71
1971-72	1.17	1.35	4.69
1972-73	7.21	4.25	9.70
1973-74	7.74	5.24	29.98
1974-75	3.94	− 1.26	26.73
1975-76	3.32	3.48	11.66
1976-77	2.53	1.98	9.24
1977-78	7.38	4.63	6.89

Source: *Pakistan Economy Through the Seventies,* by Syed Nawab Haider Naqvi and Khawaja Sarmad, published by the Pakistan Institute of Development Economics, Islamabad, 1984.

The average growth in GDP for the eight years 1970-78
—during which the Fourth Plan (1970-75) was aborted, and
there were five and a half years of Bhutto's Government,
followed by the first year of Martial Law—was 4.2 per cent.
This was not an unsatisfactory average in view of the
uncertainties produced by institutional changes and a host of
domestic and international stresses and strains. In 1971, the
country had been split into two and considerable effort was
required to restore the battered economy amidst destabilizing
international developments like the energy crisis and world-
wide inflation. In 1973, the economy was jolted by severe floods.
Transport and communications were disrupted, giving rise to
local shortages. Standing export crops were substantially
destroyed along with some of the food stocks. Consequently,
inflationary pressures gathered momentum and prices reached
peak levels.

The greatest jolt came in October 1973, when a war broke
out in the Middle East. It caused the raising of the posted price
of crude oil from $3.01 to $5.12 per barrel in October. In January
1974, the price was raised to $11.60 per barrel. This steep
escalation in oil prices placed serious strains on the economies
of developing, oil importing countries like Pakistan. Their
position was adversely affected both by the increase in oil prices
as well as the accompanying rise in the price of a number of
items such as fertilizers, chemicals and industrial machinery in
which oil enters significantly as raw material or as a source of
energy. The net result was a further deterioration in the terms of
trade of developing countries such as Pakistan. Consequently,
there was an adverse shift in the balance of payments situation,
a loss of real resources and a reduced ability to meet the
requirements of essential investments and the minimum
necessary level of social services. A difficult economic situation
was, however, made worse by some populist, erratic measures.

Fifth Five-Year Plan (1978-83)

The Fifth Five-Year Plan marked the revival of medium term planning after eight years of annual planning characterized by institutional upheaval and great economic uncertainty. This plan was conceived as a comprehensive economic effort and its principal objectives were to:

(1) meet the basic needs of the population and promote equity by providing essential consumer goods;

(2) increase employment and incomes through rapid economic growth;

(3) improve health, education, water supply and transport facilities in both urban and rural areas;

(4) develop backward regions through the expansion of infrastructure and social and technical services; and

(5) lay the foundations for long-term growth by developing basic and engineering industries and technology.

The plan proposed to rely heavily on rapid growth to achieve these objectives. It emphasized the speedy completion of large on-going projects while shifting resources to priority areas of energy, agriculture, water and the social sectors. An investment of Rs 210.22 billion was contemplated—Rs 128.22 billion in the public sector, Rs 62.00 billion in the private sector, and Rs 20 billion outside the Annual Development Programmes for the public sector. As such, the total public sector programme for the period 1978-83 was approximately 70 per cent of the plan size. Of the total public sector programme, agriculture got the largest share of 25.1 per cent, 4.1 per cent for subsidies on fertilizers and 13.4 per cent for water. The power and fuel sectors were allocated 22.7 per cent, transport and communications 16.9 per cent and minerals 11.0 per cent, and the remaining sectors received 24.3 per cent.

Public sector investment during the Fifth Plan almost attained the projected level, and private investment exceeded its target by 20.3 per cent in nominal money terms. However, in inflation adjusted real terms, public sector investment fell short by 33 per cent whereas the private sector experienced a shortfall of 13 per cent. The overall investment ratio estimated at 17.1 per cent in 1977-78 was expected to increase to 19.9 per cent by the end of the plan; it, however, declined to 16.1 per cent in 1982-83. The failure to attain the investment target was mainly due to three factors. Firstly, the disruption in resource availability and higher project costs because of increased prices of raw materials, including oil and manufactured goods. Secondly, geo-political developments within the region forcing the country to accord priority to its defence, besides incurring expenditure on a large number of Afghan refugees. Thirdly, continued world recession, restricting the growth in exports of the country.

The shortfall in investment adversely affected the achievement of targets. GDP increased by 6 per cent as against a target of 7 per cent. Similarly, growth in the agriculture sector was 4.4 per cent against the projected 6 per cent, and manufacturing grew at 9 per cent compared to a targeted rise of 12 per cent.

In the power sector, the installed capacity of power generation increased from 3,280 MW in 1977-78 to 4,780 MW at the end of the plan; 8,833 additional villages were electrified, bringing the total number of such villages to 16,433. Crude oil production increased from 9,900 to 14,311 barrels per day. The production of natural gas increased to 338,418 million cubic feet (MMCFT) as against the benchmark level of 199,920 MMCFT. In the transport and communications sectors, 5,257 kilometers of roads were added. The number of buses increased by 7,341, trucks by 20,510, telephones by 122,000 and post offices by 1,525. The population covered by radio broadcasting grew from 88 to 95 per cent and television coverage from 74 to 82 per cent.

The balance of payments position of the country showed a distinct improvement during the Fifth Plan period. The plan envisaged a real annual growth rate of 11 per cent for exports, almost twice the level of expansion in imports, which were projected at 6.3 per cent per annum. Nevertheless, since imports were over double the level of exports in 1977-78, the actual trade deficit was projected to rise from $1,503 million to $1,614 million by the end of the period. The current account deficit was expected to stabilize around $1 billion, with a substantial increase anticipated in home remittances from Pakistanis working abroad.

The Fifth Plan could not anticipate the rapid deterioration in the world economic environment which followed and, as such, the actual outcome of the balance of payments differed quite significantly from forecasts. Soon after the plan was finalized, the world economy witnessed rising inflationary pressures and mounting balance of payments disequilibria. Volatile fluctuations in the interest and exchange rates caused massive movements of speculative capital, and, above all, there was a rising trend towards protectionism. The sluggish growth in world markets causing contraction in world trade for the first time since 1958, along with a steep decline in the prices of primary products, drastically reduced export earnings of the poorer countries including Pakistan, and also caused a sharp deterioration in the terms of trade.

Although real exports grew faster than imports, the situation was reversed in nominal terms due to a sharp fall in the terms of trade. However, home remittances, an important constituent of invisible receipts, rose from $1,156 million in 1977-78 to $2,850 million in 1982-83, which helped to alleviate the situation.

Given the recessionary conditions of the world economy, real export growth of close to 9 per cent was an impressive accomplishment. Imports, on the other hand, registered an annual compound growth rate of 5 per cent against the target of 6.3 per cent per year, reflecting major import substitution efforts in wheat, fertilizers, cement, sugar, iron and steel, and engineering products. The trade balance in real terms rose by just 1 per cent compared with an annual increase of 1.4 per cent envisaged, despite the pursuit of a liberal import policy throughout the period. Some restraint in the import volume could be attributed to de-linking the rupee from the US dollar on 8 January 1982. The managed floating exchange rate and the consequent depreciation of the rupee also provided a stimulus to export earnings.

On the fiscal front, there was some improvement. The consolidated fiscal deficit fell from 8 per cent of GDP in 1977–78 to 7.1 per cent in 1982-83. Government borrowing for budgetary support from the banking system also declined from 2.8 per cent of GDP in 1977-78 to 1.7 per cent in 1982-83. Non-bank borrowing, however, financed 56 per cent of the budgetary deficit in 1982-83 as compared to about 20 per cent in 1977-78. Government revenues remained at around 16 per cent of GDP. The government's efforts to restrain public expenditure, and thereby cut the budget deficit, resulted in a significant reduction in development expenditure as a proportion of GDP, which fell from 10.5 to 7.7 per cent.

An important achievement of the Fifth Plan was the decline in the rate of inflation which was brought down to 5 per cent in 1982-83 from an average of 10.5 per cent during the first eight years of the 1970s. This was possible due to higher real growth as well as better demand management, and improved international conditions.

Sixth Five-Year Plan (1983-88)

The Sixth Plan was formulated against the background of the growth momentum established during the Fifth Plan. Its total size was proposed at Rs 495 billion which was more than twice that of the previous plan. Of this, Rs 295 billion was allocated to the public sector and Rs 200 billion for the private sector. The principal targets articulated were increases in:
(1) GDP by 6.5 per cent per annum;
(2) family income by Rs 900 per annum;
(3) agricultural production by 5 per cent annually;
(4) industrial production by 9 per cent annually; and
(5) expansion in merchandise exports from an annual level of $2.43 to $4.91 billion by the end of the period.
Furthermore, it envisaged the creation of 4 million new job opportunities, the construction of 15,000 kilometers of new roads from villages to cities, the reclamation of 3 million acres of land for cultivation

which had been destroyed by waterlogging and salinity, the reduction in the share of net external resources in the proposed gross investment from 24 to 16 per cent, and a nearly four-fold increase in private savings. It also envisaged during the plan period a rise in the literacy rate from 23.5 to 48.6 per cent, a reduction in infant mortality from 90 to 50 per 1,000 and an increase in access to clean water from 38 to 60 per cent of the total population.

The strategy of the Sixth Plan was succinctly summarized as 'development of the people, by the people and for the people'. It stressed the importance of ensuring an equitable distribution of the fruits of development to the whole population, and not restricting it to a privileged few.

As regards the sectoral allocation of development funds, energy received the largest share, almost 20 as against 17 per cent in the Fifth Plan. The share of agriculture including water, rose from 16 per cent in the previous plan to 18 per cent, while the share of social sectors, particularly education and health, rose from 7.5 to 11.5 per cent. In financial terms, the allocations for these sectors were increased three-fold over the plan period.

So far as actual implementation was concerned, it was a qualified success. It maintained the momentum of growth established in the previous plan. External resource inflows made a significant contribution to its growth performance; these inflows financed about 20 per cent of gross investment. As against the overall growth target of 6.5 per cent per annum, the actual achievement was 6.2 per cent. The annual growth rate in agriculture of 3.8 per cent was considerably below the projection of 4.9 per cent. Large scale manufacturing sector grew at an annual rate of 7.5 per cent as compared to an expected 10 per cent.

The energy situation improved, with electricity generation recording an annual growth rate of 13.6 per cent. The increase in oil and gas production was also impressive. By 1987-88, oil production was 43,000 barrels per day as against the target of 21,000 barrels. The economy, however, suffered huge losses on account of load shedding.

In the social sectors there was modest improvement although most of the targets could not be achieved. The participation rate of children in primary schools went up to 63.5 per cent as against the goal of 75 per cent. The infant mortality rate was reduced from 98.5 to 80 per 1,000, and life expectancy increased from 55 to 61 years.

The balance of payments position during the Sixth Plan highlights the fragility of Pakistan's external sector. Remittances from the Middle East fell sharply from the expectation of 10 per cent annual increase. A robust expansion of exports, however, compensated this adverse development, and the current account deficit of around 3 per cent of GNP was not unsustainably high. The country, however, remained vulnerable to external shocks on account of its narrow export base.

A disconcerting feature of the performance of the Sixth Plan was the deterioration on the fiscal front. The plan had estimated net foreign resource inflows at $4.07 billion. Actual availability was around $2.8 billion. The shortfall in external resource inflows necessitated higher domestic borrowing. The government, however, failed to broaden the tax base and to improve its elasticity and equitable imposition, mainly on account of pressure from vested interests; it was very difficult to tax the prosperous elite adequately.

Because of pressures on expenditure due to mounting debt service obligations, increased defence allocations and inadequate revenue raising efforts, there was a steep rise in domestic debt. The high interest payments on domestic debt resulted in partly 'crowding out' private investment. In the Sixth Plan period, the government started borrowing not only to cover its development budget, but also its current expenditures. This fiscal position could not be sustained for long.

The Sixth Plan had laid emphasis on reduction in income inequalities. This objective could not be achieved, and, on the contrary, all available data points to its increase. However, the average income of considerable sections of the poor did grow on account of remittances from the Middle East. According to the Household Income and Expenditure Survey of 1986, the average income of the lowest 40 per cent rose by less than 80 per cent in nominal terms between 1979 and 1985. During the same period, the average for the top 20 per cent rose by 94 per cent, and that for the top 10 per cent more than doubled.

Seventh Five-Year Plan (1988-93)

The Seventh Five-Year Plan was prepared in the context of the Second Perspective Plan spanning the period 1988-2003. This fifteen-year perspective emphasized efficient growth in output as well as improvement in the quality of life. Of the longer perspective targets, about 23.6 per cent of GDP, 22 per cent of investment, 23.8 per cent of exports, 26.2 per cent of imports and 21 per cent of revenue, were envisaged to be attained during 1988-93.

The Seventh Plan had several basic objectives:
(1) the gradual elimination of unemployment, especially among the educated;
(2) social and cultural development, with the main accent on the provision of food, housing, medical and education facilities;
(3) human resources development;
(4) self-reliance by reducing dependence on external aid and by laying the foundations for long term growth through building technological skills, and investing in basic engineering industries and scientific and technological research;
(5) maximizing the private sector's contribution to growth and carrying forward the process of privatization;
(6) reduction in fiscal deficits;
(7) stregthening of the balance of payments; and
(8) control of inflation through appropriate fiscal and monetary policies.

The original size of this plan was proposed at Rs 660.2 billion at 1987-88 prices, of which Rs 367.8 billion, or 55.7 per cent, was for the private sector. The public sector allocation included subsidies and some other non-investment expenditures treated as developmental. The public sector investment programme was accordingly placed at about Rs 350 billion, which was subsequently reduced to Rs 322.95 billion on account of resource constraints.

The plan projected an annual GDP growth rate of 6.5 per cent, which was to be sustained by an annual growth of 4.7 per cent in the agricultural sector and 8.1 per cent in the manufacturing sector. The other sectors were expected to grow at an annual rate of 6.7 per cent. In view of the annual 3 per cent increase in population, the increase in per capita income, on the basis of 6.5 per cent annual rise in domestic output, was projected at Rs 536 during the period compared to Rs 466 during the previous plan.

Table 4 shows the public sector development expenditures in the Seventh Plan and compares these with the development expenditures under the Sixth Plan. The share of agriculture and water in public sector allocations was reduced from 16.3 per cent in the Sixth Plan to 13.5 per cent. The energy sector allocation, however, was increased from 34.8 to 38.2 per cent. There was a sharp decline in the share of industry from 5.3 to 2.8 per cent. This, of course, reflected the government's desire to assign a primary role to the private sector in industrial development. The expenditures on the transport and communications sectors, an important component of infrastructure, showed a small increase from 17.3 to 18.9 per cent. A significant amount of Rs 25.3 billion was also made available in the Seventh Plan for special provincial budgetary development programmes.

The savings strategy of the 1988-93 plan envisaged a domestic savings rate of 12.6 per cent of GDP and a national savings rate of 14.4 per cent of GNP. Domestic savings in the previous decade had averaged only 8 per cent of GDP. For a significant increase in the savings rate, the plan emphasized the reorganization of the capital market, reduction in fiscal deficits and the phasing out of subsidies.

Table 4

Public sector development expenditures in Sixth and Seventh Plans		
(in Rs 000,000,000)		
Sector	Sixth Plan (1983-88)	Seventh Plan (1988-93)
Agriculture	17.3	15.6
Water	22.0	28.4
Energy	84.2	124.3
Industry	12.9	9.0
Minerals	1.1	7.0
Transport and communications	41.7	61.5
Physical planning and housing	22.7	20.0
Education and manpower	14.3	25.7
Health and nutrition	10.4	13.3
Population welfare and women's development programme	1.7	3.5
Other/miscellaneous programmes	13.3	16.3
Sub total	241.6	324.7
Plus: special provincial development programmes	2.7	25.3
Total	244.3	350.0

Source: Planning and Development Division, Government of Pakistan, Islamabad.

As regards investment strategy, the plan envisaged a gross investment rate, including changes in stocks, of 16.6 per cent of GNP, and a fixed investment rate of 15.4 per cent. The share of external finance in total investment was, however, expected to decline from 18 per cent in 1987-88 to about 11 per cent in 1992-93.

With respect to external resource inflows to bridge the savings-investment gap, the plan projected a requirement of $12.6 billion of which it hoped $10.2 billion would be received through official channels. In view of the undisbursed pipeline of $6.5 billion at the commencement of the plan period, it was hoped that an annual external commitment of $1.8 billion by way of aid and loans would ensure the availability of the required amount of external finance.

Unfortunately, the performance of the Seventh Plan was adversely affected by a variety of unforeseen factors on the domestic and international fronts. The Gulf War, the persistence of the civil war in Afghanistan, the breakup of the Soviet Union, recessionary conditions in Pakistan's export markets, frequent changes of government within the country, an uncertain political milieu, civil disturbances in Karachi and other urban areas of Sindh, and the floods of 1988-89 and 1992-93, contributed to slowing growth in the country.

The overall growth performance, because of these internal and external constraints, was limited to 5 per cent annually, agricultural production advanced at an annual rate of 3.8 per cent, and manufacturing grew by 5.9 per cent annually, while the plan had envisaged 6.5, 4.7 and 8.1 per cent respectively. Other sectors moved ahead at an annual rate of 5.3 instead of the planned 6.7 per cent. In aggregate terms, 74 per cent of the output growth targets were realized.

On the external front, the current account deficit climbed from $1.68 billion in 1987-88 to $3.69 billion in 1992-93. The principal factor responsible for this adverse development was the decline in home remittances and higher payments for services. The deterioration in the current external account occurred despite massive depreciation in the external value of the rupee. The rupee-dollar exchange rate fell from Rs 18.12 per dollar in July 1988 to Rs 27.15 in June 1993.

On the fiscal front also, the hopes visualised were not realized. Targets in respect of additional resource mobilization and the containment of current expenditures could not be achieved. Table 5 depicts the trends of fiscal deficit as a percentage of GDP.

Table 5

Fiscal deficit as percentage of GDP	
Year	Percentage
1988-89	7.4
1989-90	6.5
1990-91	8.7
1991-92	7.4
1992-93	8.0

Source: Economic Survey 1995-96: Government of Pakistan, Finance Division, Economic Advisor Wing, Islamabad.

As a consequence of these unsustainable deficits, the domestic debt increased by almost 109 per cent—from Rs 290 billion in 1987-88 to Rs 605 billion in 1992-93. At the same time, inflationary pressures during this period assumed uncomfortable proportions. This was primarily due to higher than planned expansion of monetary assets which registered an annual growth of 15.2 per cent instead of the target of 12.5. The increase in domestic credit was Rs 326.7 billion, which exceeded the projection of Rs 179.9 billion by a wide margin. The main cause of excessive credit expansion was budgetary support provided by the banking system to the government, which amounted to Rs 175.6 billion as against the plan target of Rs 51.7 billion.

Table 6 sets out changes in the twelve-month averages of the Consumer Price Index (CPI) and Sensitive Price Index (SPI) for the five years of the Seventh Plan.

Table 6

Twelve-month averages of CPI and SPI					
	1988-89	1989-90	1990-91	1991-92	1992-93
CPI	10.4	6.0	12.8	9.6	9.3
SPI	13.5	6.1	12.6	9.3	10.3

Source: State Bank of Pakistan, Karachi.

The Seventh Plan was somewhat ambitious in its targets, particularly regarding growth and resource mobilization. However, despite many internal and external constraints, it achieved respectable growth in output during the first four years. The impetus in GDP growth slowed down in the final year, 1992-93, to 2.3 per cent due to floods and crop failures. As a result of widespread flooding in the cotton and wheat producing regions of the country, and the subsequent infestation of the cotton crop by curl virus, agricultural output declined during the year by 5.3 per cent; in fact, this was the first negative growth in the agricultural sector since 1983-84. Growth in the manufacturing sector also slowed to 5.4 per cent as a result of damage to the cotton crop, which affected the textile industry.

During the Seventh Plan period, Pakistan began to implement a policy of privatizing government-owned entities. The Privatization Commission was established in January 1991 and has continued to carry out this programme despite numerous changes of government and personnel manning the Commission. The main objectives of the privatization policy of successive governments have been to reduce the demand on government resources, curtail the size of the public debt, raise funds for priority sectors, improve the efficiency of the economy through the sale of state-owned enterprises and stimulate foreign direct investment.

This period also witnessed reforms in the financial sector which were introduced in 1989 following the government's loan agreement with the World Bank. As a result of these reforms, government borrowing from the banking sector is now based on market related rates. Commercial and investment banking has been opened to the private sector and government has embarked on a programme of privatizing nationalized commercial banks. To date, two of them have been privatized. With the government borrowing at market rates, and the reduction of flows of subsidized credit, the distortions previously affecting the credit market are being phased out. Along with these reforms, the powers of the State Bank of Pakistan and the Corporate Law Authority have been enhanced through the grant of autonomy in the discharge of their functions.

Eighth Five-Year Plan (1993-98)

The Eighth Five-Year Plan was prepared within the framework of a Fifteen-Year Perspective Plan covering the period 1993-2008. The Perspective Plan had a long term vision for the country based on national objectives and the aspirations of the people. The distinguishing features of the Eighth Plan included 'a sharper focus on policy initiatives, on the management system, on the need for selectivity in sectoral programmes and on an express recognition of the fact that consolidation and rehabilitation of the political and social infrastructure is as important as new investment'.

Its proposed size at 1992-93 prices was Rs 1,700.5 billion, representing an increase of 48 per cent over the estimated actual outlays of the Seventh Plan. Public sector development expenditure was projected to climb by 36.1 per cent, and private fixed investment by 59.1 per cent, compared to the previous plan. The relative size of the Sixth, Seventh and Eighth Plans are set out in Table 7.

Table 7

	Size of the Sixth, Seventh and Eighth Plans					
					(in Rs 000,000,000)	
Plan	At current prices			At 1992-93 prices		
	Public sector outlay	Private fixed investment	Total	Public sector outlay	Private fixed investment	Total
Sixth Plan (actual)	242.4	203.3	445.7	471.6	441.3	912.9
Seventh Plan (expected)	463.2	485.6	948.8	552.8	596.2	1,149.0
Eighth Plan (target)	923.1	1168.5	2,091.6	752	·948.4	1,700.5

Source: Eighth Five-Year Plan, Government of Pakistan, Planning Commission, June 1994.

The Eighth Plan carried forward the shift in investment from the public to the private sector. It proposed a public sector development programme (PSDP) of Rs 752.1 billion. In addition to the capital formation component in PSDP, the public sector allocation also included fixed investment by local bodies and financial institutions, as well as some elements of current expenditure.

The growth target envisaged an annual increase of 7 per cent in domestic output, supported by an annual increase of 4.9 per cent in the agricultural sector, 9.9 per cent in manufacturing and 6.7 per cent in services. The plan hoped to achieve its proposed growth target in a milieu characterized by equity, stability and sustainability. For ensuring this, it aimed at reducing the fiscal deficit to half, from 8 to 4 per cent of GDP, and to bring down the current external account deficit from US $ 3.7 billion to US $1.8 billion, that is, from 7 to 2.4 per cent of GDP. It also proposed to restrict long-term external debt to 36 per cent of

GDP and keep monetary expansion below the nominal growth of GDP.

The other important macro-economic objectives of the plan included reduction in the rate of inflation from 9.3 to 6 per cent, a rise in the national savings to GDP ratio from 13.6 to 18 per cent, significant reduction in the dimensions of high cost debt by the utilization of privatization proceeds for this purpose, and the generation of 6.2 million new jobs as against 3.2 million under the Seventh Plan.

The Eighth Plan emphasized the importance of good governance for realizing its development objectives and targets. It sought to ensure equality of opportunity through merit, transparency, access to education, access to health care, and vertical mobility. It also proposed decisive action against defaulters of tax, bank loans and utility bills.

Poverty alleviation has been assigned a high priority in the 1993-98 plan. It recommended long-term measures through the Social Action Programme (SAP) and by the initiation of schemes for targeted groups such as Zakat, Baitul Maal, food stamps and self-employment. It was also ambitious in the social sectors. It proposed an increase in the participation rate for boys at the level of primary school education from 85 to 95 per cent and for girls from 54 to 82 per cent. In the health sector, it envisaged full immunization of mother and child against preventable infectious diseases. Life expectancy, the plan hoped, would go up from 61.5 years is 1992-93 to 63.5 in 1997-98. The lowering of the population growth rate was one of its primary objectives, aiming at reducing it from 2.9 to 2.7 per cent between 1992-93 and 1997-98, and 2.6 per cent by 2000. The main focus of the population welfare strategy was to expand the coverage of the population from 20 to over 80 per cent, and to improve efficiency in implementation.

In the energy sector, the Eighth Plan proposed to increase power generation capacity from 9,786 to 16,422 MW, gas production by 38 per cent, refining capacity by 183 per cent, and oil production from 60,000 to 123,300 barrels a day. An

important target in this sector is the electrification of 19,70(
villages.

The Eighth Five-Year Plan is now in its fourth year. Recently
an official mid-term review for the period 1993-96 has beer
released by the Planning Commission. It paints a discouragin;
picture of the economic performance during these three years
The overall growth of the economy has been well below th
stipulated target. Moreover, the pattern of growth an(
investment, its financing, the mobilization of domestic resources
progress on the path of self-reliance and the pace of privatizatio
have all been at considerable variance with targets visualized.

During the first three years of the Eighth Plan, GDP grew a
an average annual rate of 5 instead of the 7 per cent target. Th
performance of the agricultural sector registered an annua
growth rate of 5 per cent, just above the target. The record o
the manufacturing sector, however, was quite disappointing a
its annual growth rate of 4.5 per cent fell below the planne(
9.9 per cent. The large scale manufacturing sector grew a
only 2.6 per cent per year compared to the target of 10.5 pe
cent. This was partly due to delay in the completion of nev
projects which were envisaged to enhance the productiv
capacity of this sector, and also because of the unsatisfactor
law and order situation in the country in general and in Sindh i
particular.

As industrialization has a crucial role in accelerating growtl
and in strengthening balance of payments, its lacklustr
performance in the first thee years of the Eighth Plan is a matte
of deep concern. The shortfall experienced in these years i
unlikely to be compensated in the remaining two years o
account of capacity constraints, aging capital, high interest rates
lack of demand both at home and abroad, and the transitio
from very high protection to a relatively less protective milieu
The performance of the construction sector during the first thre
years was also quite disappointing; its annual growth rate wa
2.4 per cent as against the plan of 7 per cent.

It is heartening to note, however, that the electricity and ga
distribution sectors achieved an annual average growth rate c

9.2 per cent during this period as against the targeted 7.8 per cent. As regards the services sector, its performance was almost in line with the realized rate of aggregate growth of the economy. It achieved an annual advance of 4.7 per cent as against the planned 6.7 per cent. Within the services' sector, major shortfalls were experienced in trade, transport and communications, public administration and the defence sub-sectors. The sub-sector of financial institutions and insurance, and ownership of dwellings, however, achieved their targets.

The tempo of investment activity in the economy during the first three years of this period was disappointing. The growth rates in total fixed investment as well as in the public and private sectors were 4.6, 1.8 and 7.1 per cent respectively. The total fixed investments of Rs 255.7 billion in 1993-94, Rs 260.1 billion in 1994-95 and Rs 294.0 billion in 1995-96 (at 1992-93 prices) were below their respective targets of Rs 276.3 billion, Rs 304.5 billion and Rs 338.0 billion. As such, total fixed investment at 1992-93 prices remained 11.9 per cent short of the planned target. Private sector investment during 1993-96 stood at Rs 439.8 billion in 1992-93 prices, which represented 46.4 per cent implementation of the fixed investment target for this sector. Moreover, public sector fixed investment during the first three years of Rs 370.0 billion at 1992-93 prices was 10 per cent below the expected Rs 411.3 billion.

The share of national savings in total investment during the first three years was 70 per cent as against the target of 83.3 per cent, while that of external resource inflows was 30 per cent instead of the projected 16.7 per cent. Another disconcerting feature of economic performance during 1993-96 was the decline in national savings as a percentage of GDP from 13.6 to 12.4 per cent.

Fiscal performance during the first three years of the plan showed mixed trends. Total revenues which were projected to increase from 18 to 19.8 per cent of GDP have, in fact, averaged 17.3 per cent. The government has, however, been able to reduce its expenditure by 2.8 per cent of GDP. The overall fiscal deficit has been brought down from 8 to 6.3 per cent of GDP in the third year.

Monetary expansion during 1993-96 was significantly higher than the projected annual 12 per cent. The actual expansion during 1993-94, 1994-95 and 1995-96 was 16.9, 16.6 and 14.9 per cent respectively. This was due to excessive government borrowing for budgetary support and to build up foreign exchange reserves.

Monetary ecstasy, lower than projected real growth and persistent depreciation in the external value of the currency resulted in unleashing uncomfortable inflationary pressures in the economy. The rate of inflation, as measured by the GDP deflator, has averaged 12 per cent during the first three years compared to 6.5 per cent envisaged in macro-economic projections.

With respect to the balance of payments, the cumulative deficit on current account in nominal dollar terms exceeded the plan target mainly due to deterioration in the trade account. Exports (fob) during the first three years increased on an average by 8.9 per cent per annum as against the target of 12.5 per cent in nominal dollar terms, while at the same time imports (fob) rose by 7.1 as against an expected 7.5 per cent. The cumulative deficit in the trade account surpassed the target by 70.02 per cent.

The invisible accounts, however, showed a marked improvement. A significant increase in the inflow of foreign currency accounts (FCAs), coupled with a moderate decline in invisible payments, reduced the cumulative deficit on the invisible account to $932 billion as against the projection of $2,116 million. Consequently, the current account deficit was contained at 4.8 per cent of GDP as against the plan figure of 3.9 per cent.

The achievement on the external capital account was quite heartening. The long-term net capital inflows exceeded the target by a significant margin because of a sharp increase in the inflows of private long-term capital. Foreign investment, both direct and portfolio, increased from $443 million in 1992-93 to $1,296 million in 1995-96.

A welcome feature of the Eighth Plan during the first three years was the successful completion of Phase I of the Social Action Programme in 1995-96. During the period 1993-96, 13,356 primary schools were opened, 5,794 buildings for shelterless schools were constructed and 6,319 additional classrooms have been added to the existing primary schools. In primary health care, 141 basic health units (BHUs), 111 urban health centres and 100 rural health centres (RHCs) have been constructed, while 805 BHUs and 104 RHCs were upgraded. 14.4 million children have been immunized, 14,546 traditional birth attendants were trained, and 40,200 lady health workers were recruited, trained and deployed. The population welfare programme during 1993-96 concentrated on both the construction and expansion of services, which increased by 50 per cent, while a contraceptive prevalence rate of 22 per cent was achieved. In rural water supply 55 per cent, and in sanitation 23.3 per cent, of the population was covered.

The performance of the economy during the first three years, 1993-96, has been generally lacklustre. Only about 52.2 per cent of the gross domestic product, 48 per cent of investment and 39.1 per cent of national savings targets have been realized. To achieve the Eighth Plan GDP growth target, the economy will require an annual growth rate of 11.5 per cent during the remaining two years, which appears highly unlikely. This would require agriculture growing annually by 4 per cent, manufacturing by 21.6 per cent, construction by 21.8 per cent and commerce by 17.1 per cent.

Despite significant improvement in the provision of social services, and the reduction in rural-urban disparities, structural changes and stabilization programmes recommended in the plan have not been effectively implemented. Unemployment and inflation also remain problems of grave concern.

Table 8 sets out the GNP of Pakistan, the contribution of the various sectors to the economy and the sectoral growth rates for the ten years 1988-89 to 1996-97.

Table 8

GNP at constant factor cost of 1980-81

(in Rs 000,000)

Sector	1988-89	1989-90	1990-91	1991-92	1992-93	1993-94	1994-95	1995-96 (R)	1996-97 (P)
1. Agriculture	105,917	109,127	114,542	125,425	118,795	125,005	133,215	140,240	141,223
Major crops	51,842	51,795	54,741	63,213	53,354	54,018	58,714	62,938	60,097
Minor crops	18,205	19,147	19,820	20,290	21,092	23,754	25,395,	26,237	27,136
Livestock	30,614	32,481	34,105	36,133	38,308	40,599	42,848	45,252	48,175
Fishing	3,999	4,325	4,430	4,650	4,909	5,442	5,047	4,904	4,941
Forestry	1,257	1,379	1,446	1,139	1,132	1,192	1,211	909	874
2. Mining and quarrying	2,071	2,269	2,504	2,565	2,642	2,765	2,646	2,833	2,891
3. Manufacturing	70,300	74,324	78,969	85,324	89,889	94,734	98,228	102,554	104,381
Large scale	51,244	53,667	56,577	61,051	63,577	66,212	67,310	69,039	68,051
Small scale	19,056	20,657	22,392	24,273	26,312	28,522	30,918	33,515	36,330
4. Construction	16,937	17,466	18,462	19,566	20,701	21,040	21,253	21,944	22,475
5. Electricity and gas distribution	12,125	13,896	15,424	16,823	17,897	18,464	21,572	21,601	24,101
6. Transport, storage and communication	37,716	40,184	42,719	47,189	50,333	52,174	54,342	54,683	57,435
7. Wholesale and retail trade	67,305	69,655	73,380	78,760	81,061	83,340	87,245	92,613	95,073
8. Finance and insurance	9,743	9,793	9,913	10,343	11,065	12,629	13,426	14,694	14,912
9. Ownership of dwellings	21,928	23,086	24,305	25,588	26,939	28,361	29,858	31,435	33,095
10. Public admin. and defence	29,852	30,667	31,679	32,495	33,295	33,759	34,814	35,917	37,194
11. Services	30,054	32,017	34,108	36,335	38,708	41,236	43,929	46,798	49,854
12. GDP (fc)	403,948	422,484	446,005	480,413	491,325	513,635	540,528	565,302	582,639
13. Indirect taxes	57,269	58,359	59,345	63,722	62,156	60,458	61,584	63,431	66,404
14. Subsidies	7,351	6,741	5,390	5,004	4,026	3,234	3,847	3,014	2,026
15. GDP (mp)	453,866	474,102	499,960	539,131	549,455	570,859	598,265	625,719	647,017
16. Net factor income from abroad	14,933	17,163	9,457	4,949	3,734	1,319	4,031	-1849	
17. GNP (fc)	418,881	439,647	455,462	485,362	495,059	514,954	544,559	563,433	576,802
18. GNP (mp)	468,799	491,265	509,417	544,080	553,189	572,178	602,296	623,870	641,180
19. Population (in millions)	107,04	110,36	113,78	117,31	120,83	124,45	128,01	131,63	135,28
20. Per capita income (fc-Rs)	3,913	3,984	4,003	4,137	4,097	4,138	4,254	4,281	4,263

Government spokesmen have painted a grim picture of the performance of the economy during the current fiscal year 1996-97. According to indications, the GDP growth rate is likely to be about 3 per cent as against the target of 6.3 per cent. Growth in the important sector of agriculture would in all probability not exceed 1 per cent because of declines in the output of cotton, wheat and sugar cane as compared to the previous year. The projection for agriculture for the current year was 5 per cent growth.

The manufacturing sector is expected to register a negative growth of 1.4 per cent in large scale industry, and not the positive target of 7.2 per cent. An equally gloomy picture is provided by the country's balance of payments. The current account deficit for 1996-97 is estimated at $4.5 billion or 7 per cent of GDP as against the target of 3 per cent recommended by the International Monetary Fund. The budget deficit at the end of June 1997 is going to be over 6 per cent of GDP as against the target of 4 per cent, primarily because the increase in tax revenue has been significantly below budget projections. Inflation during 1996-97 as measured by Combined Consumer Price Index is now forecast at 12.5 per cent as against the target of 8.5 per cent, and 10.8 per cent in 1995-96.

Despite these gloomy indicators, the plan for 1997-1998, the terminal year of the Eighth Five-Year Plan, has envisaged a GDP growth rate of 6 per cent, inflation at 9 per cent and investment to grow to Rs 330.8 billion. The overall growth rate of 6 per cent is planned to be achieved as a result of 7.2 per cent growth in manufacturing, 5.1 per cent in agriculture, 6.5 per cent in electricity and gas, and 5.9 per cent in the services sector. These optimistic projections for 1997-98 are based on the assumption that the economy would respond positively to the various economic revival packages of the recently elected Nawaz Sharif Government. The task of appropriately handling the short and medium term stabilization of the economy is a formidable one. The recent economic experience of a number of developing countries clearly demonstrates that structural reforms designed to revitalize the economy do not work in the presence of large macro-economic imbalances. An inadequate and prolonged stabilization policy can fail any programme of structural reforms. The current economic situation demands both an improved diagnosis of the key problem areas as well as a set of policies designed to achieve the short and medium objectives of growth with stabilization in an environment of highly constrained financial resources.

Assessment of Pakistan's Development Record: Sunshine and Shadows

A study of Pakistan's development record reveals that there is an essential continuity between various plan and non-plan periods, notwithstanding the fact that each plan has its own approach and features conditioned strongly by a critical evaluation of the past and changing internal and external factors. The fundamental problem for planners has been how—under the severely limiting conditions of scarce financial resources and institutional inadequacies—to find some way to liberate the people from the crushing burden of poverty. Successive plans appear as stages in the nation's determined struggle to throw off the oppressive yoke of poverty which dampens the spirit, inhibits progress and which the Holy Prophet (PBUH) warned us against as likely to lead to *kufr* (disbelief).

The declared general objectives of our Five-Year Plans can be summarized as:

(1) maximum feasible increase in domestic output by accelerated industrialization and stepped up agricultural growth;
(2) improvement in balance of payments;
(3) enhanced opportunities of gainful employment;
(4) progress in provision of social services—education, health, housing and social welfare;
(5) strengthening and expansion of physical infrastructure;
(6) control of menacing growth of population;

(7) satisfaction of basic needs of the people and the promotion of equity;

(8) balanced regional development;

(9) development of human resources; and

(10) laying down long-term foundations for self-reliant growth through the build up of technological skills, investment in basic engineering industries, and scientific and technological research.

It has generally been the endeavour of Pakistani planners to produce realistic plans which the country could reasonably hope to achieve, rather than 'bold' plans. In actual practice, however, estimates of financial resources, both internal and external, have proved optimistic, primarily on account of political difficulties in mobilizing adequate domestic non-inflationary resources. The plans could also be termed as 'liberal' in so far as they have sought to make maximum use of market mechanisms, and have relied on fiscal, monetary, exchange and trade measures rather than direct controls when possible. The private sector, however, has for long been subjected to a complex and counter-productive system of controls which resulted in distortions of investment priorities. Regarding the respective roles of public and private investment, the approach has generally been pragmatic, with public investment supplementing rather than displacing private investment. Only during the period 1972-77 did the government follow a policy of extensive nationalization, without due regard to the public sector's managerial and administrative capacity.

The growth record of Pakistan's planned development has been quite commendable and compares favourably with other countries in South Asia. The flow of goods and services from economic activities within the country, measured by GDP, has expanded more than ten-fold between 1949-50 and 1995-96, that is, an annual compound rate of growth of 5.2 per cent in real terms, after adjusting for inflation. Consequently, in terms of 1959-60 prices, per capita income increased from Rs 370 in 1949-50 to Rs 1,040 in 1995-96, despite a massive increase in population from 33.4 million to over 130 million.

The growth in the economy has been associated with its structural transformation. The relative share of manufacturing has risen from 7.75 per cent of GDP in 1949-50 to 18 per cent in 1995-96, while that of agriculture has declined from 53 to around 25 per cent. Sectoral employment has also undergone changes but these have been relatively less sharp. However, agriculture still continues to absorb around 48 per cent of the labour force. During the post-1970 period, a significant increase in the relative importance of services is visible; its share rose from 37 per cent of domestic output in 1949-50 to about 49 per cent in 1995-96. Notwithstanding this apparent structural diversification, the critical and dominant role of agriculture in the economy is quite discernible as about one half of manufactured output and nearly four-fifths of Pakistan's exports are agro-based.

A noteworthy feature of Pakistan's economic progress has been the achievement of respectable growth rates with relatively modest rates of investment. This is reflected in the low rates of incremental capital-output ratios, specially in the Third and Fifth Five-Year Plans. Table 9 indicates this feature of our planned development.

Table 9

Incremental capital output ratios (ICORO)	
Plan	ICORO
Second Plan (1960-65)	3.2
Third Plan (1965-70)	2.6
Non-Plan Period (1970-78)	3.4
Fifth Plan (1978-83)	2.4
Sixth Plan (1983-88)	3.3
Seventh Plan (1988-93)	4.0

Source: Planning Commission, Government of Pakistan, Islamabad.

It cannot be denied that Pakistan, which at the time of Independence was regarded by some as an economic wasteland, has, through concerted development efforts, institutionalized growth. The country has also moved out of the first stage of industrialization focused on consumer products to more sophisticated basic and heavy engineering goods. In agriculture, the growth has kept ahead of population, an achievement which has eluded many developing countries.

In social development, where progress has been uneven and mediocre, various quality of life indices still reflect a distinct improvement over the years. Life expectancy at birth has increased from 37 years in 1950 to 62 in 1995-96. The crude death rate has dropped to one-third of the level prevalent at Independence. The public health system has developed over the years, though not at the desired pace. There has also been a marked improvement in calories and protein availability. Per capita food intake estimated at 2,618 calories per day for 1994-95 is above the recommended dietary allowance (RDA) of 2,550 calories; likewise protein intake of 67.72 grams is above the RDA of 60 grams.

The educational network has shown substantial expansion. Enrolment at the primary level has increased from 0.77 million in 1948 to 11.48 million in 1995-96. There are at present 24 universities, 157 professional colleges, 707 arts and science colleges and 687 secondary vocational institutes in the country.

These achievements, however, have been marred by shortcomings, mainly in the following five areas:

(1) growing macro-economic imbalances reflected in a huge savings-investment gap, and unsustainable budget and balance of payments deficits;
(2) physical infrastructure constraints;
(3) poor record in the field of human resources development;
(4) population explosion and rising unemployment; and
(5) decline in the quality of governance.

Pakistan's economy has for several years been experiencing baffling macro-economic imbalances which, unless effectively tackled on the basis of a well designed and properly integrated programme of economic policies and programmes, could pose a serious threat to socio-economic stability, apart from disrupting the economy's momentum of growth.

Savings and investment rates in Pakistan are unusually low, even relative to many other low income countries, averaging annually 14.8 and 19.6 per cent of GNP during the five years ending 1995-96. The average saving rates for all low income economies in 1994 was 28 per cent. At these low rates of savings and investment, it would not be possible for Pakistan to support future economic growth of 7 per cent a year, which is socially necessary, in view of Pakistan's neglected infrastructure system and low levels of investment in social sectors. Efforts to maintain a high rate of growth without mobilizing more national savings would result in a rapid accumulation of non-concessional external debt, with serious consequences for the balance of payments position of the country in the not too distant future.

Various reasons have been put forward to explain Pakistan's poor savings performance. These include: the existence of a large, unorganized underground or 'black' economy whose savings are not reflected in official statistics; a feudal outlook characterized by wasteful expenditure; conspicuous consumption and ostentatious living; a development strategy which has emphasized the production of consumer goods; rates of inflation higher than the rate of return on savings; a high population growth rate with-a concomitant high dependency ratio; low level of per capita income; and deficiencies in the methods used to prepare official statistics of savings. A frequently cited reason is, however, a culturally induced bias in favour of consumption. But while such a bias would affect the propensity to save, it cannot by itself explain all aspects of Pakistan's savings performance and, by constantly citing this factor, the importance of other determinants tend to be either disregarded or discounted. In our case it is quite clear that inadequate returns on financial savings and unequal and inefficient distribution of credit have exercised an inhibiting impact on the process of savings and investment. Admittedly, the real rate of return is not the only determinant of savings, but the evidence suggests that it is far more important than bankers and policy makers have acknowledged for a long time.

The main imbalance between savings and investment in Pakistan arises in the public sector. The issue of mobilization of domestic resources for the public sector, however, goes beyond that of raising the rate of public savings. In the public sector, domestic resources should be mobilized not only to raise the savings rate but also to meet the recurring cost of public services.

The budget deficit, that is, the gap between consolidated public revenues and expenditures, is currently one of the most serious macro problems facing Pakistan's economy. The consolidated fiscal deficit during the period 1980-81 to 1991-92 averaged 7.2 per cent of GDP. It was brought down to an annual average of 6.4 per cent during the four fiscal years ending June 1996. In 1995-96, it amounted to Rs 137.8 billion or 6.3 per cent. During the current fiscal year, 1996-97, it was hoped that it would be reduced to 4 per cent of the anticipated GDP, which it now appears was unrealistic.

As a result of persistent high budget deficits, the level of domestic and external debt, and their servicing, have been increasing sharply. The stock of domestic debt over the past five years has more than doubled, from Rs 445.1 billion in 1990-91 to Rs 908.9 billion by 1995-96. The position is similar with the public long-term external debt, which increased from Rs 376 billion in 1990-91 to Rs 809.9 billion in 1995-96. During the past five years, the government's cumulative net borrowing of Rs 520.9 billion from internal and external sources was 36.7 per cent of its total revenue receipts of Rs 1,418 billion. Total debt servicing, according to the State Bank of Pakistan's Annual Report, 1995-96, was Rs 193.1 billion in the fiscal year 1996, which was 51.7 per cent of total revenue and 46.3 per cent of current expenditure.

The budgetary gap has persisted at an unsustainably high level because of inadequately restrained expenditure policies, inelastic revenues and poor performance of public enterprises.

In particular, the tax system is characterized by a narrow base, widespread tax evasion, and low elasticity with respect to overall economic growth largely attributable to numerous tax concessions and exemptions.

It is quite obvious that Pakistan has to control firmly the disconcerting trend of large fiscal deficits, otherwise, as the experience of a number of developing countries with large and growing fiscal deficits shows, we can easily enter into a trap wherein an upward spiralling cycle of inflation, devaluation, rising wages and salaries, and high interest rates, could disrupt production and investment activity and lead to large scale capital flight. All this highlights the importance of a significant fiscal adjustment in Pakistan involving a major resource mobilization effort and measures to control and rationalize expenditure, accompanied by steps aimed at improving tax administration and collection.

Aside from the savings-investment gap and the fiscal deficit, the other significant imbalance pertains to the external payments position of the country, which continues to be under severe pressure. The protracted weaknesses of Pakistan's balance of payments stem from a narrow export base, a declining trend in workers' home remittances, mounting external debt service payments, and lax demand management which, by stimulating domestic absorption, curtails the available surplus for exports. The current account deficit during the five years up to June 1996 averaged 4.3 per cent annually. In 1995-96, despite a moderate growth in exports and increase in inflows under foreign currency accounts, this deficit stood at $4.24 billion or 6.6 per cent of GDP, as against the targeted level of 4.4 per cent. The trade gap amounted to $3.7 billion, while the deficit in the services account was $3.2 billion. There was, however, a surplus of $2.6 billion on account of net unrequited transfers, in which the contribution of home remittances was $1.46 billion.

By vigorously pursuing a policy aimed at selective import substitution and enhanced competitiveness of our exports, it should be possible for Pakistan to strengthen its external accounts. The rate of growth of our exports should be at least

7 per cent above the growth rate of our imports. For this purpose, it is necessary to establish a neutral trade regime *vis-à-vis* export promotion and import substitution. There is also a need to rationalize export incentives to promote higher value-added exports. Furthermore, there has to be greater emphasis on quality control of important export products as well as on strenghtening the institutional infrastructure for exports, such as credit insurance, trade fairs and export promotion councils. These export promotion measures, of course, have to be supported by an appropriate domestic demand management policy.

Our plans can also be faulted for being too optimistic in determining the safe limits of monetary expansion. This inevitably resulted in unleashing disconcerting inflationary pressures. The Consumer Price Index has increased more than twenty-fold between 1949-50 and 1995-96, causing acute distress to fixed income and salaried people, pensioners and unorganized labour. While no one should make a fetish of an absolutely flat price level, inflation as an aspect of development can never be condoned by anyone who has observed its consequences at first hand. These include the disorganization of public and educational services, the misallocation of resources, the distortions of incentives, and ultimately stagnation when stabilization is attempted. By then habits of saving are greatly impaired and efforts at stabilization eliminate forced savings by credit expansion and deficit financing, leaving little internal saving. Inflation corrodes confidence and thus cuts at the root of the development process.

At present, physical infrastructure bottlenecks constitute significant constraints on higher economic growth. Massive investment is needed to overcome this obstacle to economic growth. Aside from power shortages and transport inadequacies, Pakistan is facing problems of an aging irrigation system requiring investments in waterlogging and salinity control, as well as replacement and repair of irrigation works. It is clear that to remove these bottlenecks, public investment must be supplemented by growing private sector investment.

Pakistan's poor record in human resources and social development is a serious constraint to sustained growth with an equity premise. The country's literacy rate of 38 per cent is one of the lowest in the world. Educational facilities, notwithstanding the expansion registered since Independence, are still woefully inadequate, are unevenly distributed and generally favour urban areas. Mortality and life expectancy indicators are similarly disappointing for a country of Pakistan's economic standing. Health coverage is limited, heavily focused on urban areas and hospital-based curative care.

Pakistan has an explosive combination of a large population of over 130 million, and growth at one of the fastest rates in the world, about 3 per cent a year. The official open unemployment of 1.78 million people is 4.84 per cent of the labour force, and this rate will triple to around 15 per cent if the underemployed persons are also included. Within the overall employment picture, the special problem of unemployment among educated youth is socially and politically the most serious. Unfortunately, systematic planning of human resources consistent with the requirements of planned development has never been adequately done in any of our plans. While domestic output has grown at a satisfactory rate, the production and technology mix have been too capital intensive for commensurate employment growth. It is imperative to introduce employment intensive schemes, specially in the rural areas.

In the ultimate analysis, the total volume of employment in a community depends on the level of productive activity. Measures which promote the latter directly create new opportunities for employment, and incomes thus obtained constitute a demand for still more labour. Thus, an expanding and diversified economy is, in the long run, the best guarantee for high employment.

Our plans have also suffered because of our failure to mobilize the cooperation and participation of the people for the successful accomplishment of our development goals. These have been 'bureaucratic-technocratic' plans and hence there can be little wonder that the general public, especially the poor, show scant enthusiasm for the sophisticated models that are developed by high level planners. Political leaders have unfortunately not played their expected roles in articulating their strategic objectives and their 'trade-offs' between objectives. Instead, they have confined themselves to making marginal changes which were often seen by technocrats as irrational interferences. We have also failed to establish a meaningful two-way communications link between central planning and provincial and local planning. This has created resource mobilization and utilization problems, and has made the implementation of planning in the public sector inadequate. While 'planning from below' cannot take into account some major national needs, there certainly exists a wide enough area in which the people themselves can take decisions with regard to the immediate and vital needs of their lives.

Pakistan's plans have also neglected the importance of institutional factors and failed to take note of the social framework of institutions which affect the process of economic development. The links between plans and political reality have been problematic. Again, examination of the income distribution dimensions of growth in our plans has been quite weak. There is an acute awareness now that the analysis of growth, employment and distribution must be viewed integrally as one. Unfortunately, our plans have not given sufficient prominence to reducing inequalities. Indeed, the plans did not contemplate any real and direct measures to alter the distribution of existing wealth, nor to impose a more egalitarian incomes policy. Such solutions were considered too drastic to be feasible in our society given the realities of economic and political power.

Project identification, appraisal and implementation have been a particularly weak aspect of our development planning. Deficiencies and mistakes in this crucial area have resulted in imbalances and inefficiencies. Moreover, the plans have been devoid of strict criteria of universal validity, which were neither formulated nor applied consistently in the determination of priorities, and only some 'rules of thumb' were instead developed. Most of our five-year plans also made the unrealistic assumption of relative price stability and thus failed to link physical targets with prices.

To a significant extent shortfalls in the achievement of development targets envisaged in different plans can be attributed to the menacing growth of corruption in our society. In circumstances in which power and influence—attributes of excessive political and administrative authority—are widely suspected of serving private rather than public interest, the objectives of development and social change are equally endangered. As such, the maintenance of high standards of integrity, and ensuring decisive action in respect of political as well as administrative defaults once identified, have not received the attention required in the common national interest. Unhappily, ever since Independence, there has been a lack of determination and stern conscience in dealing with corruption. To establish now a new set of habits and attitudes, a refusal to tolerate corruption in any shape or form, and a readiness to punish severely those found guilty of it, requires a nation-wide moral and political crusade.

Our planning experience has highlighted the importance of establishing a mechanism to intergrate fully the current management of the economy with long-term development goals. Planning and economic management are not separate but complementary tasks, one being long-term in nature, and the other short-term. In the past, even with considerable support provided by external resources, there has been a real hiatus between shorter and longer term economic policies, the former being in nature restrictionist and the latter expansionist, each partially undercutting the purpose of the other. At present, there is an urgent need for establishing a compact machinery to design an integrated package of economic policies to ensure a measure of harmony between long-term development goals and short term crisis management. The theme of achieving the goals of economic development and change, simultaneously with those of economic stability and efficiency, has been felt with increasing sharpness in recent years. We must craft an appropriate institutional mechanism to respond effectively to this challenge.

Our inability to realize fully our development goals can also to a significant extent be attributed to the inadequacies of public administration. Measures necessary for the improvement of public administration may be considered in terms of three principal objectives, namely, greater integrity, greater efficiency and greater response to public needs. The conditions for a high level of integrity in the administration are, firstly, a determined effort on the part of the political executive, and those who support it in the legislature, to maintain a high standard of administration, just and impartial, free from influence and able to deal on merit with individual claims and grievances. Secondly, a concerted reduction of patronage both on the part of ministers and officials, for example, by insisting on appointments over as wide a range as possible through the Public Service Commissions or Special Selection Boards. Finally, the determination and provision of adequate machinery to enforce integrity in the administration as well as in public life. Improvement in public administration can only be brought about by concerted measures on the part of both the political executive and the civil services. There is need for leadership in both.

The Future Outlook

The country is currently engaged in preparing the Ninth Five-Year Plan (1998-2003). In terms of the 'approach' document to this plan, the economy should move forward on a rapid and steady path so that it can enter the twenty-first century with a GDP growth of 7 per cent annually rather than the traditional 6 per cent. The Ninth Plan is being prepared at a juncture when there is national consensus that good government must incorporate democratization, devolution, decentralization, community participation and transparency in the State's economic dispensation. If these considerations are borne in mind, it should not be difficult for the country to attain the 7 per annual growth target articulated in 'Approach to the Ninth Plan 1998-2003'.

At present there is considerable disillusionment with medium and long-term planning not only in Pakistan but in many other developing countries, because of its failure to deliver the advantages expected of it. Many political leaders and experts after the Second World War looked upon development planning mistakenly as a faultless or pristine instrument of economic growth. Oversold on its virtues as a short cut to development, as an insurance policy for a lender, and a credit asset to a borrower, there is now a danger that disillusionment with plans might cause throwing the baby out with the bath water.

Notwithstanding disenchantment with planning and its limitations in the new era of liberalization and globalization, multi-year development plans are not redundant. They are valuable instruments for a clear analysis of the inter-relationships within the national economy and for systematically tracing the effects of different policies and programmes. Again, techniques of project planning can only operate within certain parameters that multi-year macro-planning provides. Some form of macro-plan is also needed to gauge the required level and composition of external resource inflows.

It is, however, essential to achieve a large measure of agreement concerning national economic goals. The unity of purpose in national life will also help to produce coherent policies and practical measures so essential for planning sound, sustained development. A major task for the government at present is to create an earnestness of purpose which enables a nation to make sacrifices for the attainment of defined development goals.

Pakistan has the potential to become a dynamic, high growth economy, and could join the ranks of middle income countries in the twenty-first century. Not only can it generate more income but also more employment opportunities needed for mounting an effective attack on poverty. Pakistan's success in meeting its articulated development goals is, however, contingent on improving 'qualitative indicators', namely, good governance, sound short and long-term economic planning and its effective implementation, as well as appropriate fiscal, monetary and exhange rate policies designed to ensure price stability and avoid unsustainable fiscal and external account deficits. There is an obvious and urgent need to enhance 'qualitative indicators' through heavy investment in human resources, effective legislative measures and honest administration. The nation is fully aware of the daunting challenges of its development agenda, and, if these are to be satisfactorily addressed, we require both honest commitment and concerted effort.

CHAPTER 4

EDUCATION

Dr Muneer Ahmad*

Historical Background

The acquisition of knowledge is one of the main principles of Islam. Both the Holy Quran and the Holy Prophet (PBUH) repeatedly underscored it as a duty of all Muslims, and the search for knowledge of the ultimate nature of things has been declared as binding on both men and women.

The establishment of an education system is thus an inherent and integral part of Islamic society. State schools were established at quite an early stage in the history of Islam. These schools were mostly attached to mosques and their main purpose was to impart religious education. Subsequently, Islamic jurisprudence, history, logic, the physical sciences and medicine were also included. The ancient works of great authorities of the past, such as the Greek classics and, in India, some Sanskrit classics, were translated into Arabic, and became part of academia.

The teachers were usually men of learning and piety. Students lived for long periods in schools with their teachers and learned from them through individual study under their guidance, through discussion in tutorials and lectures. Many Muslim scholars undertook independent research in the fields of

* Dr Tariq Siddiqui made valuable comments on this chapter, which the author acknowledges with thanks.

geography, astronomy and medicine. The spread of such knowledge contributed in a significant way to the Renaissance in Europe.

The Muslim rulers of India took a keen interest in the promotion of education, extended patronage to scholars and men of learning, and provided scholarships to outstanding students. They granted financial assistance in the form of endowments to *madrassahs* attached to mosques and monasteries, and also founded schools, colleges and libraries.

Islamic educational institutions in India were predominantly privately sponsored and supported by philanthropists, where teachers received no salaries and students paid no tuition fees. The medium of instruction was Persian, and the study of Arabic was encouraged for Muslims. The curriculum and the duration of learning depended upon the judgement of the teachers and the ability of the students.

The first efforts at Western education in India were made by Christian missionaries. Their main objective was to civilize Indians by instructing them in Christian moral values and secular subjects. In their endeavour to convert Indians to Christianity, the missionaries acquired knowledge of Indian languages, translated the Bible and also wrote pamphlets against local religious customs which they regarded as barbarous. The missionaries had limited success and could not effect the desired social changes. The British East India Company initially tried to keep itself apart from missionary activities and adopted a policy of extending financial support to indigenous institutions. Towards the end of the eighteenth century, Company administrators in India set up oriental schools and colleges for Indian boys with the aim of producing interpreters of Muslim and Hindu law for the administration of justice. Up to the third decade of the nineteenth century the local administrators of the Company encouraged existing indigenous schools and colleges, as well as the publication of oriental works, and favoured conducting higher education through the medium of the vernacular. This approach was opposed by the policy makers in London, who favoured the diffusion of European arts and

sciences through the English language. The policy favouring
Western education became operative from 1837 when English
was formally declared the official language and the medium of
instruction in India. The objectives of Western education were
to prepare men for clerical jobs in the colonial administration;
to broaden the outlook of the 'natives' by reducing the hold of
indigenous religious beliefs and superstitions; and to create a
class of 'brown Englishmen'.

The Westernization of education cut at the roots of local
culture and tradition; the use of English as the medium of
instruction proved a handicap to original thought and research.
The Western system of education did, however, introduce
indigenous students to Western law and medicine. They became
aware of the ideals of democracy. It was Western-educated
people who pioneered the Independence movement in the
twentieth century.

The system of education which Pakistan inherited at
Independence, and which continues today with minor
modifications, was firmly in place by the end of the nineteenth
century. Education largely comprised the liberal arts, provided
by schools and colleges scattered throughout the provinces. The
medium of instruction in colleges was English. All important
examinations, including matriculation, were conducted by
universities, which were non-residential and non-teaching. They
were primarily affiliating and examining bodies. With the
provincial governors as ex-officio chancellors and government
appointed vice-chancellors, universities were deliberately placed
under direct government control.

Muslim education passed through phases ranging from the
complete rejection of Western education to its partial acceptance.
One of the experiments in the former was carried out at the
Deoband Madrassah whose main purpose was to preserve
Muslim identity, traditions and culture. Although the Deoband
Madrassah incorporated some of the innovations of the British
system of education, such as dividing students into classes,
maintaining attendance registers and setting written
examinations, its focus remained on the study of Islam and the

teaching of the *hadis*. As a matter of policy, Deoband did not accept any grant or subsidy from the government. Also, the faculty did not involve itself in sectarian controversy or in active politics.

The Aligarh Movement led by Syed Ahmed Khan adopted the view that, by not taking to Western education, Indian Muslims would be left behind in the race for political influence in British India. With this objective he campaigned persistently for years and succeeded in establishing Aligarh College in 1878. In order to counter the criticism of orthodox Muslims that Western education would alienate Muslims from their religion, he incorporated many features in the college curriculum to preserve Muslim identity, such as compulsory prayers, fasting, a Muslim dress code and oriental learning. Gradually, the Aligarh Movement won wide support among Muslims and it produced many Western-educated Muslims who pioneered the Pakistan Movement. Another contribution of the Aligarh Movement was the establishment of voluntary organizations for the promotion of Muslim education. Two leading institutions, Islamia College, Lahore, and Islamia College, Peshawar, owe their origin to such organizations.

The academy at Nadwah, set up by a splinter group of Aligarh led by Maulana Shibly Nomani, tried to give equal emphasis to the study of religious and secular subjects. Similarly, Jamia Milliah Islamia, established in 1920, also tried to integrate religious and secular knowledge with the added feature of inculcating dignity of labour by prescribing manual work for both students and professors. Still another experiment in Muslim education was conducted at Osmania University at Hyderabad, Deccan, where courses in degree classes were imparted in Urdu.

By Independence in 1947, the Muslim elite had freed themselves from their aversion to Western education. They joined public universities and colleges in large numbers and many proceeded abroad to receive higher education. The most important contribution in spreading and popularizing education among Muslims was made by non-governmental Muslim organizations such as Anjuman-e-Himayat-e-Islam which ran many high schools and colleges. However, literacy among Muslims generally, as with other Indian communities, remained low.

Overview of the Past Fifty Years

At the time of Independence the challenges were formidable. With over 87 per cent illiteracy, limited primary education, inadequate technical and high school education and few institutions of higher learning, the scene was indeed bleak.

Educational reform enjoyed high priority in the thinking of the founders of Pakistan. This was demonstrated by the fact that one of their first acts was to convene a national conference on education in November 1947. They were highly dissatisfied with the inherited colonial education system, and there was a desire to reorientate it to the history and culture of the Muslims. Uneasiness prevailed about the use of English as the medium of instruction, and there was concern about the lack of a spiritual element in colonial education and the absence of inculcation of ethical values. There was also a feeling that colonial education tended to concentrate largely on a literary type of curriculum, and neglected vocational, technical and scientific education. All these concerns were emphasized by the Quaid-i-Azam in his message to the first national conference on education. He regretted that the greatest failing of the colonial system of education was that it did not build the character of future generations in terms of integrity, selfless public service and a sense of responsibility. The chairman of the conference, the Federal Education Minister, also voiced these concerns, and stressed three elements of a good national education system, namely, the spiritual, social and technical. The spiritual element required that school children must be ingrained in the fundamental philosophy of Islam; the social element required that the virtues of good citizenship should be inculcated, particularly discipline, integrity and public service; and the technical element referred to vocational, technical and scientific education. The conference recommended the provision of universal, compulsory and free education, the extension of facilities for girls and the improvement of university education. It conceded the use of English at the university level, but favoured the use of provincial languages at the primary level and Urdu at the secondary level.

This conference created three bodies of experts to assist the government in educational planning and policy making. The first of these bodies was the Advisory Board of Education for the central Ministry of Education. It consisted of the federal and provincial education ministers, the vice-chancellors of universities, chairmen of boards of secondary education, directors of public instruction and prominent educationists. The second body was the Inter-University Board composed of vice-chancellors and two additional representatives from each university. The third was the Council of Technical Education whose main task was to advise on the reorganization of engineering, agricultural and commercial education. On the basis of the deliberations of these bodies the federal Ministry of Education prepared a six-year national plan of educational development in 1952.

During the first twelve years of Pakistan, considerable expansion took place in education. The number of universities rose from one to four. Similarly, there was a rise in the number of agricultural, engineering and medical colleges. Teachers' training institutions also increased. There was, however, no significant improvement in the quality of education. The country went on following the pattern of education left behind by the British colonial administration, which was not in conformity with the needs and requirements of local culture and tradition. It continued to neglect spiritual values and remained over-literary. The introduction of Urdu as the medium of instruction at the school stage resulted in confusion. The old system of examination remained in vogue which encouraged learning by rote and stifled creativity. Education continued to suffer from inadequate buildings and equipment because of financial constraints.

Within two months of his assumption of power as the Chief Martial Law Administrator in October 1958, Ayub Khan announced the appointment of a commission on national education. Known as the Sharif Commission, it was asked to recommend ways of improving the quality of education and of bringing it in line with the needs and requirements of the country. The commission reiterated the aims of education, namely, the preservation of the ideals of the Pakistan Movement, character building, and technical and vocational training. Its recommendations repeated some of the suggestions made earlier by the Saddler Commission, 1917, and the Sargent Report of 1944. For example, it proposed that the minimum length of university courses should be three years, and that the stage of secondary education should cover classes IX to XII, in other words, that the intermediate classes form part of high school rather than that of college education. The proposal for a three-year degree course met vociferous opposition from students, parents and teachers. The resistance was so intense that the government decided to withdraw the reform. The recommendations of the commission made religious education compulsory up to class VIII, but its content failed to inspire the younger generation to inculcate Islamic moral values. The attempt to diversify courses at the secondary stage did not take off largely because of the paucity of teachers in the newly introduced technical subjects. Some steps taken to reform the examination system also had to be withdrawn as they did not produce the desired results. Textbook boards, set up to produce high quality books, met with limited success.

Among the successes of the new educational reforms were improved administration and increases in financial allocations. Rapid expansion also took place in technical, engineering and agricultural education. There was a remarkable increase in the number of schools and enrolment at the primary, secondary and higher levels. There was, however, no perceptible improvement in the quality of education.

Apart from resistance to a three-year BA degree course, there was also opposition to the new University Ordinance which, among other things, empowered a chancellor to withdraw the degree of an offending student. Student agitation was so persistent that the government was constrained to appoint another education commission in 1964. It was headed by Justice Hamoodur Rahman and was called the Commission on Student Problems and Welfare. Its most important recommendation was to repeal the objectionable provisions of the University Ordinance. It also recommended the restoration of the University Senate and an increase in the representative element in the Syndicate and the Academic Council of universities.

In March 1969, President Ayub Khan was forced to relinquish office as a result of prolonged, country-wide agitation in which students played a prominent part. The Education Minister of the succeeding administration set up study groups to examine and suggest reforms in the educational system of the country. The new policy which emerged as a result of the deliberations of the study groups was released as the Proposals for a New Education Policy in July 1969. It recommended greater autonomy for the universities, and proposed to set up a national literacy corps in order to launch a mass literacy campaign. However, this policy was overtaken by political change.

The Pakistan People's Party Government, which took office in December 1971, announced its policy in March 1972 on the basis of the deliberations of a national conference on education to which representatives of teachers' associations and students' unions from all over the country were invited. The most significant element of these reforms was the nationalization of all private colleges and privately managed schools. The main beneficiaries of these measures were college lecturers and school teachers in these private institutions. The new education policy provided them better pay scales, pension benefits and, above all, security of service. The major setback of nationalization was the immense increase in government expenditure. It also entailed the centralization of educational administration, which resulted in inefficiency and waste.

The second important feature of the education policy of 1972 was the introduction of free education up to class X. This measure resulted in an increase in public expenditure without any commensurate improvement in the quality of education. It also could not achieve the universalization of primary education for boys or girls. The policy aimed at increasing the participation rate at the secondary level of education but was seriously constrained by limitations of financial resources. However, its endeavour to increase enrolment in science and technology at the secondary level was successful.

In the field of higher education, the new policy sought to raise the participation rate from 2 to 3 per cent in eight years. The government also set up new universities and a University Grants Commission, which had been recommended by successive education committees since 1944, Centres of Excellence, Area Study Centres and an Open University.

The education policy of the People's Party Government opened admission to elite public schools for middle class pupils on merit. However, the government's hope to spread adult literacy through the electronic media remained unfulfilled because of an undeveloped infrastructure. The number of scholarships for students at different levels was increased, selected foreign textbooks were imported and reprinted in large numbers through a newly established National Book Foundation. In order to reform the examination system, a semester system was introduced in universities. The study of Islam was made compulsory up to class X.

Like previous attempts, the 1972 policy of inculcating Islamic values through the compulsory instruction of Islamiyat did not achieve its objective. The question of the medium of instruction also remained unresolved. Two parallel streams of education— one in English and the other in the Urdu and Sindhi medium— continued producing two distinct classes of educated people. The 1972 policy also offered no way of integrating the three systems of education—the *madrassahs*, the ordinary government schools and the elite public schools. Not much headway was made in spreading mass education, nor in improving the quality of education. The primary reason for seeking education continued to be the search for a white collar job, preferably in government. Malpractices in the examination system did not decrease, while teachers continued to suffer from a lack of dedication and commitment, and their teaching thus remained uninspiring.

The Martial Law administration of General Ziaul Haq embarked upon devising a new national education policy, and convened a national conference in October 1977 to suggest ways 'to bring education in line with the people's faith and ideology'. The main emphasis of this new policy was on the aim of fostering deep loyalty to Islam and Muslim nationhood. For this purpose, a number of steps were proposed which, *inter alia,* included the revision of curricula to reorganize the content around Islamic thought, the integration of *madrassahs* with the modern school and college system, the introduction of the national language as the medium of instruction, the mobilization of community resources like mosques and *mohallah* schools for spreading basic education and functional literacy, and the establishment of separate educational institutions for women at all levels.

Apart from emphasizing the Islamic character of education, the 1978 policy's most important decision was to reverse the nationalization policy and open the education system once again to private sector initiative. At the primary level, thousands of mosques and *mohallah* schools were opened, a wider curriculum range was offered at the secondary level, a committee of experts was set up in order to integrate the curricula of *madrassahs* and modern schools, textbooks were reviewed to expunge content repugnant to Islam, and the Academy of Educational Planning and Management was established to provide in-service training to educational administrators. Another important decision taken was that the federal government would meet the entire expenditure of all the universities for which funds were to be routed through the University Grants Commission. The universities, however, remained administratively within the jurisdiction of the provincial governments.

The 1978 policy envisaged in-service training of college and university teachers. It proposed an ambitious programme for student welfare on the lines of the 1972 policy. Foreign textbooks were sold to students at subsidized rates, while some were also reprinted locally and supplied to students at cheap rates. In order to promote a feeling of common identity, a simple and inexpensive uniform was introduced for all school students. A unique feature of this policy was that the government assumed responsibility for the education of handicapped persons. It also significantly enhanced expenditure on education.

School Education[1]

Almost all successive educational policies and plans emphasized the need for universalizing primary education. Although the participation rate increased from 26 per cent in the mid-1950s to 73 per cent in the 1990s, it still varies widely over gender, region and in rural-urban areas. The participation rate of rural women is low. This situation is made worse by the high drop-out rate which is over 80 per cent in some districts in Balochistan and NWFP.

Despite limitations, primary education has expanded rapidly over the past fifty years. Starting with only a little over 8,000 primary schools in 1947 the country now has more than 115,000. Enrolment has increased from 0.77 million to 11.5 million, and the number of primary school teachers from about 18,000 to over 337,000 in the 1990s.

However, the state of primary education remains unsatisfactory in rural areas, in less developed provinces, and also in the case of women. For the country as a whole, girl students in primary schools constitute one-third of the total enrolment, and only about 12 per cent in the Federally Administered Tribal Areas (FATA) and 20 per cent in Balochistan, and, in rural Balochistan, a mere 7 per cent. Approximately one-quarter of the primary school teachers as a whole are untrained. This proportion is as high as 50 per cent in the Northern Areas, 45 per cent in Balochistan, and 42 per cent in Sindh and Azad Kashmir. The proportion of untrained teachers in relatively developed areas ranges from 10 per cent in Islamabad, to 13 per cent in the Punjab and 20 per cent in the NWFP. The proportion of untrained female teachers is exceptionally high in certain less developed areas: 53 per cent in Azad Kashmir, 51 per cent in FATA and 73 per cent in the Northern Areas. In terms of primary schools without a building of their own in the 1990s, these were overall 16 per cent, and even higher in the case of girls' primary schools. In Balochistan, nearly 50 per cent of all the primary schools and 57 per cent of the girls' primary schools were without a building of their own. The proportion of such schools was 32 and 37 per cent respectively in Azad Kashmir. Even in the relatively better off Province of the Punjab, 17 per cent of the primary schools, and 19 per cent in the case of girls' schools, were without their own buildings. The number of teachers per school is also very low in less developed areas; for example, it is 1.5 for Azad Kashmir and Balochistan, and 1.75 for the Northern Areas. Thus the ratio of students per teacher is high in such areas as Azad Kashmir where it is 98 pupils per teacher, in the Northern Areas it is 66, and in Balochistan 62. Sindh and NWFP, with 31 and 37 pupils per teacher, have somewhat better teacher-student ratios, while Punjab has 53 pupils per teacher.

The number of middle schools (classes VI, VII and VIII) was 2,190 in 1947 which has increased to over 10,000 in 1995. If private middle schools are also included the figure rises to over 12,000. Similarly, the numbers enrolled have increased from 221,000 to over 3,400,000 in 1995. The number of middle school teachers has also risen from 12,000 in 1947 to over 93,000 in 1995.

In Pakistan in 1992-93, girls constituted around 30 per cent of the total middle school pupils, while this was even lower at 23 per cent for rural female pupils. The percentage of girl students in rural middle schools was very low, in Balochistan and FATA a mere 1.5 and 2.7 respectively, while in the Northern Areas and NWFP it was 7.4 and 10 per cent respectively. It was also not very high in the relatively developed areas of Sindh at 14.7 and Punjab at 27.8 per cent.

Around one-fifth of the middle school teachers in the country as a whole were untrained in the early 1990s. This percentage was higher for middle schools for girls at 21.3, and was as high as 47 in the Northern Areas, 45 in Sindh, 32 in Balochistan and 28 for both FATA and Azad Kashmir. Even in middle schools, about 5.5 per cent were without a building of their own in 1992. The percentage of such middle schools was as high as 15 in Sindh and 8.6 in Balochistan. In Azad Kashmir and the Northern Areas relatively more of the girls' middle schools were without a building.

On the eve of Independence there were 408 high schools in the country, and this number has risen to over 9,000 in 1995. At the same time, high school enrolment increased from 58,000 to over 1.3 million, and the number of teachers from 68,000 to over 188,000. Of the total high school enrolment, girls constituted only 27 per cent in 1992, and a mere 18 per cent in rural areas. The proportion of girl students in high schools was almost non-existent in rural Balochistan at 0.08 per cent and in rural FATA with 2.2 per cent. It was extremely low in the rural Northern Areas, NWFP and Sindh with 7, 10.5 and 11.8 per cent respectively.

The position was not dissimilar for high school teachers in the country where 13 per cent were untrained. This proportion was even poorer in the Northern Areas at 36 per cent and over 23 per cent in Azad Kashmir, FATA and Sindh. Moreover, the proportion of untrained girls' high school teachers was slightly higher in the rural areas. Even in the case of infrastructure, around 2.6 per cent of the high schools in the country were without buildings of their own, the highest proportion being 8.3 per cent in Balochistan. However, more urban high schools—for both boys and girls—were without a building of their own than rural high schools.

College Education

There were 40 arts and science colleges in 1947; their number now exceeds 700. The enrolment has jumped from 14,000 to over 735,000. The number of college teachers has also increased from 8,000 in the 1970s to over 20,000 in 1994-95. In 1972, when colleges were nationalized, more than half were in the private sector. These colleges form a critical base for higher education in technical and professional colleges and universities, and for postgraduate education.

At the intermediate college level, there are separate streams for such subjects as science, engineering, medicine, commerce and the arts. Examinations are conducted by the Boards of Intermediate and Secondary Education. As the major component of students at college are those enrolled in the intermediate classes, a proposal was adopted to shift them to separate colleges or to attach them to upgraded high schools, but this has only been partially implemented. Examinations at the degree level are conducted by the affiliating universities. Technically, these universities were also responsible for ensuring academic standards but, in practice, they have found it difficult since college ownership and administration was transferred to the government after nationalization.

The existing college system ensures a better level of teaching faculty for the intermediate students than would be available in the higher secondary school system. However, shifting intermediate classes to upgraded schools will create a major problem of moving the faculty around, because MA, BA, FA, M.Sc., B.Sc. and F.Sc. are taught by the same faculty members. The number of BA and B.Sc. students is comparatively limited and colleges may not be able to evolve a system under which simple two-year BA and B.Sc. teaching can be effectively undertaken when the intake in the school system remains indifferently or inadequately educated. In the present structure, good colleges are able to attract better students, who then stay in college for four to six years under the same faculty. It is for these reasons that the prospects for reform, repeated by various expert groups since the report of the Sharif Commission, have not been implemented. This will be a major challenge for the future.

Teacher Education

There are over 110 institutions for the training of primary school teachers. Primary Teachers Certificate (PTC) training classes are also available in over 100 teacher training units attached to secondary schools. A large number of primary and secondary school teachers complete their training as private candidates or through programmes of the Open University. Teachers for high schools are trained in 11 colleges and in 6 university departments, agro-technical teachers in 7 agro-technical training centres, and technical teachers in the National Technical Teachers Training College, Islamabad. Moreover, in-service training is provided in over 13 Teachers Education Extension Centres. The Academy for Educational Planning and Management, set up in 1981, provides in-service training to education administrators.

Five major shortcomings have been identified in the existing teacher training programme: the curriculum is not relevant to the actual classroom situation, teachers have poor academic knowledge of their subjects, internal evaluation of candidate teachers tends to lower standards, the training period is inadequate, and arrangements for in-service training are insufficient. Apart from these problems, a serious deficiency is that individuals tend to opt to be primary school teachers when they cannot find other jobs. This is the result of unattractive salary scales, limited prospects of promotion and low social status. Most of the school teachers, reportedly, lack enthusiasm, dedication and preparedness. There is a need to raise the minimum qualifications for fresh entrants, to improve the management of teacher training institutions and to provide better career prospects to these teachers. Other factors are that teachers, in general, are reluctant to serve in rural areas. This is especially so in the case of female teachers. Recognizing this, some provincial governments offer them a monthly hardship allowance. Lack of provision of residential accommodation for female teachers in the rural areas acts as a further disincentive. There is also an urgent need to improve the facilities for the in-service training of these teachers.

Adult Literacy

The problem of adult illiteracy results from the lack of universal primary education. Its magnitude is staggering. Successive governments have shown awareness that illiteracy is a tremendous barrier in the way of progress, and made various efforts to spread adult education. Initially, reliance was placed on experimental adult literacy centres established by the provincial governments and operated through largely untrained voluntary workers. The aim was to teach adults to read and write. As the effort was not integrated with the day-to-day practical demands of their economic activities, the new literates tended to forget their recently learnt skills. Also, an inadequate supply of appropriate literature contributed to the failure of the adult literacy campaign.

Later, the institutions of Village-AID and local government were used to spread literacy among adults. They provided organizational facilities, while provincial education departments undertook the training of adult literacy teachers and the production of reading material. These efforts remained experimental. In the late 1970s, the Open University employed multi-media distance learning techniques. Community TV-viewing centres were also set up. However, this programme was discontinued in 1979.

The Sixth Five-Year Plan (1983-88) proposed a two-pronged strategy to improve the literacy level by accelerated expansion of primary education and through a functional literacy programme. The plan assigned higher priority to the education of women in rural areas in view of their catalytic role. It also envisaged the involvement of NGOs in the spread of functional literacy through financial assistance, the supply of instructional material and training of literacy teachers.

The Seventh (1988-93) and Eighth (1993-98) Five-Year Plans reverted to the universalization of primary education as the route to literacy, by increasing the participation rate and reducing the drop-out rate. For adult literacy, these plans urged the NGOs to launch community-based programmes linked with the socio-economic demands of the learners. One major shortcoming has been that at no stage, except during short periods, has adult literacy been considered a desirable area for the expenditure of public resources. All those who miss school add continuously to the stock of illiterates, keeping the literacy level low. A policy to address adult literacy directly, which in the short term can make the literacy percentage more acceptable, has yet to be evolved.

Technical Education

At Independence, the country had no organized public system of technical and vocational education. There were a number of government-run artisan and trade schools, and diploma courses in agricultural and engineering colleges. Skilled workers were trained almost entirely in the private sector, that is, in families, guilds and occasionally in industrial establishments. These avenues were not capable of providing the required number of trained technicians. The general education schools paid excessive attention to literary skills and training for jobs in government organizations. Occupations requiring technical skills suffered from their low social status because of prejudice against manual work.

The administration of technical education was dispersed between two different ministries, Labour and Industries, both at the centre and in the provinces. Technical education was not an integral part of the public education system. As a result of the recommendations of the Technical Education Committee of the Council of Technical Education, the government established polytechnics, trade schools and commercial training institutes. The government also set up Directorates of Technical Education at the provincial level.

During the First Five-Year Plan (1955-60) only one polytechnic was set up. In the Second Five-Year Plan (1960-65), the engineering college at Lahore was elevated to the level of an engineering university where postgraduate studies in civil, mechanical and electrical engineering were introduced. Also, the annual intake of students at degree level was raised. A number of polytechnics were established where new technologies were introduced. The annual admissions at diploma level increased and the provincial Directorate of Technical Education was reorganized and strengthened.

At present, there is a wide variety of technical training programmes both in the public and private sectors, which produce trained manpower of different categories. In the public sector, training is imparted in engineering universities and colleges, polytechnics, monotechnics, colleges of technology, technical training centres, and vocational, technical and commercial training institutes. There are now over 60 polytechnics and colleges of technology offering three-year diploma courses in about 25 technologies; 13 are for women. Their total intake capacity is about 12,000. The graduates of polytechnics serve as middle level supervisors and technicians, and self-employed professionals. There is a plan to establish one polytechnic or monotechnic for boys in each district and one women's polytechnic in each division.

Vocational training institutes for skilled workers offer a variety of courses ranging from three months to one year for middle and high school graduates. In 1993, about 200 vocational institutes, with an intake capacity of about 20,000, were functioning under the provincial education departments. In addition, vocational and technical training centres are also operating under the National Training Bureau, provincial labour departments, and semi-autonomous and private organizations which provide pre-service and in-service training in a variety of trades. The future programme is to start trade schools in local skills in existing school buildings in evening shifts, where trained teachers and skilled technicians and artisans will impart training.

In the field of commerce, there is also a post-matriculation certificate and diploma training in secretarial practices, commerce, banking and insurance offered in over 110 commercial training institutes in the public sector. Degree and postgraduate level education is offered in 20 commerce colleges. A very large training programme in commercial skills is carried out in the private sector, especially in big cities. Use of computers is being actively encouraged as an integral part of commercial education.

The *Madrassahs* and *Maktabs*

Islamic religious schools or *madrassahs* represent the continuation of the indigenous Islamic tradition of provding education entirely through non-governmental initiative. They also represent the resolve of the Muslims, since the days of British colonial rule, to preserve their Islamic identity and culture against alien influence.

According to a 1979 survey, there were 1,745 Islamic religious schools in Pakistan. Most of them have their own buildings and arrangements for the residence of scholars, for the provision of medical aid, and also libraries with textbooks and books of reference. These schools observe Islamic values of simplicity and austerity in buildings, classrooms, food and other aspects; thus they are far more economical in their operation than other modern schools. The average annual expenditure per school in 1979 worked out to approximately Rs 50,000, and Rs 432 per student.

The most distinct feature of Islamic religious schools is their policy of self-reliance in financial and material matters. They do not depend on government assistance and, instead, rely on their own resources for land, buildings, furniture, books, teachers, examinations and other academic matters. In many of these schools students sleep on the floor, and, when necessary, participate in the repair of school buildings along with the teachers through voluntary manual labour.

With the exception of a few *madrassahs* of Ahl-i-Hadis orientation, the remaining schools are almost evenly divided into the Deobandi and Barelvi. A serious defect of *madrassah* education, however, is that each institution imparts instruction in the principles of its own school of thought to the complete exclusion and rejection of others. The influence of religious education can be gauged by the enrolment levels at the *madrassahs*. In the Punjab in 1996 a total of 2,463 *Deeni Madaris* were reported with a total enrolment of 198,500. Of these 80,120 were enrolled in the Deobandi school of thought, 95,196 in Barelvi, 4,303 in Fiqh Jafria, and 18,880 in Ahl-i-Hadis. The figures for the whole country are about twice this. The numbers do not include the *maktabs* attached to the mosques from where the pupils move to the normal school system, retaining their link with their Islamic roots, and thereby becoming part of the religious oriented groups in the educational institutions and of society at large.

Scholarships

A comprehensive system of merit scholarships has been in place at all levels since the 1960s. These are awarded on the completion of classes V, VIII, X, XII, and at college and university levels. The object of the scholarship programme is to open every career to talented students irrespective of their socio-economic background. The programme also encourages the sciences and promotes education for girls. In addition, it covers foreign training of outstanding students, who, on completion of their degree or postgraduate courses, are sent abroad for further specialization in their disciplines in order to serve as teachers on their return.

A number of federal government schemes are in operation to provide overseas advanced education to junior college and university teachers. Under the Central Overseas Training Scholarship scheme, 65 scholarships are awarded annually— 43 for university and 22 for degree and professional college teachers. Under the Quaid-i-Azam Scholarship scheme, 18 are awarded annually to students who come first in their subjects, while 36 merit scholarships are granted to students who secure second and third position in order of merit. The children of government servants in the lower grades 1 to 15 are awarded merit scholarships subject to progressive performance up to Ph.D. level. Scholarships are also offered by autonomous educational agencies, foreign and local educational foundations, foreign aid agencies and philanthropic organizations. Almost all the local scholarships are given by the provincial governments.

University Education and Research

In the case of higher education, an expanded base has been created. The output ties in with the existing stage of economic development meeting a large part of the current needs of society. The state of higher education is, however, such that it does not create intellectual leadership and excellence of academic endeavour. A recent World Bank study described it as an ocean of mediocrity with a few islands of quality, hastening to add: 'It was not always so in the history of higher education in Pakistan, which in earlier days enjoyed world-wide reputation for top flight performance of many of the products of the system who graduated before the early 1970s.'[2] The study also noted institutional exceptions to the general rule, particularly places such as the HEJ Institute of Chemistry at Karachi University, the Institute of Molecular Biology at Punjab University, organizations of the Pakistan Atomic Energy Commission, some departments at Quaid-i-Azam University, and others which proved that not only quality is achievable in Pakistan, but also provided lessons on how to achieve this. The study viewed campus unrest and student indiscipline as not the cause but a symptom of the crisis of quality, calling for an integrated approach for restructuring and reform.

The number of general universities has expanded to 12. They have geographical areas assigned to them for purposes of affiliation of colleges, and are chartered to teach, affiliate institutions, examine external and regular students, and award degrees, certificates and diplomas. The universities are administratively under the provincial governments. The governor of a province is ex-officio chancellor, and the minister for education the ex-officio pro-chancellor. In the case of the federal universities, the president is the chancellor. The funding of universities since 1979 is by the federal government through the University Grant Commission. Table 1 gives the enrolment figures for the general universities.

Table 1

Enrolment at general universities 1992-93						
	BA/B.Sc.	Master	M.Phil.	Ph.D.	Dip./CA	Total
University of Punjab	4,946	3,450	29	151	1,403	9,979
University of Sindh	4,884	2,205	778	389	120	6,376
University of Peshawar	1,485	2,467	139	54	6,940	8,103
Karachi University	5,676	4,671	150	20	1,103	11,620
Quaid-i-Azam University	—	1,068	273	261	163	1,755
Balochistan University	1,168	2,687	33	9	115	4,012
Gomal University	614	1,020	—	2	1,795	3,431
Bahauddin Zakaria University	926	1,592	42	48	249	2,857
Islamia University	—	2,565	90	59	300	3,014
International Islamic University	658	313	—	22	647	1,640
AJK University	731	408	—	—	35	1,174
Shah Abdul Latif University	1,289	822	57	·8	70	2,246

Source: University Grants Commission: Handbook of Universities of Pakistan, 1994.

In 1992-93, the faculty members in these universities numbered 3,909, with 1,210 professors and associate professors. Generally, the majority of the faculty has had the benefit of education and training in good universities abroad, and those at the professor and associate professor level have doctoral qualifications and research publications to their credit. A number of Centres of Excellence have emerged where research of high quality is being conducted. Nine such centres were established by an Act of Parliament in 1974. These are in analytical chemistry at the University of Sindh, geology at the University of Peshawar, marine biology at Karachi University, mineralogy at the University of Balochistan, physical chemistry at Peshawar University, solid state physics at the University of Punjab, water resource engineering at the University of Engineering, Lahore, molecular biology at the University of Punjab and psychology at the Quaid-i-Azam University. In addition, the Pakistan Institute of Nuclear Science and Technology, the A.Q. Khan Laboratory at Kahuta, the Pakistan Council of Scientific and Industrial Research, the research organizations of the Pakistan Atomic Energy Commission, the HEJ Institute of Chemistry at Karachi and the Defence Science Laboratories have developed good research capabilities and links with international institutions as well as universities.

Seven Area Study Centres and Pakistan Study Centres were also established by Parliament in 1974 and have become part of university research facilities. The Pakistan Institute of Development Economics and the Applied Economic Research Centre at Karachi are now well recognized in their field. The Institute of Business Administration, Karachi, and the Lahore University of Management Sciences have become important institutions. A significant development at university level has been the setting up of technical universities for engineering and agriculture, by upgrading colleges and establishing new ones. This focus has helped to expand the facilities at a fast rate and has also allowed new specialities to come up in response to the needs of the economy. The Ministry of Defence has established its own specialized institutions and linked them with the universities. A large number of research centres and institutions have been established under the Ministry of Science and Technology.

Pakistan's policy makers understood the importance of establishing such institutions and took steps in that direction. The Agricultural College at Faisalabad was raised to the level of an agricultural university. This was followed by setting up two more agricultural universities, one at Peshawar, along with the Pakistan Forest Institute, and a university at Tando Jam. Independent of the universities but functionally linked institutes like the Ayub Agricultural Research Institute at Faisalabad, the National Agriculture Research Centre at Islamabad, the Barani Areas Agricultural College and other specialized field research institutes in wheat, rice, cotton, oil seeds, horticulture, livestock and fisheries, have provided valuable inputs in the agricultural sector and placed research in agriculture on a solid footing. A stronger link between the research institutions and universities would create an adequate system of education and research for the future. The output of trained manpower from these universities and agricultural colleges has been sufficient to meet the public sector needs while making reasonable numbers available for private sector employment. The faculty at these universities and research institutions is well qualified, has international links and has, at most of the senior levels, acquired the services of those with M.Sc. degrees and doctorates from good foreign universities. Large numbers of those with M.Phil. and Ph.D. degrees have also been produced domestically. The agricultural universities had an enrolment of 10,414 with 954 faculty members in 1992-93. There were 200 M.Phil. and 536 Ph.D. students. The number of professors and associate professors in the faculties was 382.

In the field of engineering, development has followed a similar path with the setting up of four universities of engineering and technology at Lahore, Jamshoro, Karachi and Peshawar. Moreover, a campus at Taxila has recently been upgraded to university level, and a college established at Quetta. A private sector GIK Institute of Technology has also been established at Swabi, NWFP. The growth of public sector engineering institutions placed large demands upon these universities for trained manpower. The Water and Power Development Authority, Pakistan Steel Mills and its allied industries, the Heavy Electrical and Mechanical complexes, the Federal Chemical and Ceramics Corporation, Ministry of Defence Production industries, the Pakistan Telecommunication Corporation, together with civil engineering, construction, roads and irrigation systems, expanded at a fast rate and became large employers of engineering and technical manpower. A corresponding private sector increase in manufacturers and suppliers created important growth centres in a number of urban areas. The creation of technical manpower, except for short periods of mismatch when shortages or surpluses appeared in the market, remained reasonably well tuned to demand. A large number also took advantage of external markets which developed during the 1970s and 1980s and worked in the Gulf and the Middle East in construction and other engineering works. This was especially true in the case of technical manpower coming out of polytechnics and vocational institutions who were not readily absorbed in the domestic market. The traditional on-the-job production of semi-skilled and skilled manpower continued to provide important support. Overall, the engineering universities had an enrolment of 17,474 in 1992-93, with a faculty of 917. Of the students, 1,742 were enrolled for M.Sc., 69 for M.Phil. and 49 for Ph.D.; and of the faculty, 355 were either professors or associate professors.

In medical education also there has been important development. The number of medical colleges has expanded sufficiently to meet the needs at the graduate level, and postgraduate institutes have been set up at Peshawar, Islamabad, and two at Lahore as well as in Karachi. The College of Physicians and Surgeons is responsible for conducting examinations and the award of degrees at the masters and fellowship levels. In addition, the Aga Khan University at Karachi has emerged as an important institution in the field of health and medicine.

It is noteworthy that enrolment at university level shows a large, substantial shift to scientific and professional education. Out of a total of 67,927 students in 1986-87, as many as 54 per cent were in the scientific and technical fields, 13 per cent in professional subjects and 33 per cent in the arts. The numbers in the sciences and technical fields would be larger if additional places were available. Table 2 illustrates the position.

Table 2

Subject-wise enrolment in universities in 1986			
	General universities	Agricultural universities	Engineering universities	Total
Arts	13,802	0	0	13,802
Science	12,152	0	0	12,152
Education	2,488	0	0	2,488
Commerce	3,110	0	0	3,110
Law	3,207	0	0	3,207
Pharmacy	1,372	0	0	1,372
Agriculture	207	7,568	0	7,775
Engineering	623	0	14,970	15,593
Other	8,428	0	0	8,428
Total	45,389	7,568	14,970	67,927

Source: Higher Education and Scientific Research for Development in Pakistan, World Bank, 1990, Vol. II, p. 174.

The traditional system of public examinations in Pakistani universities was introduced by the British colonial administration about a hundred and forty years ago. It is essay-type. It is externally administered at the end of a long course, extending over two or more years, and its results are used for a variety of educational and social purposes. Despite its demonstrable unrealiability, the essay-type examination system continues to remain entrenched. To make matters worse, this inherited system has also deteriorated in practice. Many students feel that it is not a reliable form of examination, and both teachers and parents are worried about the malpractices that have crept in. Occasional attempts were made to reform the system but without much success. The Commission on National Education, 1959, introduced a weightage of 25 per cent marks in each paper for internal evaluation. This was designed to balance the entirely external evaluation and also to induce the students to apply themselves to study all the year round. The reform failed because of, among other reasons, the unfavourable teacher-student ratio and the lack of teacher training in internal evaluation.

The subsequent 1966 Commission on Student Problems and Welfare favoured an entirely external system of public examination up to the first degree level, and internal evaluation only to determine whether a student was fit to take such an examination. For postgraduate courses it favoured a double examiner system, both internal and external.

In 1970, the National Committee on Examinations recommended the use of internal along with external examination. It also proposed that the marks for both the evaluations be entered in separate columns in the degree certificates of the students. It recommended that answer scripts be shown to the students for their feedback.

In the case of the general universities the bulk of students are enrolled in degree colleges which teach and present the students for examination. The university itself has little academic or administrative role apart from laying down the syllabus and setting the examination. The colleges are administered by the government. A large number of students also take university examinations privately, without the benefit of formal teaching. Tables 3 and 4 illustrate the low standards at which BA and B.Sc. students are being instructed; the results of the Punjab

University in 1996 show a pass rate of 25.5 per cent in BA and 34.9 per cent in B.Sc. examinations.

Table 3

BA results of Punjab University in 1996						
		Number			Pass %	
		Boys	Girls	Total	Boys	Girls
Appeared	54,219	26,601	27,618	25.5	19.7	31.1
College enrolled	25,807	8,939	16,868	34.8	24.6	46.3
Private	28,412	17,662	10,770	17.1	17.3	16.8

Table 4

B.Sc. results of Punjab University in 1996						
		Number			Pass %	
		Boys	Girls	Total	Boys	Girls
Appeared	9,321	6,744	2,577	34.9	26.9	55.8
College enrolled	6,405	4,278	2,127	40.8	30.6	61.3
Private	2,916	2,466	450	21.0	20.4	29.5

No educational system can afford such a waste of resources and human endeavours. In a well-administered system, inadequately prepared students would not be allowed to take the examination. The high failure rates create the environment for demands for easy examinations, pressures to postpone them, the search for guides and notes, the approaching of examiners, the temptation to tamper with results and downright dishonesty. These are symptoms. The cause is inadequate preparation and poor teaching standards. The better colleges tend to have over

60 per cent success rates; they also attract better students. The poorer colleges have results below 20 per cent down to zero. Universities which teach their own MA, M.Sc. and higher level students perform much better. The same is the case in the professional universities which teach their own students, and where the semester system has taken root, for example in the Quaid-i-Azam University, the institutes of business administration, and engineering and agricultural universities.

Future development in higher education would require a number of reforms, including a move towards teaching universities, the conversion of larger and better colleges into degree awarding institutions, and a strong policy on admissions and adequate preparation before taking university examinations. Furthermore, an increased involvement and greater control over teaching in the colleges, which remain affiliated to universities, would be desirable.

The creation of specialized research institutions linked to the universities needs to be carried forward, as it has proved successful. The appearance of M.Phil. and Ph.D. students on the campus has a healthy academic influence and creates the environment for greater faculty involvement, and challenges for learning and research. Universities require much greater support than has been given to convert them into institutions of higher learning at the M.Phil. and Ph.D. level. The conversion of the existing subsidy into tuition fee support programmes, made conditional on good performance by the students, and the simultaneous raising of fees to reasonable levels, that is, to about half the operational cost, would allow considerable flexibility for designing new programmes.

And, finally, the academic and administrative autonomy of colleges and universities need to be accepted and respected by government, thus delinking current attitudes from the colonial legacy. The liberation of the institutions of higher learning from short term political expediency would require charters in which the president, governors, ministers of education and governmental bureaucracy have no role to play, where the institutions are governed as corporate bodies by men of learning and experience, and where the selection of such men is in the hands of people who can exercise intellectual and academic leadership.

Progress Made and Some Conclusions

On Independence, Pakistan faced a number of challenges which included: the need to develop a philosophical basis for education while integrating its Islamic heritage, local culture and modern requirements in order to eliminate the dichotomy which had developed in the education system during a hundred years of foreign domination; the integration of indigenous religious systems of education in the national system; and the introduction in the curricula of moral, ethical and religious values in consonance with the beliefs of the population and national ideals, so as to develop national character and recreate a moral and ethical basis for education. A second set of challenges related to the need to provide mass education to the population through adult literacy programmes, to improve female participation in education at all levels so as to create a literate home environment and provide opportunities to women to take an active part in the economy and development programmes. Other major areas requiring attention included the rapid expansion of the school system at the primary level to achieve universal primary education; the expansion of middle schools to keep pace with growth from the primary level; the expansion of high schools and secondary education in arts and science, technology, trades and agriculture to meet the development needs of the economy; the training of manpower for trade and industry in polytechnics, commercial institutes, vocational institutes, and specialized agriculture, including livestock, fishery and forest institutes; and the creation of health workers, nurses and health technicians. In all these cases, problems relating to the training of teachers were formidable. Another important area related to the modernization of the curriculum, syllabi and the production of textbooks to lift standards of education to international levels.

The issues relating to the medium of instruction and the reform of the examination and certification system also required the attention of policy makers.

The critical issues for the public at large were the immediate and rapid expansion of the education system. The ground covered in terms of numbers during the past nearly fifty years is impressive. Tables 5 and 6 compare the 1947-48 position with that of 1994-95 in terms of enrolment.

Table 5

Enrolment by level of education in 1947-48 and 1994-95						
	Total		Multi-plication factor	Female		Multi-plication factor
	1947-48	1994-95		1947-48	1994-95	
Primary (000)	770	11,484	14.9	110	4,566	41.5
Middle (000)	221	3,472	15.7	21	1,066	50.8
High (000)	58	1,347	23.2	7	396	56.6
Secondary Vocational (000)	4	94	23.5	1	23	23.0
Arts and Science Colleges (000)	14	735	52.5	1	274	274.0
Professional Colleges	4,368	147,218	33.7	327	23,849	72.9
Universities	644	71,441	110.9	56	17,692	315.99

Source: Economic Survey 1985-86 and 1995-96, Tables on Education, Government of Pakistan.

Table 6

Male-female participation ratio by level of education for 1947-48 and 1994-95						
	Primary	Middle	High	Secondary vocation	Colleges	Profes- sional colleges	Univer- sities
1947-48	6.0	9.5	7.2	3.0	13.0	12.3	10.5
1994-95	1.5	2.2	2.4	3.0	1.7	5.2	3.0

Source: Economic Survey 1985-86 and 1995-96, Tables on Education, Government of Pakistan.

During the period 1947-48 to 1994-95, the population has increased over four-fold. The multiplication for enrolment between 1947-48 and 1994-95 at the primary level is 15 times; at the middle school level 15.7; at the high school level 23.2 times; for secondary and vocational level 23.5; in the arts and science colleges 52.5 times; and in the professional colleges and universities 33.7 and 110.9 times respectively. The direction has been set and the rate of growth in the future is bound to be faster because of insistent public demand.

The male-female (M-F) ratio has also changed very substantially. At the primary level female enrolment increased by 41.5 times and the ratio was reduced from 6 to 1.5; at the middle school level the increase is 50.8 times and the M-F ratio came down from 9.5 to 2.2; in high schools the increase is 56.6 times and the M-F ratio came down from 7.2 to 2.5; at the secondary and vocational levels the increase is 23 times, while the M-F ratio remained stable at 3. In the arts and science colleges, female enrolment increased by 274 times and the M-F ratio came down from 13 to 1.7; in the professional colleges the increase in female enrolment is 72.9 times while the ratio has come down from 12.3 to 5.2. In the universities the increase is 315 times and the M-F ratio has come down from 10.5 to 3.

This high rate of expansion has created many problems in the public education system. The opportunity to obtain additional resources for education from the community was lost, the fees were kept low and limited resources were spread out too thinly. This resulted in overcrowding, inadequate buildings and the employment of poorly qualified, untrained teachers. These inadequacies, however, are not uniform across the whole of the country. There are bad schools, good schools and very good schools; poor colleges, well provided for colleges and excellent colleges; well provided for universities and institutes and indifferently financed and staffed universities and institutes. There is a mixture of highly qualified and poorly qualified staff, highly gifted and well trained students and poorly prepared ones. As such, generalized statements are bound to be misleading.

The dramatic expansion of education is shown when the 1951 census is compared with that of 1981. It has not taken place at all levels. As a result, the educational composition of the population has changed. In the absence of any current census figures we can only compare the change over thirty years between 1951 to 1981, the year of the last census. Table 7, shows that, while population increased about 2.5 times, the number of those with primary education increased 4.7 times, those with middle education 5.1, and those with high school or intermediate level education 9.2 times. Those with degree qualifications increased 9.2 times, and with higher than Bachelors degrees by 11 times.

Despite the increase in education compared to 1951, 80 per cent of the working population in 1981 was reported to be illiterate. The distribution of education in the urban and rural work force is shown in Table 8.

Table 7

Population by levels of education in the 1951 and 1981 Census			
(in 000s)	1951	1981	Increase X
Population	33,779	84,253	2.5
Primary	1,255	5,944	4.7
Middle	542	2,981	5.1
Matric/Intermediate	240	2,568 882	9.2
Degree	44	497	9.2
Higher	14	147	
Other	—	12	11.0

Source: Census of Pakistan 1951 and Census of Pakistan 1981, Tables on Levels of Education, Government of Pakistan,.

Table 8

Working population by level of education in rural and urban areas, 1981							
(in 000s)	Popu-lation	Illiterate	Literate	Below Matric	Matric/ Inter.	Degree	Others
Total	21,924	16,001	5,922	3,722	1,696	444	5
Urban	5,728	2,961	2,766	1,408	997	357	3
Rural	16,196	13,039	3,156	2,368	699	86	2

Source: Census of Pakistan, Government of Pakistan, 1981.

Illiteracy in the rural work force was particularly high, over 80 per cent, while about half the work force in the urban areas was also illiterate. In the urban areas, only about a quarter had qualifications of matriculation or above. The effect on productivity of such a distribution of education in the work force needs no elaboration.

The numerical position of schools, colleges and universities, enrolment and teachers from 1947-48 to 1995-96 is given in Table 9. At the primary level, 20 per cent of the existing popu-

Table 9

Number of school educational institutions, enrolment, teachers, 1947-1995						
Level	1947-48	1959-60	1971-72	1976-77	1987-88	1995-96(E)
Primary:						
Schools	8,413	17,901	45,854	53,162	105,884	115,744
Enrolment (in 000s)	770	1,890	4,210	5,611	7,959	11,484 **
Teachers (in 000s)	17.8	44.8	105.7	133.3	196.2	337.4
Middle:						
Schools	2,190	1,974	4,110	4,490	6,993	10,586
Enrolment (in 000s)	221	422	963	1,298	2,053	3,472 **
Teachers (in 000s)	12	13	36	46	61.6	93.6
High Schools:						
Number	408	1,069	2,247	3,214	5,492	9,657
Enrolment (in 000s)	58	149	366	509	745	1,347 **
Teachers (in 000s)	6.8	18.3	37.9	59.6	99.8	188.1
Colleges: Arts and Science						
Number	40	126	339	433	548	707
Enrolment (in 000s)	14	76	186	233	420	735 **
Teacher	—	–	8,313	11,834	16,490	20,837
Universities:						
Number	2	4	8	12	22	24
Enrolment	644	4,092	17,507	37,711	65,340	71,441 **
Teachers	—	382	1,640	2,916	4,020	6,797

E: Estimated
** Figures for 1994-95
Source: Economic Survey of Pakistan, 1990-91 and 1995-96.

lation still needs to be covered and a large provision for future expansion would be required based upon the rate of population growth. At the middle school level the uncovered population is large and a major investment would be needed if eight years of elementary education is adopted as a target. At the high school level the position would be unmanageable for quite sometime to come, and the majority of students would continue to leave education and move to semi-skilled or skilled jobs.

The expansion of the education system, though large, has been far below requirement. The participation rates at different levels of the school system and the male-female ratio in Table 10 (see p. 274) show the ground which still needs to be covered to achieve eight years universal elementary education. Those who have had no education will continue to form a large part of the population, and those with inadequate education would still be there for a number of decades into the twenty-first century.

Nevertheless, a breakthrough can be achieved in the field of education. The challenge in the future is for upgradation and the introduction of modern management coupled with extensive investment. After fifty years, the education system is very large, but it has only overcome a part of the legacy inherited and its handicaps. It is still not healthy. It is geared for the present not the future. It needs a big revolutionary push towards autonomy at every level, links with the community, and public funding for support—not bureaucratic and administration controls, but creativity and growth. Education requires national attention.

Table 10

Participation rates by level and sex, 1989-90, 1991-92, 1993-94 and 1995-96				
Level	1989-90	1991-92	1993-94	1995-96
Primary (Class I-V) Overall participation	68.5	66.3	70.8	73.0
Boys	84.2	83.0	86.3	89.0
Girls	51.4	49.2	54.9	57.0
Ratio of boys and girls participation	NA	NA	63.6	64.0
Middle (Class VI-VIII) Overall participation	33.9	44.6	44.7	46.0
Boys	45.0	58.9	58.0	59.2
Girls	21.6	29.4	30.5	32.3
Ratio of boys and girls participation	NA	NA	52.6	54.6
High (Class IX-X) Overall participation	21.1	27.2	29.1	32.0
Boys	28.7	36.6	37.9	41.6
Girls	12.7	17.7	19.4	22.0
Ratio of boys and girls participation	NA	NA	51.2	52.9

Source: Economic Survey of Pakistan, 1990-91 to 1995-96.

NOTES

1. The source for the figures in the first paragraph of the section on School Education is the *National Education Policy 1992-2002*, Ministry of Education, Government of Pakistan, while it is *Pakistan Education Statistics 1992-93* for the remaining paragraphs on School Education.
2. World Bank, *Higher Education and Scientific Research for Development in Pakistan,* 1990.

REFERENCES

Iqbal, M., *Education in Pakistan*, Aziz Publishers, Lahore, 1977.

Qureshi, I.H., *Education in Pakistan*, Maarif Printers, Karachi, 1975.

Ministry of Interior, Education Division, *Pakistan Education Conference: Proceedings,* Karachi, 1947.

Government of Pakistan, Education Division, *Proceedings of the Educational Conference held in December 1951,* Karachi, 1956.

Ministry of Education, *Report of the Commission on National Education,* Karachi, 1959.

Ministry of Education and Scientific Research, *Proposals for a New Educational Policy,* Karachi, 1969.

Ministry of Education, *The Education Policy: 1972-80,* Islamabad, 1972.

Ministry of Education, *National Education Policy: Salient Features,* Islamabad, 1979.

Ministry of Education, *Pakistan Education Statistics, 1992-93,* Islamabbad, 1995.

Planning Commission, *Five Year Plans.* Finance Division, Economic Advisor's Wing, Economic Survey.

University Grants Commission, *Report of Study Group on Examination in Universities,* Islamabad, 1995.

Government of Punjab, *Evaluation of Examination System and Eradication of Malpractices,* Lahore, 1992.

Government of Pakistan, Ministry of Religious Affairs, *Report of the National Educational Committee for Deeni Madaris,* Islamabad, 1979.

Government of Pakistan, University Grants Commission, *Handbook of Universities of Pakistan,* 1994.

World Bank, *Higher Education and Scientific Research for Development in Pakistan,*1990.

World Bank, *Pakistan Education Education Sector Strategy Review,* 1986.

Government of Pakistan, *Census Reports, 1951, 1961, 1971, 1981.*

CHAPTER 5

TOWARDS A MORE FOCUSED POPULATION POLICY

Dr Nafis Sadik

The Population Situation: 1950-2015

The population of Pakistan has grown from 33 million at the time of Independence in 1947 to about 145 million in 1996. During this period, population growth has varied from an annual rate of 2.2 per cent during the 1950-55 period to a high of 3.7 per cent during 1980-85. The current rate of population growth is estimated to be 2.8 per cent a year, which, if it continues, would lead to a doubling of the population by the year 2021—close to 300 million. This high rate of population growth is the result of rapidly declining mortality, with little change in fertility. The crude death rate (CDR) has declined dramatically by 72 per cent, from a high of 29 per 1,000 population per year during 1950-55 to about 8 today. During the same period, the total fertility rate (TFR) declined by only 14 per cent, from 6.5 in 1950-55 to an estimated 5.6 in 1995-2000. Not only are further reductions in mortality projected to take place, it is also anticipated that reductions in fertility will proceed more rapidly, and the rate of population growth will decline to 1.04 per cent by 2050. Pakistan currently adds about four million people to its population each year. As with other rapidly growing developing countries, its population is young, with 44 per cent under the age of 15. The large number of young people at the threshold of their reproductive years will result in continued rapid population growth in the future even though fertility is expected to fall substantially.

Life expectancy at birth in 1995-2000 is estimated to be 63 years for males and 65 for females—a major improvement over the situation 25 years earlier, when combined life expectancy for males and females was only 51 years. The infant mortality rate, which is a useful indicator of the Reproductive Health (RH) programme performance and a key determinant of fertility, is still high at 74 infant deaths per 1,000 live births. Yet, it represents considerable progress compared to its level in 1960-65, when it was 155, more than double the current rate.

Maternal mortality is another important indicator to measure the mortality and morbidity situation, and has clear implications for the acceptability, quality and level of reproductive health services. Given its importance to both reproductive health and mortality, the maternal mortality ratio (MMR) is an important indicator to measure a country's progress in improving women's health status. The current MMR in Pakistan is very high at 270 maternal deaths per 100,000 live births. It is crucial for Pakistan to make considerable efforts, on a priority basis, to reduce those preventable maternal deaths.

The government perceives the rate of population growth and the fertility rate as too high, and thus not satisfactory. It also regards mortality levels as unacceptable. Immigration is viewed as significant and too high, while emigration is viewed as significant and satisfactory. The government also perceives the spatial pattern of internal population distribution as appropriate.

The Socio-Economic Situation

Gross national product (GNP) per capita in Pakistan remains low at $440 in 1994. The average annual rate of increase of GNP has been relatively high, averaging about 6 per cent per annum, but the rapid rate of population growth has dampened the increase in GNP per capita, and the benefits of economic growth have not touched all segments of the population.

Educational levels are low, especially for females. Gross primary enrolment is 53 per cent for males and only 28 per cent among females. Secondary enrolment is 32 per cent for males and only 14 per cent for females. Literacy rate is 47 per cent for males and only 21 per cent for females. Female literacy has improved very slowly, by about 16 percentage points over 25 years—from a low of 5 per cent in 1970 to the current low level of 21 per cent. Given the importance of education for individuals to address their own personal needs and concerns, urgent action will be required to dramatically raise these very low education levels, especially for girls and women.

As of 1993-94, there was, on an average, one doctor for every 1,918 persons, one hospital bed for 1,548 persons, and one nurse serving a population of 5,969. The shortage of service providers and supplies is even more acute in rural areas, as most of the infrastructure is concentrated in the urban areas. Various indicators of the health and sanitation situation in Pakistan underscore the urgent action required for improvement. 62 per cent of children under the age of 5 suffer from malnutrition, only 55 per cent of the population has access to health facilities, 69 per cent of the population has access to safe drinking water, and only 40 per cent to sanitation.

Pakistan's investment in the health sector declined from one per cent of GNP during 1987-88 to 0.8 per cent in 1993-94. Although there is a large infrastructure of *hakeems* (local medicine men) and homeopaths in the private sector which fills gaps to some extent, large scale investment in the health sector is required both to improve access to and the quality of health services. The 1994-98 programme, through which 33,000 village health workers are being trained and engaged in a phased manner to provide primary health and family planning services at the community level in the rural areas, will meet some of the requirements of the rapidly growing population.

Pakistan should strive to make reproductive health services accessible to all individuals of appropriate ages through the primary health care system. The unmet need for quality family planning services in the country should be assessed within the context of a reproductive health framework. Universal access to a full range of safe and reliable family planning methods and to related reproductive health services should be provided. The degree to which deliveries are attended by trained health personnel is an important aspect of RH services. In Pakistan today, only about 35 per cent of births are attended by trained personnel. Raising this very low rate would require considerable investment in the health care sector.

Another important element of reproductive health is the access to quality family planning services. A measure of access and utilization of these services is the prevalence of contraceptive use which is very low at 14 per cent and needs to be increased; such services are also an important element of reproductive health. The proportion of the population that has access to basic health services is a good indicator to measure progress on this component of reproductive health. Currently, only 55 per cent of the population has basic health services.

Despite the religious, constitutional and legal rights of women, their position remains weak due to an ineffective framework for enforcing these provisions. Female infant mortality and maternal mortality rates are high, and the rates of labour force participation, literacy, and primary and secondary school enrolment for females are very low. The patriarchal structure of Pakistani society greatly limits the possibilities for women to be active outside the home. Gender disparities exist in the availability of food, and in education and employment. Women suffer additional constraints because their spatial mobility is sharply limited. Moreover, they have little control over resources, enjoy limited decision making power, are hardly aware of their civil rights and, in combination with their overall low status, often have limited aspirations.

Population Programme of Pakistan: 1953-1995

The founding of the private Family Planning Association of Pakistan in 1953, as part of the international family planning movement, marked the beginning of the country's organized family planning effort. In 1960, government health clinics began providing some family planning (FP) services, and in 1965 the government articulated for the first time an explicit population policy, noting that high rates of population growth 'would defeat any attempt to raise per capita income by a significant amount'. The same year, a national family planning programme was launched. Despite high political commitment, implementation of the new programme was hampered for various reasons. The programme was introduced on a large scale without the groundwork needed to overcome cultural and social constraints; its managers had unrealistic expectations, spread resources too thinly, and overestimated the demand for contraception. In 1969, after four years of effort, just 6 per cent of couples were using contraception and only 21 per cent of women had met a programme worker.

In 1971, the government changed its strategy to a continuous motivation system which tried to address the deficiencies of the earlier effort by shifting the focus from targets to client motivation and follow-up. In view of the limited impact of this approach, the government launched in 1974 another strategy —the contraceptive inundation scheme—which sought to distribute contraceptives through shopkeepers, clinics and field workers. Like the previous initiatives, the inundation strategy was poorly conceived and implemented. A 1975 survey documented that contraceptive use and knowledge about sources of services were almost the same as in 1969. In 1977, the family planning programme was virtually shut down due to the policy which sought to contain Pakistani women to traditional roles. In 1980, the programme was restarted with a multi-sectoral approach emphasizing links with health and other sectors. This approach also had little impact—with contraceptive use rising only to 9 per cent in 1985—primarily due to under-funding, poor organization, and a lack of administrative support and political commitment.

The results of the 1991 Pakistan Demographic and Health Survey showed the rather poor state of the FP programme— only 12 per cent contraceptive use among Pakistani women; the number of children desired at 4.1 with only a 2 per cent decline from the World Fertility Survey findings of 1975; a decline in TFR from 6 in 1975 to only 4.9; and even a slight increase in 'Wanted TFR' from 4.3 to 4.4. This survey further revealed that more than one-quarter of currently married women were found to have an unmet need for family planning services (11 per cent for birth spacing and 18 per cent for limiting births). It also showed that the high level of unmet need for family planning services was approximately the same by type of residence with rural areas reporting about 28 per cent and urban areas reporting 29 per cent. Analysis of unmet need by education level also indicated that the need for family planning services ranged only from about 26 to 30 per cent. These results indicate that unmet need is very high regardless of a person's education or type of residence. There are, however, regional differences in unmet need, with Balochistan reporting the lowest level at 11 per cent, Sindh at 24 per cent, and the Punjab and NWFP at about 30 per cent.

A major turning point in the programme came in 1991, when the government began to strongly support the FP programme, with the realization that lagging social investment was a constraint to development. The government in 1993 embarked on a massive investment programme in health, family planning, education and rural development, aimed at providing a coherent framework for improving the coverage and quality of basic social services, with emphasis on primary education, basic health care, family planning, rural water supply and sanitation. Total national spending on social action sectors rose from 1.7 per cent of GDP in 1993 to 2 per cent in 1994, and again to 2.6 per cent in 1995, a cumulative increase of 53 per cent.

Pakistan continues to grapple with difficult political, social, cultural and economic issues that affect the pace and effective ness of its development efforts. The ongoing structural reform and development programmes concentrate on four broad goals —poverty reduction and human resource development, strengthening the environment for the private sector, a major restructuring of the roles of the public and private sectors, and improving the allocation and use of public expenditures.

A Strategically Focused Population Programme

The Programme of Action adopted at the 1994 International Conference on Population and Development (ICPD POA), fully endorsed by the Government of Pakistan at the Conference, advocates a new strategy that emphasizes the inextricable linkages between population and development. It focuses on addressing the needs of individual women and men, rather than on just achieving demographic targets, as a way to resolve major demographic and development issues. The key to this new approach is the empowerment of women and of providing them with greater choices through expanded access to education and health services, skills development and employment, and through their full involvement in the policy and decision making process at all levels.

The ICPD POA enunciates general principles, objectives and actions, the implementation of these recommendations remaining clearly the sovereign right of each country, consistent with its own national laws and development priorities, and with the religious, ethical and cultural values of its people, and in conformity with universally recognized international human rights. Pakistan's strategy should include sustained political commitment, mobilizing religious support, formulating and implementing an effective national programme that recognizes the linkages amongst gender, population and development, as well as paying attention to the youth and promoting male involvement, as well as, enhancing resource mobilization and allocation to the programme.

Even with an accelerated effort to improve and expand basic services, educate women, and strengthen reproductive health and family planning, Pakistan's population could reach 262 million by 2020. The investment required to close the existing large gaps in physical and social infrastructure and, at the same time, meet the basic needs of this rapidly expanding population, will be massive. The level of investment and savings in the economy remains too low to meet requirements for sustained higher growth, and, to make matters worse, Pakistan's natural resource base is coming under increasing pressure from rapid population growth, poor management of water resources, and a lack of attention to urban environmental problems.

Given the government's views on population growth, mortality, immigration and spatial population distribution and the goals enunciated in the Cairo Programme of Action, Pakistan needs to focus on developing and implementing an effective population programme, rooted within the framework of a broad-based population policy, which would reduce the currently unacceptable rates of population growth and high mortality rates, and the current inequities that women suffer in society.

Although Pakistan has had a Population Welfare Programme for about 35 years, its progress has been hindered by fluctuations in political support and frequent changes in administrative arrangements. However, the programme is now strongly endorsed by the government at the highest level and the challenge ahead lies in sustaining this political commitment at all levels (national, provincial and local) and translating it into effective programmatic action at the field level. For the population programme to succeed, this is imperative, as is the need to span the full spectrum of political leaders.

Two important policy issues need urgent resolution. First, priority should be given to addressing programmatic and political commitment issues at the provincial levels; and, second, a rationalization of service delivery points supported by both federal and provincial programmes must be undertaken quickly.

Mobilizing religious support is also essential to the success of the population programme. In view of the importance of religion in people's lives, the issue of family planning in the context of Islam needs to be addressed. The basic source of guidance on all matters in Islam, the predominant religion in Pakistan, is the Holy Quran. According to various authorities, 'there is no text in the Holy Quran prohibiting prevention of pregnancy or the diminution of the number of children'. The inclusion of religious leaders, as partners with the government to promote family planning and reproductive health, will facilitate the implementation of an effective population programme, based upon concepts, precepts and practices which are not incompatible with religion.

A more effective programme can be achieved through adopting a broader approach. The Cairo Programme of Action defines reproductive health care in the context of primary health care as including, *inter alia,* the following components: family planning counselling, information, education, and communcation services; education and services for pre-natal care, safe delivery and post-natal care, especially breast feeding and infant and women's health care; prevention and appropriate treatment of infertility; prevention of abortion and the management of the consequences of abortion; treatment of reproductive tract infections, sexually transmitted diseases (STDs) and other reproductive health conditions; and information, education and counselling, as appropriate, on human sexuality, reproductive health and responsible parenthood. Innovative programmes must be developed to educate and enable men to share more equally in family planning and in domestic and child rearing responsibilities, and to accept the major responsibility for the prevention of STDs.

In developing this broader reproductive health approach, a number of basic programming concepts need to be underscored (1) involve women, women's organizations, and other group working for women's needs in the planning, implementatio and monitoring of reproductive health services and programmes (2) promote men's participation in reproductive healt programmes, and create awareness of responsibility for the sexual and reproductive behavior; (3) assure the highest level c quality of care in providing information and services; (4) promote an approach that provides a constellation of linked or integrated services to meet the needs of clients; (5) make available as wide a range as possible of safe and effective modern methods of family planning; (6) create a better understanding of the social, cultural and behavioral context within which reproductive ill health occurs; and (7) improve coordination of the reproductive health programme among governmental, multinational and bilateral agencies, NGOs and the private sector.

In order to achieve this end, Pakistan must use all available channels to increase the availability and quality of reproductive health services and continue to invest heavily in expanding its inadequate social infrastructure. The international community also has a responsibility to help by providing financial and technical assistance. Since family planning services are currently accessible to only a quarter of the population, and in view of the inadequate quality of services, there is an urgent need to expand the number of facilities and of trained personnel providing services. Given the scarcity of resources, the most cost-effective way to increase access to reproductive health services is to improve coordination between the federally administered Ministry of Population Welfare Programme and the health systems administered by the provinces. The population programme must also ensure that sufficient focus is given to preventive care and follow-up services.

The information, education and communication (IEC) component of the population programme has suffered from the same cyclical policy shifts and inconsistencies that have plagued the overall programme for years. In fact, because of the sensitiveness of mass media and other forms of publicity to political changes, the IEC component was often the first to be shelved when the population programme became controversial. While the IEC programme has made significant strides in raising awareness of the small family size norm and of the salience of family planning services, it has not sufficiently contributed to helping potential clients develop confidence in the safety, efficacy and acceptability of methods or in helping them to know where and when services can be obtained. A more focused IEC programme, based on sound research, continuous review and evaluation is urgently needed in the country.

The linkage of gender, population and development is indisputable. There can be no sustainable development without the full and equal participation of women, and empowerment of women is a fundamental prerequisite to sound reproductive health. This means that women must have increased access to resources, education and employment, and that their human rights and fundamental freedoms are promoted and protected so as to enable them to make choices free from coercion or discrimination. Family life education and public information for young people that encourages responsible sexuality, respect for women and gender equity are also fundamental to improving the status and role of women in Pakistan.

Since discrimination on the basis of sex often starts at the earliest stages of life, greater equality for the girl child is a necessary first step in ensuring that women realize their full potential and become equal partners in development. The value of girl children to both their family and society must be expanded beyond their definition as potential child-bearers and care-takers, and reinforced through the adoption' and implementation of educational and social policies that encourage their full participation in the development process. Leaders at all levels must speak out and act forcefully against patterns of gender discrimination within the family, based on preference for sons. Special education and public information efforts are needed to promote equal treatment of girls and boys with respect to nutrition, health care and education, as well as social, economic and political activity.

While women will remain the focus of reproductive health activities since the burden of ill health associated with reproduction affects women to a larger extent than it does men, all programmes and services should also pay attention to the roles and responsibilities of men. Men have a stake in reproductive health through their multiple roles as sexual partners, husbands, fathers, family and household members, community leaders and gatekeepers to health information and services; they must be urged and supported to take responsibility for their sexual and reproductive behavior and for their social and family needs. In view of the power exercised by men in nearly every sphere of life in society, ranging from personal decisions regarding the size of families to the policy and programme decisions taken at all levels of government and the private sector, it is essential that men understand their responsibilities well and actively support women in their efforts to improve reproductive health.

Reproductive health services for men also need to be developed. Such services can be provided as a constellation or package of various services or an array of interventions. Services can be provided in a variety of settings, including primary health care facilities, maternal and child health and family planning clinics, male-only clinics, clinics for treatment of STDs, mobile units and military hospitals. Other major sources of services and information are subsidized commercial sales, community outreach, employment-based programmes, youth programmes and organized groups. Given the social and cultural context and the pronatalist attitudes of Pakistani males, it is crucial to enlist them for supporting family planning through educational campaigns and other approaches. Information, education and communication campaigns aimed at men should encourage them to take greater responsibility for family planning, including supporting their wives to seek and obtain reproductive health services. Such campaigns should aim to enhance men's self-esteem, while emphasizing the benefits of family planning to men, their wives and children. Educational materials should also promote the use of male-specific methods of contraception like condoms and vasectomy.

Another important area for attention is the youth of the country, particularly as 27 per cent of Pakistan's population is between 5 to 14 years of age and another 18 per cent is between ages 15 to 24. Given this large proportion of youth and adolescents at the threshold of reproductive age, it is crucial to address the needs of this segment of the population as they relate to reproductive health information, education and services. The population programme must develop culturally appropriate, accessible information and services that recognize the important linkages between human sexuality, family planning and the transmission of sexually transmitted diseases including HIV/ AIDS. IEC programmes stressing peer counselling and family life education are urgently required.

The goals of national family planning and reproductive health should be defined in terms of unmet needs for information and services; and demographic goals, while legitimately the subject of the government's development strategy, should not be imposed on family planning providers in the form of targets or quotas for the recruitment of clients. Pakistan's population and reproductive health programme has to be based on a pragmatic and participatory approach which: (1) responds to the needs of the individuals and involves them in the programming process; (2) promotes sustainability; and (3) identifies interventions that have the greatest impact for the largest number of people, at an affordable price. The programme should encourage partnerships between the government, NGOs and the private sector to maximize both coverage and quality of services and to stimulate innovative ideas.

Building national capacity to promote sustainable programmes requires the retention, motivation and participation of appropriately trained personnel working within effective institutional arrangements, as well as involvement of the private sector and non-governmental organizations. The lack of adequate management skills critically reduces the ability for strategic planning, weakens programme execution, hampers the quality of services and thus diminishes the usefulness of programmes to their intended beneficiaries. The recent trend towards decentralization of authority in population and development programmes significantly increases the requirement for trained staff to meet new and expanded responsibilities at the lower administrative levels. It also modifies the 'skills mix' required in central institutions, with policy analysis, evaluation and strategic planning demanding higher priority than previously.

Future population growth could vary substantially depending on the extent to which the ICPD POA is implemented. Under the United Nations medium variant, or the most likely scenario, the population of Pakistan is projected to grow to 262 million by the year 2020. However, if the population and development programmes are not successfully implemented, the population could grow to the high variant of 271 million people by the year 2020. Conversely, if the POA is successfully implemented, population growth would approximate the United Nations low variant scenario where, by the year 2020, it would be 253 million.

Due to the built-in momentum of population growth, even a few years' delay in investing in RH/FP will significantly increase the future size of the population, which will require even larger investments in the future just to maintain the current levels of service and quality of life. An effective population planning programme ultimately will generate savings. It is estimated by the National Institute of Population Studies that, for every rupee spent on the population programme, the government would save Rs 2.5 in primary education and health care alone within 10 years. Thus, the population planning programme more than pays for itself through savings in investments which are required in other sectors; and the freed, scarce resources could be invested to enhance generally the quality of life.

Allocation of resources for population and development and other sectors is an extremely important policy issue, reflecting not only the country's social, economic, cultural and political realities, but also its policy and programme priorities. The quality and success of programmes are, to a great extent, influenced by a balanced allocation of resources. In particular, population-related programmes play an important role in enabling, facilitating and accelerating progress in sustainable human development programmes, especially by contributing to the empowerment of women, improving the health of the people, slowing the rate of growth in the demand for social services, mobilizing community action and stressing the long-term importance of social sector investments.

The mobilization of domestic resources, which provide the largest proportion of funds for attaining development objectives, is one of the highest priority areas for focused attention to ensure the timely actions required to meet the objectives of the POA. Based on the current large unmet demands for reproductive health services, including family planning, and the expected growth in future in numbers of women and men of reproductive age, demand for services will continue to grow very rapidly over the next decades. This demand will be accelerated by increasing interest in delayed child-bearing, better spacing of births and earlier completion of desired family size, and by the desire for easier access to services. Intensification of efforts to generate and make available higher levels of domestic resources and to ensure their effective utilization in support of service-delivery programmes and of associated information, education and communication activities, is urgently required.

The Government of Pakistan now recognizes the need for an effective population planning policy and the Eighth Five-Year Development Plan for 1993-98 calls for special attention to be given to increasing the level of investment, and the budgetary allocations for the country's Population Planning Programme for the 1994-95 financial year were raised from the original budget of Rs 996 million to Rs 1,200 million, an increase of 20 per cent. The government's commitment to increase allocations to the social sector in general and the population programme in particular will no doubt help improve the country's lagging social indicators and improve the welfare of the people.

Conclusion

The population programme of Pakistan, although being one of the oldest, has suffered from a lack of consistent support and policy focus. The social enabling environment has also been weak, educational and literacy levels have been low, especially for girls, and health infrastructure and related support are not adequate. In addition, poor planning, organization and management of social sectors have further weakened its effectiveness in the country. The programme now stands at a crossroads. Its future success will clearly depend upon what and how rapidly changes in direction and management will be introduced. The full commitment to the ICPD approach of the centrality of addressing the needs of individuals and couples is paramount. The programme should be rooted within the framework of poverty alleviation, sustained economic growth and sustainable development, and the social sectors must find a central place within it. The government's Social Action Programme offers a window of opportunity to redirect the population programme and should be fully utilized.

At the policy level, signs of commitment must be clear, continuous and coordinated, and should prevail at all levels of the government and bureaucracy. There is an urgent need to help promote and sustain a broad-based policy coalition among NGOs, the academic community, religious leaders and organizations, and the bureaucracy. Moreover, a higher level of budgetary allocations to the programme should be ensured; the functionaries of the programme need to be augmented, motivated and supported; flexibility and innovation should be used to revamp the supervisory and accountability dimensions; the large unmet need for services should be met as soon as possible; community and grass roots level action are urgently needed to generate additional self-sustaining demand for services and local accountability; logistics and monitoring systems should be strengthened to assure an uninterrupted supply and appropriate mix of contraceptive methods; and, finally, the various training programmes in existence should be reviewed and revised to reflect the new directions and the centrality of meeting the needs of individuals and couples by emphasizing the quality of care dimensions and clients' perceptions and perspectives.

The entire programme should be supported by a societal mobilization effort. The cost of not resolving the population and reproductive health issues in the country is enormous. It can weaken the very foundation of civil society. The annual rate of population growth, an indicator of the population situation, continues to persist at close to 3 per cent. If it is not reduced in the future, the population of the country could become a staggering 650 million people by the middle of the next century—a sixteen-fold increase since the founding of the country. The economic, social, environmental and even the political consequences of such a demographic scenario are very serious.

The way forward is very clear. With boldness in vision, clarity of priorities, consistency in policy, redirection of the reproductive health and family planning programme and commitment to address the needs of couples, especially by creating an enabling environment for their decision-making, the rate of population growth can indeed be decelerated. In combination with an increased focus on social investment and poverty eradication, the revised strategy on population, reproductive health and family planning programme can ensure the future generations of population yet to be born with a life of improved opportunities and self-fulfillment.

ANNEXES

Population size and growth, 1950-2050

	1950	1960	1970	1980	1990	1996	2000	2050
Population (in thousands)	39,513	49,955	65,706	85,299	121,933	144,517	161,827	381,488
	1950-55	1960-65	1970-75	1980-85	1990-95	1995-2000	2000-10	2040-50
Pop. growth rate (in per cent)	2.24	2.69	2.57	3.67	2.83	2.83	2.61	1.04

Health and mortality

	1950	1960-65	1970-75	1980-85	1990-95	1995-2000	2000-10
IMR	190	155	140	120	91	74	61
MMR					270*	.	

*latest available

Components of population growth

	1950-55	1960-65	1970-75	1980-85	1990-95	1995-2000	2000-10
Life expectancy (in years)	38.9	45.0	47.8	56.2	61.5	63.9	67.2
TFR (per woman)	6.50	7.00	7.00	7.00	6.17	5.59	4.69
CBR (per 1,000)	49.5	48.4	47.5	44.5	40.9	37.3	32.8
CDR (per 1,000)	28.5	21.6	17.7	12.4	9.3	7.8	6.4

Source:United Nations, World Population Prospects: The 1994 Revision, ST/ESA/ SER.A/145, New York, 1995.

Fertility and FP

	WFS-1975	DHS II-1990-91
Numer of children desired	4.2	4.1
Desire for no more children (%)	43	39
% of currently married women who have more children than they desire	26	10
TFR	6.0	4.9
Wanted TFR	4.3	4.4

Source: Bankole, Akinrinole and Charles F. Weston, 1995, *Childbearing Attitudes and Intentions*, DHS Comparative Studies No. 17, Calverton, Maryland. Macro International Inc.

Meeting the ICPD challenge

ICPD Goals

Year	Life expectancy	IMR	MMR
2005	>70	<50	<125
2015	>75	<35	<75
UN projections			
2005	68	61	NA
2015	71	47	
1996	64	74	270

United Nations, Population and Development: Programme of Action adopted at the International Conference on Population and Development, ST/ESA/SER.A/149, New York, 1995.

Selected indicators for ICPD goals—1995

Percentage of pop. with access to basic health services	Births attended by trained personnel	Contraceptive prevalence rate CPR	Female literacy rate	Female enrolment rate at primary level
55%	35%	12%	21%	28%

Sources: World Health Organization, *Coverage of Maternity Care*, 3rd edition, Geneva, 1993.
         United Nations Population Division, *World Contraceptive Use 1994*, ST/ESA/SER.A/143,
         United Nations Children's Fund (UNICEF), *The State of the World's Children, 1995*.
         United Nations Statistical Division, *Women's Indicators and Statistics Database*, Version
         3 (CD-ROM), 1994, based on data compiled by UNESCO.

Trends in the Total Fertility Rates (TFR) for Pakistan, India and Bangladesh, 1950-2020

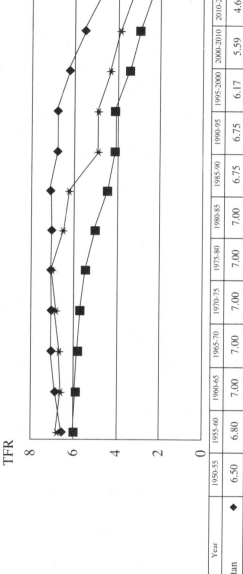

Year	1950-55	1955-60	1960-65	1965-70	1970-75	1975-80	1980-85	1985-90	1990-95	1995-2000	2000-2010	2010-2020
Pakistan ◆	6.50	6.80	7.00	7.00	7.00	7.00	7.00	6.75	6.75	6.17	5.59	4.69
India ■	5.97	5.92	5.81	5.69	5.43	4.83	4.47	4.07	4.07	3.42	2.92	2.26
Bangladesh ✳	6.66	6.62	6.68	6.91	7.02	6.66	6.15	4.80	4.80	4.35	3.90	3.21

Source: United Nations, World Population Prospects: The 1994 Revision, New York, United Nations.

Trends in the Infant Mortality Rate (IMR) for Pakistan, India and Bangladesh, 1950-2020 (United Nations medium variant)

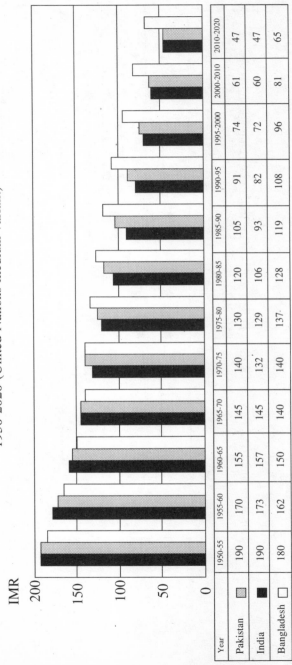

Year		1950-55	1955-60	1960-65	1965-70	1970-75	1975-80	1980-85	1985-90	1990-95	1995-2000	2000-2010	2010-2020
Pakistan		190	170	155	145	140	130	120	105	91	74	61	47
India		190	173	157	145	132	129	106	93	82	72	60	47
Bangladesh		180	162	150	140	140	137	128	119	108	96	81	65

Source: United Nations, World Population Prospects: The 1994 Revision, New York 1995, United Nations.

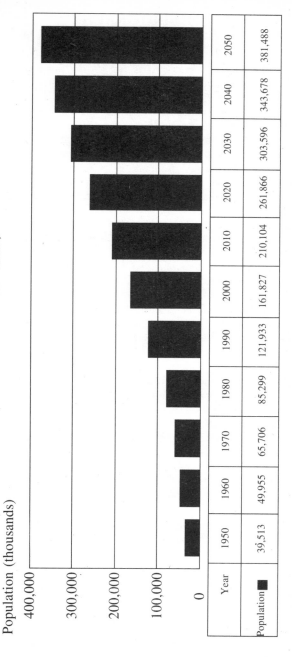

Pakistan's population size and projected growth, 1950–2050
(United Nations medium variant)

Population (thousands)

Year	1950	1960	1970	1980	1990	2000	2010	2020	2030	2040	2050
Population	39,513	49,955	65,706	85,299	121,933	161,827	210,104	261,866	303,596	343,678	381,488

Source: United Nations, World Population Prospects: The 1994 Revision, New York 1995, United Nations.

BIBLIOGRAPHY

Ahmad, Mahbub, *Experiences of Selected Muslim Countries with Planning and Implementing RH/FP Programmes,* unpublished draft monograph, 1996.

Bankole, Akinrinola and Charles F. Westoff, *Childbearing Attitudes and Intentions,* DHS Comparative Studies No. 17. Calverton, Maryland, Macro International Inc., 1995.

Government of Pakistan, Ministry of Population Welfare, *National Report on Population of Pakistan,* International Conference on Population and Development, 1994.

———, Ministry of Population Welfare, *Eighth Five-Year Plan,* Population Welfare Programme 1993-98.

National Institute of Population Studies (NIPS), compiled by Dr Abdul Hakim, *Basic Indicators (Demographic and Socio-Economic Variables),* Islamabad, 1994.

———, *Demographic Situation and its Socio-Economic Implications for Pakistan* (updated facts), Islamabad, 1994.

———, *Effects of Rapid Population Growth on Social and Economic Development in Pakistan,* Islamabad, 1994.

Rosen, James E, and Conly, Shanti R, Pakistan's, *Pakistan's Population Programme: The Challenge Ahead,* Country Study Series # 3, Population Action International, Washington DC, 1996.

United Nations, *World Population Prospects: The 1994 Revision,* ST/ESA/ SER.A/145, New York, 1995.

———, *Population and Development,* Programme of Action adopted at the International Conference on Population and Development, ST/ESA/SER.A/ 149, New York, 1995.

———, *World Population Policies,* Volume III, ST/ESA/SER.A/102/Add. 2.

United Nations Population Fund (UNFPA), *Population Policies and Development Strategies, Post-ICPD Perspectives,* Technical Report Number 27, New York, 1995.

———, *Pakistan: Programme Review and Strategy Development Report,* New York, 1993.

———, *Male Involvement in Reproductive Health, Including Family Planning and Sexual Health,* Technical Report Number 28, New York, 1995.

CHAPTER 6

HUMAN RIGHTS

I. A. Rehman

Concern for human rights has always occupied a prominent place in the political discourse of Pakistan. Some consciousness of the fundamental rights of all individuals formed part of the legacy of the struggle against colonial masters. Pakistan came into existence about 20 months after the signing of the United Nations Charter, and its first constitutional document arrived a few months after the adoption of the Universal Declaration of Human Rights (UDHR). Respect for human rights was considered an essential attribute of a modern democratic state, as visualized by Pakistan's founders. Accordingly, there were intermittent efforts between 1949 and 1973 to define and to some extent enlarge the scope of fundamental rights in Pakistan. A long period of regression followed, beginning in 1979, when the Martial Law regime, in its zeal for Islamization and reinforcement of its version of the State's ideology, made a series of deviations from human rights' norms. Although this phase ended in 1985, subsequent democratic civilian governments have not been able to resolve the contradictions between universal human rights and the fundamental rights guaranteed in the Constitution, on the one hand, and the post-1979 constitutional amendments, laws and practices on the other. As a result, Pakistan has fallen into the unenviable category of countries where not only has progress towards higher grades of human rights been stalled, but the people face serious difficulties in enjoying the human rights the State has not expressly disowned, or even the fundamental rights enshrined in the Constitution.

The Roots of Human Rights in Pakistan

All anti-colonial movements have been founded, consciously or unconsciously, on the rights of a people to be free in their homeland. The South Asian people were aware of some rights, as sanctioned by their religious beliefs, and indigenous theories of benevolent rule, before the struggle began against the British. However, while the Queen's Proclamation of 1858, by which the Crown assumed direct rule over the subcontinent, did refer to the colony's 'ancient rights',[1] the British largely blocked the emergence of demands for freedom based on the theory of rights, by starting as early as 1861 the slow progress towards self-governing status. For more than 80 years of British rule that followed, the struggle for freedom was conducted within the framework of proposals for constitutional advance which the colonial rulers drew up from time to time. The masses were deprived of the possibility of appreciating the demand for independence as of right. This reduced the element of passion for freedom in their struggle, and also delayed their education in the theory of human rights.

The leaders of the struggle against colonial rule, however, did not fail to invoke the theory of the right to freedom, because they were not unfamiliar with the principles of democracy and self-determination enunciated in the American Bill of Rights and the French Declaration of the Rights of Man, which had been elaborated by a number of European writers, especially in England. Gopal Krishna Gokhale, for instance, sought in 1905 the right to self-governance by quoting John Stuart Mill on the evils of colonialism and, two years later, defined the subcontinental people's aspiration in terms of their desire 'to be in their own country what other people are in theirs'.[2] Some others were more forthright; Annie Besant in 1917 defended the Indian demand for home rule on the basis of freedom being the birthright of every nation.[3] Likewise, when Maulana Mohammad Ali declared that no nation had a right to rule over another, and denied an ethical basis to the British purpose in the subcontinent, he was arguing for freedom as of right.[4] It is true that the expression 'inalienable right to freedom' started gaining currency in 1930 but, by 1928, when the Nehru Report was compiled, the Indian nationalist leadership had acquired a fair understanding of the theory of rights. A Declaration of Rights recommended by this Report for inclusion in the constitution of a free India embraced the following rights: freedom of conscience and religious belief and practice; freedom of expression, assembly and association; the right to free elementary education and freedom from discrimination on the basis of caste or creed in admission to state-aided educational institutions; equality before the law and equal civic rights; equal access to public utilities and resorts; and the equality of men and women as citizens.[5] Seven months before Pakistan came into being, the Constituent Assembly of India had adopted an Objectives Resolution which promised to all the people of the country 'justice, social, economic and political, equality of status, of opportunity and before the law; freedom of thought, expression, belief, faith, worship, vocation, association and action, subject to law and public morality'.[6]

The Indian Muslims' freedom struggle ran in conjunction with the nationalist movement for decades till it began charting a different course on the issue of safeguards for the Muslim community. This demand for safeguards itself was derived from the belief in rights, especially religious and cultural, and Muslim leaders often incorporated references to these rights in their rhetoric, as evident from the numerous resolutions adopted at the Muslim League's annual sessions, where they emphasized religious rights. For instance, the 1925 session of the Muslim League adopted a resolution demanding full religious liberty and the subsequent Fourteen Points offered by Mohammad Ali Jinnah as a counter to the Nehru Report contained the pledge that full religious liberty, that is, 'liberty of belief, worship and observance, propaganda, association and education, shall be guaranteed to all communities'.[7] Zafrulla Khan elaborated the point further when he said 'the constitution should contain a clause defining fundamental rights such as freedom of profession, practice and propagation of religion, education, language, articles of food, cultural and social usages, etc., and that it should devise means whereby these matters may be fully safeguarded'. Like other Muslim Leaguers, he believed the theory of rights to be beyond debate and said, 'this is a matter with regard to which there can be no possible difference of opinion and its consideration need, therefore, detain us no longer'.[8]

Besides the anti-colonial struggle, in which political rights came under focus in the pre-independence period, two other factors contributed to the people's consciousness of rights. The first was the system of the rule of law created by the British. For example, the Criminal Procedure Code of 1898 provided safeguards against unlawful encroachments on the right to personal liberty. Section 61 of the Code allowed the police to keep in custody a person arrested without a court warrant for a maximum period of 24 hours unless a magistrate had authorized his detention under Section 167. Section 340 recognized the right of an accused facing trial to be defended by a lawyer and extended immunity against self-incrimination. Above all, Section 491 empowered the High Courts to direct 'that a person within the limits of its appellate criminal jurisdiction be brought up before the court to be dealt with according to law' and 'that a person illegally or improperly detained in public or private custody within such limits be set at liberty'.

These provisions gave rise to the concept of individual right to due protection of law and to be treated in accordance with the Constitution. The defence of personal liberty and resistance to laws of preventive detention became a special forte of leading lawyers who were also prominent on the political stage. The Quaid-i-Azam was at his eloquent best when he denounced the Rowlatt Bill in 1919 on the ground that 'it is against the fundamental principles of law and justice, namely, that no man should lose his liberty or be deprived of his liberty without a judicial trial in accordance with the accepted rules of evidence and procedure'.[9] He freely drew upon the observations of Blackstone and Lord Shaw, eminent jurists, to underscore the sanctity of the Constitution and limits to state authority; and declared in his letter of resignation from the Imperial Assembly that the adoption of the Rowlatt Act amounted to a violation of the constitutional rights of the people. On other occasions he declared that 'the liberty of a man is the dearest thing in the law of any constitution', and vigorously defended the right to freedom of speech.[10] Similarly, while starting his movement against the Rowlatt Act, Mahatma Gandhi described the measure as 'destructive of elementary rights of individuals'.[11] Nor was consciousness of the right to be treated in accordance with law confined to the topmost leaders of the freedom movement. Commenting on the Bengal Criminal Law Amendment Ordinance in his presidential address to the 1924 session of the Muslim League, Syed Riza Ali declared: 'the Ordinance sets up special tribunals, introduces a different set of procedure and curtails, in some cases takes away, the right of His Majesty's subjects to the protection of the highest court of law in the land, the High Court. All these are encroachments on some of the most cherished and elementary rights of the subject.'[12] There was nothing extraordinary about what was said at another session of the Muslim League that 'in England the question of elementary and fundamental rights of the people was regarded as most sacred, yet it was denied in a part of its Empire'.[13] Finally, the civil disobedience movement launched by the Muslim League in Punjab in the spring of 1947 was rooted in the concept of people's civil rights. The view that individuals had the right to equal protection of law had become well established before Independence.

The second factor which contributed to the people's awareness of rights before 1947 was the recognition of labour's rights. Although a non-self governing colony, India became a member of the League of Nations when this was founded after the First World War. It also became a party to the International

Labour Organization. As a result, the Indian Trade Unions Act of 1926 recognized labour's rights to form trade unions and protected their deliberations against the charge of criminal conspiracy. Besides, between 1921 and 1938 the government of undivided India ratified 14 ILO Conventions including: Hours of Work (Industry) Convention, 1919; Night Work (Women) Convention, 1919, and its revision in 1934; Night Work of Young Persons (Industry) Convention, 1919; Right of Association (Agriculture) Convention, 1921; Weekly Rest (Industry) Convention, 1921; Minimum Age (Trimmers and Stokers) Convention, 1921; Medical Examination of Young Persons (Sea) Convention, 1921; Workmen's Compensation (Occupational Diseases) Convention, 1925; Equality of Treatment (Accident Compensation) Convention, 1925; Seamen's Articles of Agreement Convention, 1926; and Underground Work (Women) Convention, 1935. These Conventions and the work of trade unions in the years before Independence added to public awareness of citizens' rights.

In the final years of the freedom struggle, the leaders of the Pakistan Movement had advanced their position on the right to safeguards for a minority to their nation's right to self-determination. They were exposed to such developments as the Atlantic Charter, the Declaration of the United Nations of 1 January 1942, in which protection of human rights in all countries was mentioned as one of the results expected of victory over the Axis Powers, and the signing of the United Nations Charter on 26 June 1945, which had declared that one of its purposes was to promote and encourage respect for human rights and for fundamental freedoms for all without distinction as to race, sex, language or religion. Pakistan's founding fathers also did not wish to ignore the commitment to human rights the Congress Party in India had made in its Objectives Resolution in December 1946.

The Evolution of Human Rights in Pakistan

In March 1949, less than three months after the UN General
Assembly approved the Universal Declaration of Human Rights,
Pakistan took the first step towards framing a new constitution
when the Constituent Assembly adopted the Objectives
Resolution. It contained the leadership's acknowledgement of
two pressures on them. First, the Islamic lobby had begun to
exploit the religious argument in the Pakistan demand and by
its agitation had suggested a counter-weight to the political,
economic and linguistic demands of the more numerous East
Bengal Province. Second, the commitments made to democracy
and people's sovereignty during the movement for Pakistan had
made reaffirmation of these ideals unavoidable. Under the cover
of an assertion that the ultimate sovereign, Allah Almighty, had
delegated His authority to the State of Pakistan, which was to
be exercised through the chosen representatives of the people,
this Resolution promised respect for the principles of
democracy, freedom, equality, tolerance and social justice as
enunciated by Islam. It also guaranteed fundamental rights
including equality of status, of opportunity and before law,
social, economic and political justice, and freedom of thought,
expression, belief, faith, worship and association, subject to
law and public morality. The minorities were promised freedom
to profess and practise their religions and develop their cultures.

Several committees were constituted to deal with specific
aspects of the proposed constitution. The one charged with
working on fundamental rights and minorities' interests
apparently had no difficulty and the Constituent Assembly was
able to adopt its report on 6 October 1950. The 15 point draft
on fundamental rights contained the following: equality of all
citizens before law, equal protection of law to all persons, and
protection to all persons against deprivation of life or liberty,
save in accordance with law; protection against retrospective
application of laws; guarantees that a citizen's right to move a
High Court for a writ of *habeas corpus* would not be suspended

except under grave emergency; guarantees against discrimination on grounds only of religion, race, caste, sex or place of birth with regard to access to places of public entertainment, recreation or welfare; protection against slavery, servitude and forced labour; protection against torture, or cruel or inhuman treatment or punishment; prohibition against employment of children under 14 in a factory or a mine, or in occupations involving danger to life or injury to health; the right to employment in the service of the state irrespective of religion, race, caste, sex, descent or place of birth; guarantees of protection to property rights; guarantees to all citizens of freedom of speech, expression, association, profession, trade or business; the right to acquisition and disposal of property and peaceful assembly; the right to move freely throughout Pakistan and to reside or settle in any part thereof; the right to equal pay for equal work; freedom of conscience and belief; freedom to religious denominations to run religious and charitable institutions and to procure articles of religious worship or rites; protection to students against religious instruction other than in their own belief; a declaration that the practice of untouchability is an offence; and guarantees to the effect that laws repugnant to fundamental rights would be void.[14]

On 7 September 1954 the Constitutent Assembly of Pakistan accepted a few more recommendations of the committee on fundamental rights. These were a prohibition against denial of admission into any state-run educational institution on the ground only of religion, race or caste, and a bar to discrimination against any community in the matter of exemption from or concession in taxes granted with respect to religious institutions. The most significant addition was the creation of a right to move the Supreme Court for the enforcement of fundamental rights, and a reaffirmation of the powers of High Courts to enforce fundamental rights through writs of *habeas corpus*, *mandamus*, prohibition, *quo warranto* or *certiorari*.

When the Constitution of 1956 was adopted, the recommendations of the committee were substantially incorporated in the chapter on fundamental rights. The committee had manifestly drawn upon the Universal Declaration of Human Rights and so had the Constituent Assembly while adopting this chapter. However, there were some significant departures from the committee's report in the text finally adopted; and either the committee's report or the Constitution's final draft, or both, ignored some rights included in the UDHR. For instance, while both the report and the Constitution guaranteed the right to life and liberty, the right to security of the person contained in the UDHR was ignored. Restrictions on child labour contained in the report were dropped from the Constitution. Freedom of conscience, prohibition against torture, cruel or inhuman treatment and punishment, and the right to equal pay for equal work — all derived from the UDHR — were included in the report but not in the Constitution. Both the report and the Constitution ignored the UDHR articles relating to the right to leave one's country and return to it; the right to marry and found a family and the right to marry of one's free will; the right to freedom of thought and freedom to change one's religion; the right to take part in government and cultural activities; and the right to work, education, and a standard of living adequate for one's health and well-being. Some notable changes to the recommendations of the committee made at the time of the Constitution's adoption were: the laws relating to the armed forces and other forces charged with maintenance of public order were exempted from being held void in the event of conflict with fundamental rights; those arrested were given the right to be told of their offence, to be defended by counsel of their choice, and to be produced before a magistrate within 24 hours of arrest, except in cases of enemy aliens or those held under a preventive detention law. Preventive detention could be ordered for three months only unless a board of judges justified further detention.

The Constitution of 1962, which represented the will of President Ayub Khan alone, did not in the beginning recognize fundamental rights as these were placed in an unenforceable chapter on the Principles of Law-Making. The position was rectified by a constitutional amendment in 1963, and the chapter on fundamental rights contained in the 1956 Constitution was restored. In this process no reference to the UDHR was made. A significant change over the 1956 Constitution was the deletion of the provision which guaranteed the right to move the Supreme Court for the enforcement of fundamental rights.

While retaining the scheme of fundamental rights contained in the 1962 Constitution, the authors of the 1973 Constitution made some significant additions. In Article 11, restrictions on child labour, as recommended by the committee in 1950, were introduced. In the article on protection against retrospective punishment, an exception was made for any law designed to punish the abrogation or subversion of the Constitution. A new provision offering protection against double punishment was added as well as protection against self-incrimination, as suggested in the earlier committee's report of 1950. A new article was added to guarantee the inviolability of the dignity of man and the privacy of home, and to provide for protection against torture for extracting evidence. In the article on freedom of speech and expression, freedom of the press was made explicit. In the article guaranteeing equality of citizens before law and their entitlement to equal protection of law, a clause was added to prohibit any discrimination on the basis of sex alone. And the prohibition of untouchability was dropped.

An area of special concern for the authors of the 1973 Constitution, and the government that worked it till 1977, was the provision relating to preventive detention. Originally there was a movement towards a relaxation of the constitutional provision regarding preventive detention. The scope of a preventive detention law was defined and limited to dealing with 'persons acting in a manner prejudicial to the integrity, security or defence of Pakistan or any part thereof, or external affairs of Pakistan, or public order, or the maintenance of supplies or services'. The period of first detention was reduced from the three months specified in the 1956 and 1962

Constitutions to one month, after which further detention was made subject to the approval of a Review Board, and the maximum period of detention was fixed at 8 to 12 months, except for an enemy agent. A detainee had to be informed of the grounds of detention 'as soon as may be, but not later than one week'. However, in 1975 the government chose to stiffen these provisions. The time of first detention was extended to three months, the period in which a detainee was to be informed of the grounds of detention was increased to 15 days, and the list of those who could be detained for more than 12 months was enlarged to include any person 'who is acting or attempting to act in a manner prejudicial to the integrity, security or defence of Pakistan or any part thereof or who commits or attempts to commit any act which amounts to an anti-national activity as defined in a Federal law or is a member of any association which has for its objects, or which indulges in, any such anti-national activity.'[15]

Effect of Religious Belief on Fundamental Rights

The framers of the Constitutions from Independence to 1973 did not ignore the Universal Declaration of Human Rights but, nevertheless, did not wholly incorporate it into the chapter on fundamental rights. The reasons were varied. A firm commitment to social rights, for instauce education and health, was avoided on the ground of shortage of resources. Economic rights, for example the right to work and to equal pay for equal work, were underplayed in deference to economic reality. The right to protection against cruel or inhuman treatment or punishment was not recognized perhaps as a concession to the tradition of colonial rule. The right to participate in government, directly or through freely chosen representatives elected on universal and equal suffrage, was not included in fundamental rights, presumably because democracy was viewed as a slogan and not as a matter of right.

However, some of the reservations against total acceptance of the UDHR were plainly rooted in religious belief. Neglect of the basic human right to freedom of conscience, of the right to change one's religion, and of prohibition of marriage without the consent of intending spouses was unmistakabaly due to the problem of recognizing these rights in a Muslim society. This has prevented Pakistan from ratifying the 1966 Covenants on Social, Economic and Cultural Rights and Civil and Political Rights, and it has only signed the Convention on the Rights of the Child and the Convention on the Elimination of all Forms of Discrimination Against Women subject to reservations on religious grounds. Yet, up to 1973, the effect of religion on fundamental rights did not pose serious problems.

The liberal minded leaders of the Pakistan Movement believed that while their ideal was the creation of a state in which the Muslims would be able to mould their lives according to their belief, they saw no contradiction between Islam and the modern concepts of democracy and the equality of human beings. Not only that, they often argued that Islam offered higher values of democracy and equality. Theocracy was explicitly rejected. This approach was reaffirmed by the mover of the Objectives Resolution, Prime Minister Liaquat Ali Khan. Theocracy was pointedly repudiated, and all sects in Islam as well as non-Muslim citizens were promised equal rights and protection. While sovereignty belonged to God Almighty it had been delegated to the people: 'This is the very essence of democracy, because the people have been recognized as the recipients of all authority and it is in them that the power to wield it has been vested'.[16] During the debate on the 1949 Resolution, Hindu members of the Constituent Assembly expressed the fear that it would open the way to a theocratic dictatorship. Quite a few Muslim members rejected these apprehensions. Some of them apparently believed that mentioning God's sovereignty would interfere as little with the working of a democratic system in Pakistan as had similar references in some Western constitutions.[17] Subsequent events did not vindicate the latter view as the Constitution gradually acquired theocratic features and these did not leave fundamental rights unscathed. The first issues involving fundamental rights that arose in the constitutional debate related to the name of the State, the religion of its chief executive, and the Islamization of laws.

The first two reports of the Basic Principles Committee (BPC), in 1950 and 1952, recommended simply 'Pakistan' as the name of the State. It was only in the 1954 report of the committee that 'Islamic Republic of Pakistan' was suggested, and all Constitutions have accepted this nomenclature except for a brief period in 1962-63 when the State's name under the original version of the Constitution of 1962 was 'Republic of Pakistan'. Similarly, the first report of the Basic Principles Committee did not bar a non-Muslim from becoming the head of state but subsequent constitutional proposals and texts reserved the office for a Muslim, all the time ignoring the problem that would arise when a Senate Chairman or a National Assembly Speaker, both offices open to non-Muslims, became acting head of state with full powers. As regards Islamization of laws, the first BPC report was silent on the issue. Its second report prohibited the making of laws repugnant to Islamic injunctions, but by the time the Constitution of 1956 was adopted a commitment to bring all laws into harmony with Islamic injunctions had been written into the basic law, and to this day the Constitution retains this feature. However, till 1979 the power to change any law found repugnant to Islam vested exclusively with Parliament.

The Constitution of 1973 not only retained the provisions of the earlier Constitutions in respect of the State's name, the exclusion of non-Muslims from Presidential election, and the Islamization of laws, it offered further concessions to the religious lobby. A new Article 2 declared Islam to be the State religion of Pakistan, and Article 91 reserved the office of Prime Minister for Muslims. Through the Constitution (Second Amendment) Act of 1974, anyone 'who does not believe in the absolute and unqualified finality of the Prophethood of Muhammad (peace be upon him), the last of the Prophets, or claims to be a Prophet in any sense of the word or of any description whatsoever after Muhammad (peace be upon him), or recognizes such a claimant as a prophet or a religious reformer', was placed outside the definition of a Muslim. While this amendment to Article 260 kept the door open to Qadianis to avoid being branded non-Muslims by affirming their faith in the finality of the Holy Prophet (PBUH), the matter was settled by a simultaneous amendment which included all members of the Qadiani groups in the category of non-Muslims for whom seats were reserved in the assemblies.

However, the position till the Islamization campaign of General Ziaul Haq, who was President between 1977-88, was that, except for the declaration of Qadianis as non-Muslims, the concessions to the faith of the population's majority did not materially affect the availability of fundamental rights to the general body of citizens. The title of the State had no effect on fundamental rights. The Objectives Resolution was not enforceable. The exclusion of non-Muslims from the offices of the President and the Prime Minister did in theory smack of discrimination on the basis of belief but in practical terms the impossibility of a non-Muslim becoming head of state or government was generally conceded. The process of Islamization of laws through the agency of elected representatives was not considered in conflict with fundamental rights. Even the proclamation of Islam as the State religion was not seen to undermine fundamental rights because at that time no conflict was perceived between Islam and socialism, and the provision was viewed to be as inconsequential as the one written down by a secular-nationalist Jamal Abdel Nasser in the Constitution of the United Arab Republic.[18] However, all these provisions were exploited by General Ziaul Haq to create a quasi-theocratic order that considerably eroded both fundamental rights and the Pakistani people's entitlement to enjoy rights enumerated in the UDHR.

Regression under Ziaul Haq

The regime of General Ziaul Haq gravely undermined the Pakistani people's basic human rights and the fundamental rights contained in the Constitution by arbitrary changes. Quite a few constitutional amendments carried out by his regime hit both fundamental rights and the UDHR. The powers of the newly created Federal Shariat Court to strike down any law it held repugnant to Islam, and now to similarly deal with any provision of the Constitution, along with authority to devise legislation, is in conflict with the provision in the Objectives Resolution which stated that authority belongs to the people, and also with Article 21 of the UDHR, namely, that state authority is derived from the will of the people. The amendment to Article 51 which reintroduced separate electorates is also violative of Article 21 of the UDHR in that it denies universal and equal suffrage. The earlier provision about reservations of seats for non-Muslims did not attract this criticism for it amounted to giving the minorities an extra privilege. Above all, Article 2A was added to the basic law thereby making the Objectives Resolution a substantive and thus enforceable part of the Constitution and giving rise to controversies in courts whether fundamental rights could stand the test of repugnancy to Islamic injunctions.[19] While adding the original text of the Objectives Resolution as an annexure to the Constitution, to be read with Article 2A, General Zia arbitrarily deleted the expression 'freely' that had been used to define the minorities' right to profess and practise their beliefs, thus indicating his reservations on one of their fundamental rights.

The Zia regime also introduced a considerable body of legislation that discriminates between citizens on the basis of both belief and gender. The *Hudood* laws of 1979 have been widely assailed for discrimination against minorities and women. The exercise in deception carried out while rearranging the provisions of the Evidence Act and re-naming it as *Qanun-e-Shahadat* introduced an element of discrimination against women.[20] Extremely controversial additions were made to the Penal Code concerning offences against religion. Under Section 295C, death or life imprisonment was provided for defiling the name of the Holy Prophet (PBUH). Later, under orders of the Federal Shariat Court, the offence became punishable specifically with death. Sections 298B and 298C were specifically designed to prohibit the use of Islamic symbols, nomenclature and rituals by Qadianis and to deny them freedom to propagate their belief. All of these additions are in blatant violation of fundamental rights in the Constitution and the UDHR.

Post-Zia Trends

The first civilian government after the withdrawal of Martial Law in 1985 allowed General Zia's Constitution (Ninth Amendment) Bill to lapse, though it had been adopted by the Senate. This would otherwise have consolidated plan to turn Pakistan into a theocracy. However, succeeding governments have not been able to salvage fundamental rights from the effect of the Zia regime's inroads. The PPP governments of Benazir Bhutto (1988-90 and 1993-96) failed to honour their pledges to rescind separate electorates or to revise the *Hudood* laws. The Muslim League governments of Nawaz Sharif have not recognised the problems created by these laws. Besides, the Muslim League government of 1990-93 revived the Ninth Amendment in the form of the Enforcement of Shariah Act of 1991, which formally proclaims the injunctions of Islam as the supreme law of Pakistan. While this law does prohibit any challenge to the political system on the ground of repugnancy to Islam and also protects the rights of non-Muslims guaranteed by or under the Constitution, it leaves a large body of fundamental rights, women's rights in particular, exposed and vulnerable. The law of *Qisas* and *Diyat*, kept in force from 1988 to 1997 through Ordinances of dubious validity and made into a regular Act early in 1997, has provisions that discriminate against women and minorities, in terms of *diyat* (compensation). It also hits the fundamental right to security of life and liberty, in view of the judgment of foreign courts holding security of life to include security of a person's physical organs and limbs.[21]

Questions of Enforceability and Access

Human rights become meaningful only when mechanisms exist for their enforcement. A formal adherence to the UDHR or inclusion of fundamental rights, however gloriously worded, in a country's constitution offers no guarantee of respect for human rights. Pakistan's record in the area of human rights over the past five decades has suffered, apart from inadequacies in the chapter on fundamental rights itself, because of several factors. Firstly, for two decades, fundamental rights remained suspended under Proclamations of Emergency or Martial Law that restricted the courts' powers to enforce them. Secondly, some of the fundamental rights could not be enforced for lack of laws and procedures required for their implementation. For instance, there was no law to enforce the right to protection against forced labour until the Bonded Labour Abolition Act of 1991. Likewise, the prohibition against child labour has not yet been fully enforced because of a deficiency in the supporting legislation on children's employment. Thirdly, the authors of fundamental rights in Pakistan ignored the need for affirmative action to establish the individual's rights in a society still governed by institutions, custom and social thought that were indifferent, if not hostile, to these concepts and was certainly ill-equipped to enforce them. It took girl students years of battle in courts before they could win their right to admission in medical colleges on merit, a principle yet to be uniformly accepted in all institutions.

In these circumstances it fell to the courts to defend and promote human rights. As suggested earlier, the courts began with a tradition of respecting certain rights, such as the right to due process of law, fair trial, *habeas corpus*, freedom of expression, which the Civil and Criminal Procedure Codes and the Law of Evidence had recognized before Independence despite the absence of any reference to such rights in the Government of India Act of 1935. Even before the introduction of fundamental rights under the Constitution of 1956, the High Courts had been given, with effect from 1955, the power to issue writs in the nature of *habeas corpus*, *mandamus*, prohibition, *quo warranto* and *certiorari*.[22]

However, the conduct of the judiciary in upholding human or fundamental rights has run parallel to dominant trends in the political arena. For instance, during the first 20 years after Independence the courts moved from a preference for state's rights to recognition of an individual's rights against the state and offered relief particularly in cases of illegal detention and attacks on freedom of expression and political belief; they did not hesitate to invoke fundamental rights even when Martial Law regulations stood in the way, although no court tested the validity of Martial Law on the touchstone of the people's basic human right to be governed by elected representatives. It was not till 1993 that the Supreme Court admitted a petition challenging the dismissal of a government on the grounds of fundamental rights.[23]

Besides, the courts' effectiveness in enforcing fundamental rights has been more in evidence in cases involving attacks on civil rights in transgression of law. Except for the Supreme Court verdict in the case of brick-kiln workers' bondage, the courts have tended to be less than forward looking while dealing with economic rights or labour's trade union rights.[24] The fact that the practice of denying labour its rights through its employment under the contract system has spread under a court verdict is most disturbing. Above all, the courts have been found wanting in upholding fundamental rights in the face of their perceptions of the State's belief or their own religious inclinations. It is true that they have declined to accept Article 2A as the article in command of the entire Constitution, but on other occasions they have held that what is repugnant to Islam cannot be claimed under fundamental rights.[25] A Christian leader's petition challenging separate electorates in provincial elections has remained undisposed for years by the Supreme Court, although it had granted interim relief at the first hearing. The Supreme Court's upholding of the restrictions on the basic right of Qadianis, despite clear provisions in the fundamental rights chapter, highlights the limitations the judiciary has imposed on itself.

As in several other countries, Pakistan's legal system has come under great strain while dealing with waves of lawlessness or spurts in the incidence of heinous crimes. The government also has a well-entrenched tendency to deal with organized violence by political, ethnic or sectarian militants purely as a law and order problem. For many years, security forces have enjoyed a free hand in dealing with suspects in this category and exploited the executive's blinking at their freedom to use violence. As a result, Pakistan has invited strong censure at home and abroad for a spate of extra-legal killings and deaths in so-called police encounters which amount to a systematic negation of human and fundamental rights.

In an underdeveloped society, the enjoyment of human rights by ordinary citizens obviously depends on their access to enforcement machinery. The fact that fundamental rights can only be secured through the writs of superior courts in effect means a denial of these rights to a vast section of the population, especially in rural areas, that still has difficulty in gaining access to courts. Further, undemocratic regimes in Pakistan have bequeathed a tradition of denying the people the protection of fundamental rights by suspending or curtailing the courts' powers, a tactic effectively employed by General Ziaul Haq. Access to fundamental rights has also been affected by the rise of a parallel system of judiciary in the form of religious courts, and the creation of special tribunals whose procedures do not conform to the minimum requirements of the due process of law and fair trial. Training courses for the judiciary and lawyers do not include their due sensitization to human rights' norms, and the citizens' ability to invoke guarantees of fundamental rights is adversely affected by the lack of supportive services from the bench and the bar.

Conclusion

In contrast with the period 1947-73, when some movement towards harmonizing the fundamental rights in the Constitution with universal human rights was visible, however spasmodic or inadequate it seemed, the last two decades have witnessed a palpable indifference to the universal experience in the evolution of human rights, as well as some steps in the nature of retrogression. As a result, the State has not only failed to notice the new additions to the roster of universal rights, such as the right to development and the right to environment, it has shown little interest in strengthening human rights' norms by ratifying the Covenants of 1966 or such international treaties of fundamental import as the Convention against torture and cruel or inhuman treatment and punishments. There is no indication as to when rights, such as those to education, health cover and social security, relegated to the chapter on unenforceable principles of policy, will be accepted as fundamental. Even the requirement of an annual Presidential report on progress towards these objectives is not honoured. The introduction of constitutional provisions and laws that apparently conflict with the provisions of fundamental rights, and the executive's tendency to set no limits to laws that can be used to curtail fundamental rights, have created a situation in which it is difficult to claim that fundamental or human rights enjoy the same sanctity as they did in the 1950s or that the present order represents a genuine advance on the legacy with which Pakistan had started. Finally, the hiatus generated by the introduction of religious belief not only into law-making processes but also into the interpretation and implementation of statutes casts ominous shadows on the future of human rights in Pakistan.

Pakistan's experience over the first 50 years of its existence as a State brings out the fact that human rights flourish only in an environment of democratic governance, where implementation mechanisms are adequate and free to translate human rights' values into routine practices, and where respect for human rights increases by the same measure as the people's awareness of them and their ability to assert them rises. If the law-makers, custodians of power, dispensers of justice, opinion-makers and the conscious sections of citizenry could join hands to create such an environment in the future, the wounds inflicted during the past decades might be forgotten and the sufferings of countless Pakistanis as a result of denial of human rights would not have been in vain. This is the agenda for human rights activists in Pakistan who will need stronger than normal crutches of optimism to chart their steps across what at the moment appears to be a forbidding landscape.

NOTES

1. C.H. Philips, *Evolution of India and Pakistan (1858-1947)*, ELB Society and Oxford University Press, London, 1965, p. 11.
2. Ibid, pp. 158-59, 163.
3. Syed Sharifuddin Pirzada, ed., *Foundations of Pakistan: All India Muslim League Documents, 1906-47*, National Publication House, Karachi, 1970, p. 118.
4. Ibid., p. 117.
5. C.H. Philips op. cit., 231.
6. Ibid., p. 343.
7. I. H. Qureshi, *The Struggle for Pakistan*, University of Karachi, 1984 edition, p. 318.
8. Syed Sharifuddin Pirzada, op. cit., p. 184; Zafrulla Khan's presidential address at the Muslim League session in Delhi, 1931.
9. Mohammad Jafar, I. A. Rehman and Ghani Jafar, eds., *Jinnah as a Parliamentarian*, Azfar Associates, Islamabad, 1977, p. 39.
10. Ibid, pp. 119 and 285.
11. C.H. Philips, op. cit., p. 212.
12. Syed Sharifuddin Pirzada, op. cit., p. 10; Syed Riza Ali's presidential address at the Muslim League session, Bombay, 1924.
13. Ibid, p. 99 (Chagla while speaking on his resolution calling for the release of Bengal detainees, Muslim League session, Delhi, 1926).
14. Safdar Mahmood, *Constitutional Foundations of Pakistan*, Jang Publishers, Lahore, 1990, pp. 240-42 and 244.

15. Makhdoom Ali Khan, *Constituion of Pakistan*, Pakistan Law House, Karachi, 1989, pp. 11-12.
16. Safdar Mahmood, op. cit., pp. 47-51.
17. See Mian Iftikharuddin's speech on the Objectives Resoultion in *Selected Speeches and Statements,* ed., Abdullah Malik, Nigarishat, Lahore, 1971, pp. 364-70
18. Browne, ed., *Basic Documents of Human Rights*, Clarendon Press, Oxford, 1971, p. 51.
19. Zaheeruddin v State 1993 CSCMR 1718, quoted in M. Munir, *The Constitution of the Islamic Republic of Pakistan*, PLD Publications, Lahore, 1996, Vol I. p. 231.
20. For instance, Sections 3 and 17 of Qanun-i-Shahadat discriminate against women.
21. The U.S. Supremen Court has held that the provision regarding the right to life prohibits the mutilation of human body by the amputation of an arm or a leg. The Indian Supreme Court has taken a similar view. See M. Munir, op. cit., p. 246.
22. The High Courts were granted powers to issue writs by the addition of Article 223-A to the provisional constitution in 1954, and this amendment became operative in 1955.
23. Mohammad Nawaz Sharif v President of Pakistan, PLD 1993 Supreme Court, p. 473.
24. Makhdoom Ali Khan, 'The Many Causes of Delay', in *Justice Delayed*, Human Rights Commission of Pakistan, Lahore, 1991, pp. 36-37.
25. M. Munir, op. cit., p. 231.